DOING TIME
INSIDE

APPRENTICESHIP AND TRAINING IN GWR'S SWINDON WORKS

ROSA MATHESON

The
History
Press

Iron Foundry – North Bay. North Bay was the part of the foundry where the heavy castings were made. In the background can be seen the gantry for the overhead crane that carried the ladle full of molten metal up from the cupola. Working here meant physically hard labour.

First published 2011

The History Press
The Mill, Brimscombe Port
Stroud, Gloucestershire, GL5 2QG
www.thehistorypress.co.uk

British Library Cataloguing in Publication Data.
A catalogue record for this book is available from the British Library.

ISBN 978 07524 5301 9

Typesetting and origination by The History Press
Printed in Great Britain

Contents

Acknowledgements

I always look on my books as 'team efforts' because undoubtedly that is what so many of these people who help are – part of the book-writing team – in some form or other. I count myself immensely lucky to have them – as I do with my editorial team led by Amy Rigg. They are all always patient and supportive.

Whilst there are many to thanks some deserve particular attention: as always Brian Arman; Ken Gibbs for use of materials, advice and textual input; Roy Hazell for invaluable input on the ATS and use of archive; David Hyde for materials, editorial support and always being at the end of a telephone line; Bob Townsend for all sorts of help so generously given; Alan Philpott who is always as helpful as he can be; Elaine Arthurs, archivist at STEAM Museum for the Great Western Railway, for her patience and generous assistance; Roger Trayhurn, Daryl and all the team at Swindon Central Library; Dr Diane Drummond for advice and discussion; Jack Willcock for editorial scrutiny; and, of course, Jack Hayward for friendship, moral support, research, and collation of pictures, graphics and index.

A very special thanks to Ken Tanner, Dave Ellis and the railwaymen and women of Thursday Morning Club and all the railwaymen and women, too numerous to name, who over the years have generously and enthusiastically shared their stories and knowledge with me; especially those who are in this book, particularly Andrew Binks, Tony Tucker, Geoffrey Fletcher, Nigel Hockin and Trevor Tremblin.

Lastly, but not least, thanks to my family, whose love, interest and pride in my work keeps me going through the tiresome times.

Other titles by the author:

The GWR Story	9780752456249
Railway Voices: 'Inside' Swindon Works	9780752445267
Women and the Great Western Railway	9780752444192
Trip: The Annual Holiday of GWR's Swindon Works	9780752439099

Introduction

Writing this book has been both fascinating and frustrating. The subject outgrew its place as a chapter in the previous book *Railway Voices 'Inside' Swindon Works* and has had to be shoehorned into the available space allowed for this book. It has been frustrating because it has raised almost as many questions as it has answered, and it would take many more months or years sifting through scant evidence and material to find those answers.

Today, apprenticeship is no longer part of the national psyche as it was in previous centuries. In the early nineteenth century, however, industrial Britain was on the rise and hungry to grow. 'Apprenticeship' was a fundamental building block of the brave new industrial world, particularly the world of railways. The demand for skilled men – 'mechanics' or 'mechanicians' as they were called then – was insatiable. Because of their skills and craftsmanship and because of the amazing outcomes of their endeavours, 'mechanicians' then came to hold a place of high status in the hierarchy of working men.

However, there was also still a need for many traditional craftsmen to take their skills into this brave new world. Coach builders, carpenters, wheelwrights, tinsmiths, all had a place in Swindon Works' apprenticeship story, and became part of the 'legend'.

Alongside those who were apprenticed were those who were 'trained' until, in the end, everyone was a trainee and had training, as apprenticeship underwent radical changes and restructuring in the mid-twentieth century.

From its very beginnings to its final demise, apprenticeship was a continuous thread that shaped the identity of GWR's and later BR's Swindon Works. The Works without apprentices would have been like a fitter or carpenter without his tools – unable to do his job.

So, what was apprenticeship as was traditionally understood and what made it so valued? Well that depends from which side you are looking.

Great Western Railway.

Locomotive, Carriage & Wagon Department,

ENGINEER'S OFFICE,

Swindon, Wilts,

20th Feb. 1905.

WHEN REPLYING

71.741.

REFER TO

Certificate of Apprenticeship.

I hereby certify that F. W. Hawksworth

has been employed as an Apprentice in this

Department as follows:-

Name in full Frederick William Hawksworth

Date of Birth 10th February 1884.

Period of Apprenticeship Six years,

from 10th Feb. 1899 to 9th Feb. 1905

Trade Engine Fitting & Turning.

Works at which employed Locomotive Works, Swindon.

Geo Churchward

CHIEF SUPERINTENDENT.

G. W. R. Loco. & Carr. Department.

Not one but two famous names on this Certificate of Apprenticeship – Churchward and Hawkesworth. F.W. Hawkesworth, the apprentice. Hawkesworth was the only one of the Works' 'top-men' to do his apprenticeship at Swindon. We can see from his certificate that, surprisingly, his six-year apprenticeship was in Fitting and Turning, but not Erecting!

1

Apprenticeship: An Evolution

There are few these days who are not familiar with the term 'apprentice' thanks to the television series of that name. Unfortunately this series will have given its modern-day viewers a somewhat corrupted or inappropriate appreciation of what an apprentice actually was/is or does. The dictionary defines an apprentice as: 'someone who works for or with a qualified or skilled person, for an agreed period, in order to learn a trade' or, as the *National Apprentice Services 2009* puts it, 'an apprentice learns on the job, building up knowledge and skills, gaining qualifications and earning money all at the same time'. 'Apprenticeship' is, interestingly, omitted from *The Oxford Companion to British Railway History*, although they offer a limited explanation under 'mechanical engineering', stating: 'what might be termed a mechanical engineering apprenticeship ... involved moving round the various departments of a railway works, learning how to make, build or repair things.' Alan Wild's engineering apprenticeship at Swindon Works (1958–63) would very much bear this out:

As an apprentice I worked in AE, AM, BD, E, G, H1, J, L2, O, P1, R, T, U & V Shops:
with E Shop I did maintenance work in almost all Carriage & Wagon shops including the
Oil & Grease Works and the Laundry, also pump houses at Kemble, Rodbourne & Newburn
Crescent.

Even before industrialisation apprenticeship was a tried-and-tested formula for training young boys (and young girls) into the secrets, understanding and mastery of the skills of their chosen trade. It is known that from the earliest times in Egypt and Babylon training in craft skills was organised in order to maintain an adequate number of craftsmen. The Code of Hammurabi, who was King of Babylon, is said to be the oldest set of law directives laid down. It dates from *c.*1760 BC, and dictates some 282 codes of behaviour, one of which decrees 'apprentices cannot be taken away from their artisan masters if they are being taught a craft'; this was in order to ensure that craft skills were passed on to the next generation.[1]

In Britain, around the twelfth century, artisans began to organise formally to protect themselves and their own particular trades. Different craftsmen joined together to form mutual interest groups which became known as 'gilds' or, now, 'guilds'. These guilds established their own rules and standards as well as protective practices, jealously guarding the 'mysteries of their art', which were only passed on through their own apprenticeship schemes. Once qualified, journeymen, i.e. *journee*[2] or 'day' men (paid by the day), who could not afford to set up on their own would work for a 'master'. Interestingly, this term, 'journeyman', was still used in Swindon Works right up to its end.

A master could have several journeymen working for him, but only of his trade. He was not allowed to employ or use a craftsman of another skill in which he had no qualification himself. This stringent protectionist practice stifled wider entrepreneurial development. Only guild members could sell within a town (unless on market day or annual fair), thus preventing 'untrained' persons setting up business and upsetting the status quo. Guilds provided

Journeymen in the 'age of steam' and broad-gauge engines in Brunel's B Shed at Swindon Works, as photographed by William Hooper in the early 1900s. Note the different headwear denoting the power structures in the workplace. *Paul Williams' Hooper Collection*

a framework for everyday businesses in everyday life – carpenters, masons, shoemakers, tailors, brewers – but over time these structures became much abused and misused, especially in respect of their apprenticeships. The craftsmen were held in the highest esteem, as this small piece from the *Red Book of Hergest*, a fourteenth-century Welsh bardic manuscript shows:

> 'Open the door!' 'I will not open it.' 'Wherefore not?' 'The knife is in the meat, and the drink is in the horn, and there is revelry in Arthur's Hall; and none may enter therein but the son of a King of a privileged country, or a craftsman bringing his craft.'[3]

However, not all behaved in a manner becoming their status and position in society and, in the matter of apprenticeships, many master craftsmen were found to be extremely wanting. Such matters needed to be addressed. The Elizabethan Statute of Artificers 1563, 'an act containing diverse orders for artificers, labourers etc.', is held to be the clearest starting date for statutory apprenticeship; from then pre-modern Britain apprenticeship 'operated in a distinctive legal and institutional framework'.[4] The Statute (a striking early example of state policy intervention and regulation of industry) was an extraordinarily comprehensive document reducing all previous such laws 'into one sole law and statute … concerning the retaining, departing, wages and orders of apprentices, labourers etc.' Its aim was to 'banish idleness, advance husbandry, and yield unto the hired person both in time of scarcity and in the time of plenty a convenient proportion of wages'.[5] Previously, training had been under the control of the many guilds and although they continued to monitor and implement its regulation, it was now no longer within their monopoly. The Statute laid down that it was 'unlawful' to 'set up, occupy, use or exercise any craft, mystery or occupation except he shall have been brought up there in seven years at the least as an apprentice' and that 'the terms and years of such apprentice do not expire afore such apprentice shall be four and twenty years'.[6]

Apprenticeship was, at this time, a costly undertaking for the parents of the would-be apprentice. They would have had to bear the upfront and ongoing costs over the long term.

Apprenticeship was therefore, broadly speaking, a relatively affluent affair and definitely not an opportunity for poor families to improve their economic situation or status.[7] That said, apprenticeship was also used as a means of social management, a simple solution to local economic and social troubles, whereby 'the poor children' under the protection of 'the Parish' would be apprenticed out in order to defray costs of upkeep or, as stipulated in the Elizabethan Poor Law (1597), to prevent any likely 'to fall into evil ways'. Various charities would support poor children or orphans by paying their premiums for them and examples can be found in the GWR apprentices record books, such as the Ramsey Charity, who supported A.C. Felton in 1872 in the 'Loco Works' premium £20, and Broad Farm Charity, who supported C.R. Gilbey, apprenticed in 'carpentry and joining' in 1873, premium £20. Yet another charity, the Broad Town Trust, established in 1686 by the will of Sarah, Duchess of Somerset, supported several poor 'county' or 'manor' boys with apprenticeships in the Works over a number of decades. Records show that several were apprenticed to William Gooch and Joseph Armstrong during the 1860s and 1870s, mostly as engineers, but others as carpenters and joiners.[8] Even in the mid-twentieth century the Broad Town Trust and other charities were supporting premium apprentices through the Works. Derek Fellows, apprenticed as a coach body builder in 1949, had his premiums paid by them. His payments were handled by solicitors in Old Town, Swindon, and so the Fellows family 'never saw any money', as he puts it. Interestingly, after having paid just two premiums the money was returned to the solicitors as, as the railways had been nationalised, apprenticeships became 'free'.

There were many aspects to apprenticeship and many will argue that it was a multifaceted process in that it carried hidden agendas. James Foreman-Peck, in his paper 'Spontaneous

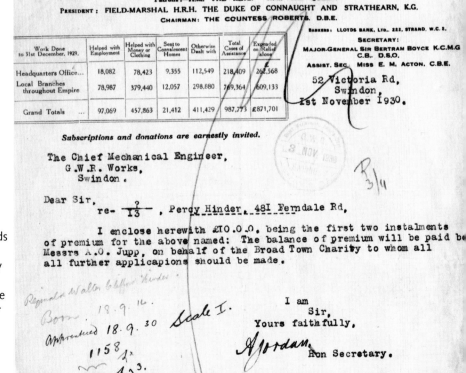

Many charities sponsored the apprenticeship of children from poor backgrounds by paying their premiums. Many such children went through the Works until after nationalisation, when all apprenticeships were free.

Disorder? A Very Short History of British Vocational Education and Training, 1563–1973', cites it as 'an instrument of social control in the face of the disorders created by a market economy and the undirected energy of young males'. Indeed, 'apprentice' was often synonymous with 'disorder' or 'misdemeanours', as Anne Yarbrough's research of *Apprentices as Adolescents in Sixteenth Century Bristol* highlights:

> Apprenticed boys were a conspicuous and often troublesome presence in 16th century Bristol. They were rude and lewd, heedless and immature, and their behaviour excited the constant worry of their elders. But the apprenticeship was an economic and social necessity for Bristol as it was for pre-industrial towns in general.[9]

Such lawlessness was not confined to Bristol. William Hogarth's moralistic engravings – *Industry and Idleness* (1747) – are related to London. They illustrate the worst excesses of the idle apprentice, with plate 11 showing the luckless lad on his way to be hanged at Tyburn. Interestingly, Foreman-Peck found that 40 per cent of those hanged at Tyburn in the first half of the eighteenth century had been apprentices – a somewhat macabre statistic.

Dr Diane Drummond, in her study of *Crewe: Railway Town, Company and People* during the nineteenth and twentieth centuries, also maintains that apprenticeship, even at this later stage, and especially in railway workshops, was still an instrument of regulation. She states: 'Apprenticeship represented a period of ritual servitude where boys learnt to obey their betters.' Whilst apprenticeship was essentially about needful and necessary learning, i.e. acquiring a set of needed skills and necessary knowledge to use in a specific way in the workplace, Drummond also suggests that apprenticeship was the place 'where the meanings of working-class manhood were more fully discovered'. In other words, the boy had to learn about the workplace, its culture, its hierarchy and *his* changing place in it along the way. He had to

Hats were *de rigueur* in the nineteenth and early twentieth centuries, but those who worked in Swindon Works had to be mindful of what they chose to wear and where they wore it. Flat caps were the usual work and day wear, but straw boaters were not only *a la mode* on TRIP but were also acceptable, whilst foremen and those of more senior ranks kept to their bowlers and homburgs to show off their authority and rank.

learn the codes of conduct which defined what was acceptable and what was not in terms of his thinking, appearance and practices. In the early times of Swindon Works this could even extend to what hat to wear. Flat caps for the workshop men (although straw boaters were okay on TRIP, the annual holiday); however, trilbys, bowlers or even homburgs were only for the high-and-mighty foreman and managers, at any time. Also decreed was which public house he should drink in and what church/chapel it would be best for him and his family to attend. The apprentice was, in fact, also serving an 'apprenticeship for life' and it would determine what type of railwayman the boy would become.

Harold Holcroft's 'apprenticeship for life' was in GWR's Stafford Road, Wolverhampton Works, starting in the late 1890s. Writing about his working life in *Locomotive Adventure: Fifty Years With Steam*, he remembers acutely how the end of short-time working brought to him a new realisation about the realities of life for the workshop men. For him the return to normal hours was merely the loss of a lie-in and a long weekend, but for the men in the Works, who greeted it with 'cheers of jubilation', it was something much more – it meant more food on the table, more comfort, they were more able to pay their bills and there was less anxiety in their families lives, because it meant more money in their take-home pay. It meant the difference between managing or real distress. It was, said Holcroft, a 'turning point' in his thinking and views on life: 'I now had to see their viewpoint on the problems of existence … This was all part of my education in learning more about my fellow men in other social planes.' Alfred Williams, the now famous and respected literary 'hammerman' who worked in GWR's Swindon Works' hot shops at the turn of the nineteenth century, saw first hand how the boys learned a lot more than trade skills – and, according to him, not always for the best. He writes in his book *Life in a Railway Factory* (1915) about the 'change in character and morals' that occurred, 'particularly in those from the country', as the lads are 'speedily initiated into the vices prevalent in the factory and taught the current slang phrases and expressions'. These 'expressions' are part of what he calls the 'filthy language commonly used by workmen and foremen alike'. Not only did these workshop men inform the language of the young lads in their charge, they also shaped the thinking in respect of their 'attitudes, beliefs and future political stance'.[10] Alfred Williams would have agreed with this. He recognised the role a good foreman could play and tells of the foreman of the 'boy turners'. He describes him as:

> a very good formative agent, one who will exercise a healthy restraint on the intractables and encourage the timid … he very often furnished [the boy] with hints of a personal nature which – whatever the lad may think of them at the time – bear fruit in later life. If the youngster is inclined to be wild and incorrigible he tries his best to reform him and gives him sound advice … [as well as] a corrective cuff in the ear and a vigorous boot in the posterior, but he usually succeeds in bringing out the good points and suppressing, if not eradicating, the bad.

John Walter started his apprenticeship in 'fitting, turning and erecting' in June 1945, joining his grandfathers Alfred and Fred, father John, uncles Stan, Vic, Bert, Fred, Harry, William and Wilf, and numerous cousins already in the Works. Knowing that such family members were 'ever present' severely reflected on how he conducted himself within the Works. He also recalls an early novel learning experience in life relationships: 'This was war time days so there were also women working on adjacent machines, the first real contact in those days of 16-year-old boys with REAL women. My education started there.' This 'wider' learning transferred down the decades so that in the 1970s Andy Binks, apprenticed at that time, remembers: 'those men taught me a whole lot more than my job. I learned a lot about how things work in life.'

Part of this life-forming process was forging relationships. Apprenticeship was the period of the boy's life, when friendships were made that would often last a lifetime – with their master, with other apprentices and with the older men who mentored them over the years. Here is where the foundations were laid for that 'camaraderie', 'companionship' and 'being part of

The boilermakers were very much 'a separate group' with a particular identity, even within their trade. There were two classes of boilermakers – the platers and the riveters – and each kept to his own area of work as the trade was jealously guarded and protected.

Left to right: Ken Johns, Dougie Lovelock, Lionel Voller and Brian Phillips. This now non-pc photograph of a night gang of fitter-turner-erectors sitting happily in front of the 'Pin-Up' board in the AE Shop during the 'swinging sixties' shows how changing attitudes informed 'what goes' and what was acceptable in the workplace.

one big family' that all Swindon Works' workers talked of. This 'big family' identity was very much part of the Works' cultural character and psyche, so much so that it pervaded into the socio-cultural context of Swindon itself, in that if you were not in the Works, you were not an 'insider' and therefore, by definition, an 'outsider' and not one of 'the family'.[11] Apprentices learned to adopt this identity very quickly and use it to their own advantage. Friendship and camaraderie were essential ingredients in the apprenticeship formula, as they provided the glue that helped many a lad through the less pleasant side of being an apprentice – the dreariness, the drudgery, the poor pay, the rotten jobs and being 'on the butt end of the older men's temper or supposed and sometimes cruel humour', as one man described it. Such black humour and practices became part of the tradition in many engineering factories up and down the country, and especially inside Swindon Works. Alfred Williams records one such black joke:

> The boys were always frightened at the thought of one painful ordeal, which they were told they would have to undergo. They were seriously informed by their new mates in the shed that they would have to be branded on the back parts with a hot iron stamp containing the initials of the railway company [GWR] and very many youngsters would believe the tale and awaited the operation with dreadful suspense. As time went on, however, and they were not sent for to the offices, they came to discredit the story and smiled at their former credulity.

Yet, whilst apprenticeship was tough and scary, it was made bearable by the fact that you were not on your own (at least not in Swindon Works) – there were always a good number of other young lads doing the same thing (and probably feeling the same thing) as you. Pat Sullivan remembers of his time in the Scragerry in the 1950s:

> Although it was a hard job and it was dirty … thing was it wasn't quite so bad because the place was full of lads the same age. All the people that were working in the Scragerry at that time were fifteen, sixteen. It was quite strict really. You could understand the chap in charge he had to be quite strict really otherwise with all those lads he wouldn't have got anything done would he?

Views on apprenticeships were not all one-sided or constant. Adam Smith in his treatise on the *Wealth of Nations* had a very unsympathetic outlook on them, believing them to be over-long, that they made the young lazy, hindered outsiders from using their own abilities and, above all, they were a conspiracy to raise wages and prices to the benefit of the masters.[12] Views of those who formulated the policies changed over the hundreds of years that they were in operation, particularly in the latter part of the twentieth century. Views of those who have actually gone through the system seem to be split into two opposing camps, one holding that: 'it was the best possible way of learning a trade', as did Ken Gibbs who says, 'an apprenticeship in Swindon Works was the best possible training'; whilst the other perspective describes it bluntly as 'cheap labour'. A survey conducted by the Ministry of Labour in 1928 puts it almost as directly: 'In the earlier years of apprenticeship the apprentices receives more by the way of training than he gives in production and his wages in consequence are determined on the basis of his being a liability rather than an asset during that time.'

A.E. 'Dusty' Durrant, remembering his experience of apprenticeship in the Works in the following decade, dryly remarked: 'there was a period in which apprentices seemed to be used as cheap labour rather than learning much of use – other than patience!' Whilst Paul Warren, who did his in the 1950s (showing that such sentiments were not confined to just one era), speaks more strongly of his time: 'It was slave labour. I did five years and it could have been completed in two. For three of them I was just cheap labour. I got 19s. 6d for the first three months and £1. 19s. 6d after. I got £4. 19s. 6d in my last year.' James Foreman-Peck explains the latter perception perhaps more objectively as:

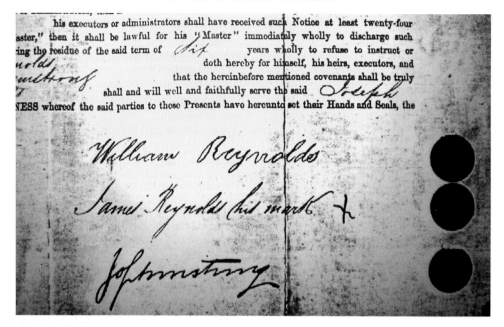

his executors or administrators shall have received such Notice at least twenty-four ~~aster,"~~ then it shall be lawful for his "Master" immediately wholly to discharge such ~~ing the residue~~ of the said term of *Six* years wholly to refuse to instruct or *holds,* doth hereby for himself, his heirs, executors, and *unstrong* that the hereinbefore mentioned covenants shall be truly *7* shall and will well and faithfully serve the said *Joseph* ~~NESS~~ whereof the said parties to these Presents have hereunto set their Hands and Seals, the

William Reynolds

James Reynolds (his mark) +

J. Armstrong

Many adults in the nineteenth century could not read or write and in order to give their official or legal consent would make their 'mark' (usually an X) against their name written for them, as is here, when James Reynolds signed his agreement for his son William's apprenticeship in 1868.

> Apprenticeship allows an initially very low-productivity worker first to be paid more than they are worth to the employer in terms of extra output. Subsequently, as the training given takes effect, productivity rises above the wage so that the employer recoups the 'investment' or 'loan' to the worker.

This is a standard and generally accepted explanation for the modern two-stage model of apprenticeship, and certainly the one commonly experienced in Swindon Works. For many of the many thousands of apprentices over the centuries, however, being an 'investment' felt more like 'serving a sentence'. Perhaps what gives us a deeper insight into the thinking regarding the period served as an apprentice is the language used. 'I did my time' is the phrase most often used to start a conversation about individual apprenticeships. In Swindon Works (as in many other factories around the country) it was spoken of as 'doing my time' or 'serving my time'. When one was finished and the 'bound time' was ended, it was joyfully described as 'coming out of my time', whilst the GWR recorded this event in their early apprentice record books as the boys being 'given up', i.e. being 'released' from their 'bindings'.

Early apprenticeships, although regulated by the guilds, were still often a hit-and-miss affair and one of the aims of the 1563 Statute had been to regulate a system that had become much abused by both parties – the master and the apprentice. At that time apprentices commonly lived in the household of the master and were vulnerable to abuses such as no provision of food, no clothing, no accommodation and sometimes no wages either. The masters lost out when apprentices wouldn't work the hours, did poor work, stole the household's food and drink, got drunk and were unable to work, disappeared for days on end or just totally absconded. It has been recorded that between 1540 and 1590 nearly 45 per cent of apprentices to London cabinet-makers were listed as 'gone' or 'run away'.[13] The Master and Servants Act 1747 sought to regulate relations between employers and their employees by enforcing contracts before a court of law, thereby ensuring payments of wages due and punishing servants or labourers for 'misdemeanors or ill behaviour' by stopping wages or even sending them to the 'house of correction'. Later, in 1766, it also became a punishable offence for employees to quit before the agreed term, while in 1823 the new crime of absconding (a popular option for many apprentices, some even in GWR years), punishable by three months' imprisonment, was included and they had to make up any time lost whilst absconding. Later still, in the 1860s, union officials' activity came within its jurisdiction.[14] Most hold that the implementation of these acts was heavily biased on the side of the employer to the extent that the contract seemed to work one way.

The contract, or indenture as it was then, between an apprentice and his master was a legal document which set out the 'binding' terms and conditions to which all those parties identified within and covered by the indenture; i.e. the master, the apprentice and the guardian agreed and put their signatures to or, for those who could not write, their 'mark' (finger/thumbprint), as with James Reynolds who put his mark as witness to his son, William Reynolds' indenture with Joseph Armstrong in March 1868.

Signatures on the indenture were recorded as being 'Signed, Sealed [with melted wax] and Delivered', as if to drive home the full weight of them. They were then verified by the signature of a further independent witness of high standing.

So important was this document that in its earliest days it was made on only one sheet which was then torn in two. Each party took one part of the document. Should a dispute arise between them, the validity of their contract could be confirmed by matching up the two halves

An indenture was a legally binding document. It placed responsibilities and conditions on both shoulders – the master's and the apprentice's. Early indentures were particularly onerous and, to modern-day eyes, very intrusive into one's private habits.

on the torn line (the indenture), thereby proving whether either part had been tampered with. Indentures, once written, were in terms of the law unassailable and stood for the term agreed and signed to. Apprenticeships were, in general, (apart from those instigated by the authorities on behalf of Poor Law or orphaned children) applied for and negotiated by the parent on behalf of the child who, at the time of signing over himself to the person and/or the company, was legally a minor and so the legal document had to be agreed to and witnessed by the parent but also signed by the child/would-be apprentice. Records of nineteenth-century indentures, such as those of William Reynolds and Matthew Dickson, bear witness to this, but many if not most of the men interviewed who undertook an apprenticeship with the GWR in the twentieth century, and later with the nationalised British Railways, claimed not to recollect signing any document at all. William Bullock, a premium apprentice in the 1930s, however, remembers how he walked down the Works tunnel on a Monday in November in 1931 'to sign my agreement forms with the GWR' and how later, having being taken into B Shed, he wanted to 'turn away and leave the building but you could not do this as you had just "signed on"',[15] whilst Ken Gibbs, apprenticed in 1944, recalls in his book *Swindon Works: Apprentice in Steam*, 'several of us had a call to the Manager's Office where we were given a little induction chat and signed for the Apprenticeship'. Such a written contract was essential in terms of pupil or premium apprenticeships, as monies were exchanged in payment for 'pupillage' or the services of instruction given.

The simple concept of the indenture was that of setting out an agreement between the parties of what was expected of each of them, i.e. a set of rules and obligations which they were both bound to observe and fulfil. For the master this was providing 'care' (in terms of accommodation and nourishment, but also, in the early days and even in the nineteenth and early twentieth century, in the widest sense, religious, moral and social welfare too) as well as good instruction. Interestingly, an early Swindon Works' indenture between Philip Williams, indentured to Minard Christian Rea, the then Works' manager, dated 5 May 1854, includes the words 'sufficient … meat and drink and lodging and other [then something illegible]' but this has then been crossed through. It does, however, suggest that at one time lodging and sustenance provision had been made for some such apprentices, perhaps in the home of Minard Rea himself, as he had lived in the railway village. For the apprentice, the agreement required complete servitude, utter obedience, loyalty, hard work and staying the course. That, however, was not all that was demanded of him. The conditions of the indenture for these young apprentices were, to modern-day eyes, extremely oppressive. These early indentures carried stipulations that would be looked on as an infringement of human rights in this day and age, as we can see if we look at that of Philip Williams:

This Indenture Witnesseth that Philip Williams son of George Williams of New Swindon in the County of Wilts, Smith, now aged seventeen years or thereabouts of his own free will and accord as by and with the consent of his father as testified by his being a party to and executing these pretents … doth put bind and place himself **Apprentice** to Minard Christian Rea Manager of the Works of the Great Western Railway Company at New Swindon aforesaid as Agent for and on behalf of the said Company … wherein to learn the Art of a Smith and with him in the manner of apprentice to serve from the day of the date thereof for and following and to the full End and Term of four years from thence and following to be fully complete and ended. *During which term the said apprentice his Master shall faithfully serve, his secrets keep, his lawful commands everywhere gladly do, he shall do no damage to his said Master nor see to be done of others but to his Power shall tell or forthwith give warning to his said Master of the same, he shall not waste the goods of his said Master nor lend them unlawfully to any, he shall not commit fornication nor contract Matrimony within the said term, he shall not play at Cards or Dice Tables or any other unlawful Games whereby his said Master may have any loss or others during the said terms without Licence of his said Master, he shall neither buy nor sale , nor shall he haunt Taverns or Playhouses nor*

absent himself from his said Master's service day [– or night – is crossed through] unlawfully, but in all
things as a faithful Apprentice he shall behave himself towards his said Master and all his during the said
term. **And** the said Minard Christian Rea as such Agent as aforesaid in consideration thereof
doth Covenant promise and agree that he the said Minard Christian Rea as such Agent as
aforesaid … in consideration of his said **Apprentice** in the Art of a Smith … which he useth
by the best means that he can shall teach and Instruct or cause to be taught and Instructed
Paying unto the said Apprentice such wages as the said Minard Christian Rea as Manager of
the said Works and as such Agent as foresaid, shall think fit having regard to the ability of the
said apprentice and the execution of the work performed by him and having regard to the
scale of wages adopted by the said Company for the Apprentices at the said Works …

And for the time performance of all and every said Covenants and Agreements either of
the said Parties bindeth himself unto the other by these Pretents **Indentures** whereof the
Parties above named therein these Indentures interchangeably have put their Hands and Seals
the third day of May and in the seventeenth year of the Reign of our Sovereign Lady Queen
Victoria by the Grace of God of the United Kingdom of **Great Britain** and Ireland **Queen**
Defender of the Faith and in the year of our Lord one thousand eight hundred and fifty four.

Signed Sealed and delivered by the said Parties   Philip Williams
In the presence of Frederick   Miller George Williams
Clerks to Messrs Bradford   Minard C Rea
Solicitors Swindon[16]

—⟨ᴏᴏᴏ⟩—

Interestingly, the wording on this document and one found for a Richard Selman 'to be
taught and instructed in the trade Art Science or Occupacion of a Broadweaver', dated 1291,
which I came across in my research, are almost identical.

Unquestionably, no apprentice nowadays would agree not to go to the pub, theatre or
cinema, and especially would not agree to forfeit sexual relationships! The early indenture was
a momentous requirement that placed a heavy load upon young shoulders and appeared to sign
the young lad's life away for the next umpteen years. It would have taken a brave, young soul to
put his signature to such a document without some qualms or feelings of anxiety. Undoubtedly,
apprentices had to believe in the long term. They had to hold on to the knowledge that
eventually all the onerous conditions, drudgery and low pay would be worthwhile, for, whilst
unskilled boys would often initially earn more than apprentices, later the dividend was that, as
skilled craftsmen, they would earn twice as much as unskilled labourers.

Early indentures were all handwritten with embellished script, such as that of Phillip
William's, but that of William Reynolds' just fourteen years later in 1868 is a formatted printed
document with appropriate gaps left for the individual details to be handwritten in. The
significant difference between the two (apart from the fact that Queen Victoria is not included)
is that Reynolds' indenture includes penalties and forfeitures of rights to the apprenticeship:

… **PROVIDED ALWAYS** nevertheless and it is hereby covenanted and agreed by and
between the said parties that in the case of the said *William Reynolds* shall at any times hereafter
be wilfully guilty of disobedience or misconduct towards his 'Master' and his 'Master' shall
give notice thereof in writing to the said *James Reynolds* [William's father] his executors or
administrators then if the said *William Reynolds* shall after the said *James Reynolds* … have
received such notice at least twenty four hours, again be guilty of the like, or any other
misconduct towards his 'Master' then it shall be lawful for his 'Master' immediately wholly to
discharge such Apprentice from his service and it shall be lawful for him thenceforth during
the residue of the term of *Six* years to wholly refuse to instruct or receive the said Apprentice.

Along with all their other hardships and drudgery, apprentices had to cope with low wages at a time when their unskilled peers were often earning much more. The payback was that in later years the tables would be reversed: as qualified journeymen, they would earn a much better wage.

Compared to these early indentures the 'agreements' or 'regulations' of later GWR (and then BR) years seem very lightweight, yet they were still held in awe by those that signed on the dotted line.

The premium apprenticeship agreement that Joseph Smith and his son Stanley Smith had to sign to was a modified and more explanatory one, put together originally by George Jackson Churchward in February 1892 (figures in brackets), but updated by Samuel Collet in August 1908, with certain details crossed out and handwritten in:

APPLICATION FOR APPRENTICESHIP AT GWR CARRIAGE WORKS SWINDON
Engineer's Office Swindon

February 17th 1892 C J Churchward
Revised August 5th 1908 C B Collett

Regulations under which APPRENTICES are employed
1. Apprentices are taken on when vacancies arise.

2. A full term of Apprenticeship is five years but the engagement is terminable on either side at the expiration of any period of six months dating from the commencement of Apprenticeship. Apprentices are not taken on under 15 years nor over 16 ½ years. [These are both crossed out and 15½ years and 17 years respectively are written in for the revision.]

3. … It is particularly requested that no application be made on behalf of any youth who is not of sound constitution and of good bodily health and strength as otherwise he would not be able to carry out satisfactorily obligations specified in this Memorandum.

4. Apprentices are subject to the Rules and Regulations in force as to the Management of the Works … they are liable to dismissal at anytime if they fail to keep good time, or to give proper attention to their work, or if they otherwise misconduct themselves.

5. It must be understood being in receipt of wages for work performed apprentices must necessarily be kept for some considerable time upon work in which they have become tolerably proficient. Variety of work will be given from time to time ... but it is impracticable to remove them from one class of work to another at frequent intervals.

6. Before any youth is accepted as an Apprentice he will be employed in the Workshops on trial for one month without any wages. During this period he will be required to commence work at 6.0. am and to work the ordinary hours as given in para 11 . If he is found satisfactory he will be entered on the Register of Apprentices and receive wages under the conditions in para 10.

9. A Premium of £5 is payable in advance for each period of six months. 2.6d. Stamp duty is payable on the registration of the application ...

10. Scale of Wages represents the maximum rates for the respective years of service but advances year from year will be dependant on good conduct, any grounds for complaint ... they may be withheld or lower rates given
    First Year (10d)★   1. 9d per day
    Second (1. 2d)   2. 1d
    Third (1. 6d)   2. 2d
    Fourth (2. 0d)   2. 6d
    Fifth (2. 6d)   2.10d

11. Payment is made by the hour for actual number of hours worked 9 hours or being reckoned as one day.
    The ordinary hours of work are as follows:
    Monday to Friday
    (6.0 am to 8.15 am – 9.00 am to 1.0 pm and 2.0 pm to 5.30 pm)★
    8.00 am to 12.30pm and 1.30 pm to 5.30 pm
    Saturday
    (6.00 am to 8.15 am – 9.00 am to 12.00noon)★
    7.30 to 12 noon
    All apprentices are expected to commence work punctually at 8.0 am and to make, as a rule, full time hours (54)★ 47 hours during the week

12. The usual holidays are:
    Easter 3–4 days
    Annual Works Holiday about July – 7 days
    Christmas 4 to 7 days

13. Every applicant for Apprenticeships must produce a certificate of registration of birth, a medical certificate of his suitability for following the employment, on registration he will be required to become a Member of the Medical and Sick Fund Societies in accordance with GWR Co Rules.

14. Every Apprentice is required to become a Member of the Science and Art Classes in connection with the Technical Schools at Swindon and to attend the Winter Sessions course of theoretical instruction which may be prescribed for him.

Note: ★ *denotes 1892 rates and hours*

Industrialisation in the nineteenth century saw a growth in apprenticeships and with more boys (and girls) now working in factories and being paid wages, the 'outdoor' apprenticeship, i.e. apprentices not living with the master in his home nor being given 'sustenance and lodging', began to gather momentum. This was not popular amongst many of the guilds as one element of the 'control' of apprentices was relinquished: if they were at large outside for a good part of the day and night, how did one control them so that they stayed out of places of ill repute, turned up in good order and in time for working the next day? The realities and practicalities, however, made the change inevitable and with it came a change in the relationship between master and boy; now it was more 'boss' and 'employee' – and what factory owner wanted his house filled with his 'employees'? By this time apprenticeships in common trades and in modern trades, which had not existed in the sixteenth century, were often undertaken without any formal indenture and compulsory apprenticeship was finally repealed in 1814. In the railways, however, and in particular in the GWR, apprenticeships were de rigueur and very much sought after. The railway companies used apprenticeships to bind their workers and their progeny to the company and ensure company loyalty, compliance and a continuous supply of young labour. This was an effective way of controlling the workforce and of particular significance when Swindon was a 'one-industry' town. Young boys who misbehaved put their future job prospects in jeopardy, as William Gooch (Works' manager) brought emphatically, with underlining, to their attention in June 1869: 'Boys brought before my notice as committing such depredations [damage in the village] will not in the future <u>at any time</u> be employed in the Works.'[17]

From the earliest of times apprenticeship was a 'controlled' enterprise in many ways, one element of which was that, whilst it was an entry into the workplace, it was also a barrier. It guarded entry to skills-specific labour markets. The 1563 Elizabethan statute made apprenticeship compulsory and prerequisite, decreeing that no one who had failed to serve an appropriate apprenticeship for a specified number of years (then seven) was allowed to enter or practise a trade. Up until then the guilds had operated their own systems of 'barriers' but in 1563 these became universal. Later this barrier controlling system was fully utilised to their own advantage by the many trade societies and clubs, by unions and by the companies, especially the GWR. Whilst Mr Holden, Superintendent of the Carriage Department, might proclaim in 1874 that 'boys fell naturally into their places, and filled up the vacant places in the Works',[18] in fact the GWR manipulated their apprenticeship system to provide a steady supply of the 'right kind' of tradesmen to meet the company's needs by dictating which boy could do what trade and when, and also by declaring that only skilled men's sons could enter into skilled trades (unless they were prepared to pay). Once again a 'poor man's son', i.e. the lower grades, could not expect to improve his lot in life through bettering himself in the workplace. As Roy Blackford, a Swindon Works' apprentice coach finisher in the 1940s, graphically described it, 'the boys were "food" for the Works generally'. For the boys there was little real choice. New Swindon and subsequently Swindon had always been a one-industry town, even, as Hugh Freebury recalls in the middle of the twentieth century: 'The GWR had a virtual monopoly in the Borough. In fact Swindon was more of a complete railway town than any other in the country since the complete rolling stock, locomotives, carriages and wagons were all built and repaired there.'

By the turn of the twentieth century apprenticeships were, in many trades and commerce, in a state of flummox. The demands of capital versus labour were becoming more strident and the relationship between the men and the bosses or the management became even more distanced. Unions and not individuals were now the channels of negotiation for employment terms and conditions; apprentices were, however, still outside this machinery for collective bargaining. Apprentices' wages were still generally well below the level of other young workers who were not bound, and by the early 1900s apprenticeships were out of favour with boys and employers alike – why be bound to a long service period for low wages when there was also no guarantee of a job anyway? Many employers, GWR amongst them, found the indenture onerous, legally tying their hands, limiting their ability to be flexible in a rapidly changing economic and technology specific workplace, and so they decided to do away with this formality and 'employer certificated' apprenticeships came in. These became common practice in GWR and Swindon Works. The first company evidence I have found of this is a Certificate of Apprenticeship on company-headed paper for a James George Saunders, date of birth 12 March 1873, whose apprenticeship in boiler-making was from 12 March 1888 to 10 March 1894. The certificate was signed by William Dean. Godfrey J. Dibsdall also received a certificate when he finished his 'fitting' apprenticeship in September 1899. Harold Holcroft, who had started his 'new kind' of premium apprenticeship at Stafford Road in 1898 and finished in 1906, remembers:

> From Swindon came a Certificate signed by Churchward himself to the effect that I had served an apprenticeship of five years in the shops and had attended the specified evening classes, that my conduct and timekeeping had been good and that it was considered that I was a good workman.

It would appear that 'certificated' apprenticeships were common practice and indentures were being done away with, yet there is a document dated August 1912 in respect of the 'National Insurance Act 1911 Part 2 Unemployment Insurance', which raises vexing questions. Under the heading 'List of grades of workmen in respect of which it is believed that contributions are NOT PAYABLE' (and it is a long list covering three pages), there was listed: 'Apprentices over 16 years of age (not indentured) and boys and youths over 16 years of age employed in connection with the grades mentioned ... Apprentices (indentured) all grades.'

Obviously this is significant in terms of apprentices paying for or receiving 'contributions' under the Act, but what is perhaps more interesting here is – which apprentices are indentured and which are not, and why not? My rationale for this situation would have been that those identified as indentured are ones that had been previously agreed and were merely serving out their time; however, because of the earlier certifications, this is not likely. It would appear that

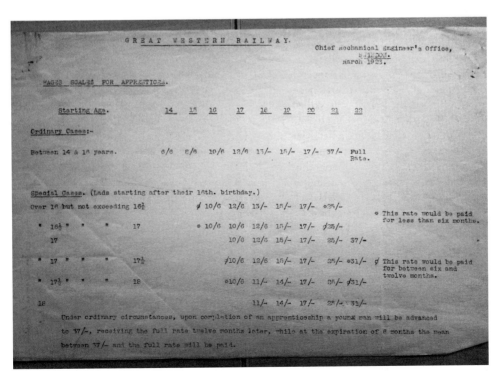

No matter what the era, apprentices' wages were always a 'bone of contention', with many grumbling they were just 'cheap labour'.

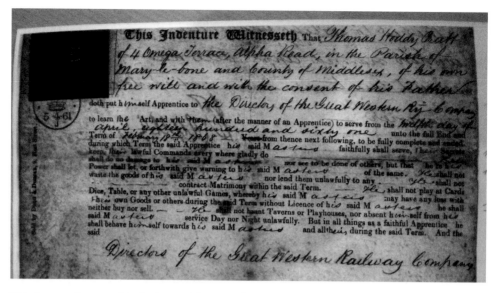

This is a most unusual Indenture in that it is the only one that I have come across where the apprentice is apprenticed to *the Directors of the Great Western Railway Company* rather than to just an individual such as the Superintendent or the Manager or to 'the Company'. Thomas Hoddy Pratt must have had very good connections.

Whilst I have seen the front of many indentures, I have only come across this one example of 'completion' written on the back of one, which makes this whole document of Thomas Hoddy Pratt something rather special indeed. *STEAM Museum of the Great Western Railway Collection*

they were co-existing side by side – but why? The amended regulations for apprenticeship signed by Collett in 1908 do not make mention of the indentured nor the not indentured, but those of 1926 (the next earliest document I can find) very specifically do; Regulation No. 12 states: 'Apprentices are *not* bound by Indentures but if …'

The change from indentures to non-indentures is of significance. Whilst it would appear that the daily practice of apprenticeship did not change (apart from the fact that the tenure was now generally five years), the essence of it had. As explained by a solicitor friend, 'An Indenture is an Indenture. It is as it is. Whole and complete.' Now, however, an apprenticeship was no longer immutable. No longer was there guaranteed tenure for the apprenticeship period. Whilst the terms on other agreement or regulation forms stated that the apprenticeship *should* be for a period of five years, a full sixty months, it was now subject to termination at each six-month period, by either side.

Also, significantly, no longer was the indenture proof of a served apprenticeship; now, should the apprentice fulfil his work satisfactorily and for the full time, he would receive a certificate on company-headed paper. What strikes me as interesting is, having interviewed a great number of men over a period of years, I found that whilst the practice of indentured apprenticeships had gone, the belief in its presence remained; without exception all men interviewed believed their final certificates equated to an indenture and spoke of them as such. What had not changed was that the now unindentured apprentices were expected to follow the same training paths through the workshops, to attend night school and to attain their City and Guilds certificates – whether they did these two latter things or not is another matter (see Chapter 4).

Through the decades the tried and tested GWR apprenticeship scheme was known to be sound and solid and it achieved a high reputation around the world. Swindon Works was always being asked about the application of its scheme. In 1941 the technical instructor of the Nigerian Railways wrote that he was undertaking to 'formulate some common system and plan' and would appreciate 'facilities for examining your apprenticeship training scheme'. Following the visit he wrote again in November 1942: 'I have learned of a meeting recently held by all the Main Line Companies to investigate the whole question of apprenticeship training and to formulate some common system and plan', and could he have a copy. In 1946 the Institution of Professional Civil Servants wrote outlining their intention to prepare 'a report on the training of apprentices in government employ' requesting copies of booklets of the scheme operated at the Works for their perusal.[19]

Even after nationalisation apprenticeships (apart from the length of tenure) remained pretty constant over the decades, but there were times when they had to modified to fit current needs, such as in periods of crisis. War work affected apprenticeships (see Chapter 6) and call-up for National Service also had an impact. The 1948 National Service Act, effective from 1 January 1949, fixed the period of National Service to eighteen months, but this was extended to two years in 1950. Normal age for call-up was 18, but some apprentices, e.g. those in engineering, were allowed the option of deferring until they had completed their apprenticeship at 21. Many were more than happy to go – 'it was an opportunity to go and see the world', several men told me. One of those who went and had a most happy time was John Charlesworth:

> I went into the Forces from 1957–59 because it was National Service. I was lucky, I played an instrument so I got in a band. I had an audition and got in RAF Fighter Command Band which was based up at Stanmore in Middlesex. I play trumpet but I played a cornet in the military band. I went all over the place, mostly it was in England but I went to Scotland too.

Pat Sullivan was also happy to join up at 18 to do his two-year National Service with the RAF. At the end he returned to the Works, his apprenticeship still not finished. He remembers the arrangement was that 'you weren't classed as a journeyman when you were twenty one, when you should have finished your apprenticeship, instead you had a year as an "improver", but you were on top money anyway'.

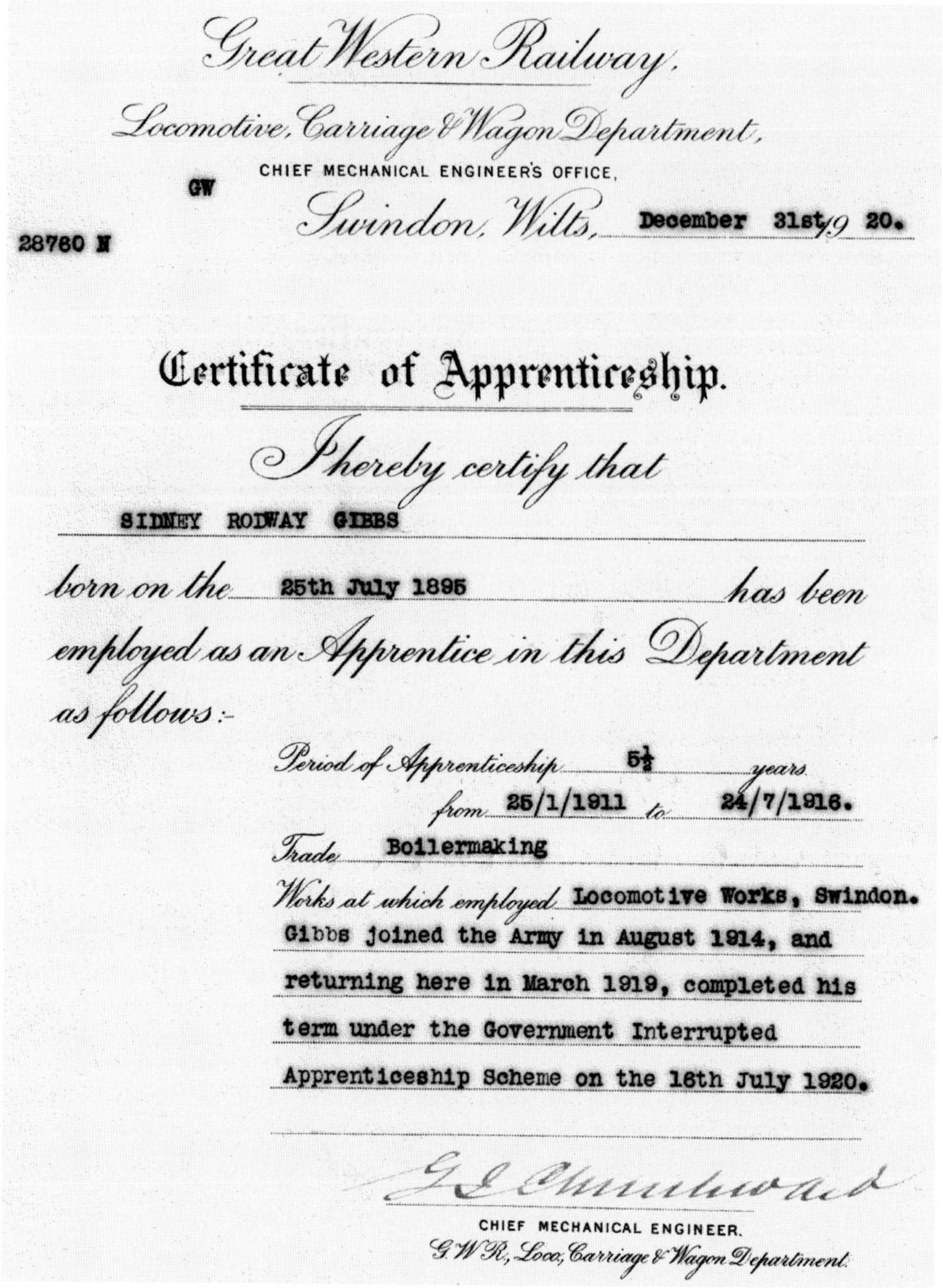

Great Western Railway.

Locomotive, Carriage & Wagon Department,

CHIEF MECHANICAL ENGINEER'S OFFICE,

GW

Swindon, Wilts, December 31st/9 20.

28760 N

Certificate of Apprenticeship.

I hereby certify that

SIDNEY RODWAY GIBBS

born on the 25th July 1895 *has been employed as an Apprentice in this Department as follows:-*

Period of Apprenticeship 5½ *years*

from 25/1/1911 *to* 24/7/1916.

Trade Boilermaking

Works at which employed Locomotive Works, Swindon.
Gibbs joined the Army in August 1914, and
returning here in March 1919, completed his
term under the Government Interrupted
Apprenticeship Scheme on the 16th July 1920.

G J Churchward

CHIEF MECHANICAL ENGINEER.
G.W.R., Loco, Carriage & Wagon Department.

It is interesting to compare the style of wording and presentation of the two certificates within the Gibbs family, separated by thirty-one years and a huge change in railway ownership. Note that Kenneth Gibbs' is issued by The Railway Executive (Western Region), and, just one year later, Tony Tucker's certificate is issued by 'British Transport Commission' (page 108), as are others thereafter.

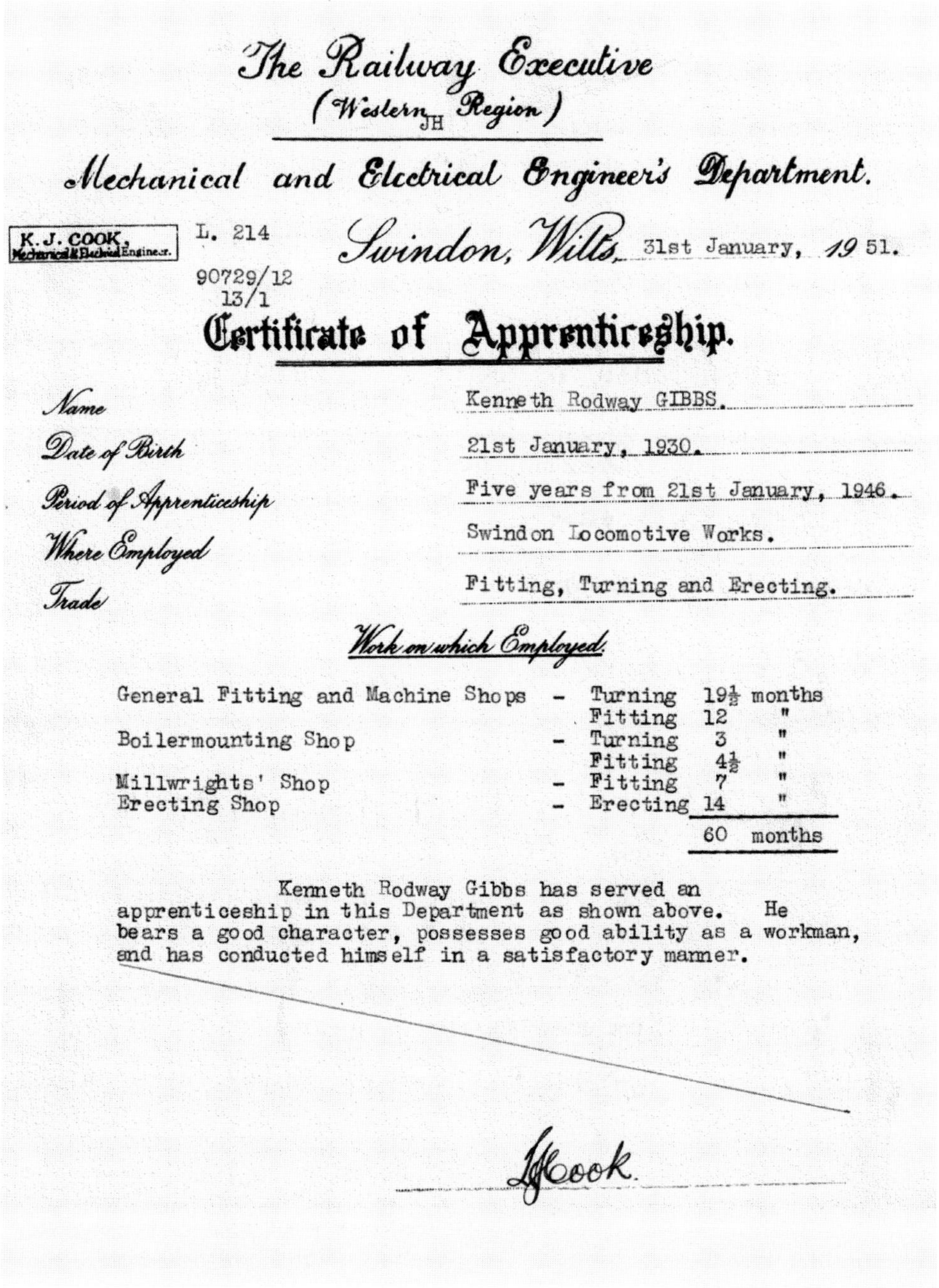

The Railway Executive
(Western Region)
JH

Mechanical and Electrical Engineer's Department.

K. J. COOK,
Mechanical & Electrical Engineer.

L. 214

90729/12
13/1

Swindon, Wilts, 31st January, *19* 51.

Certificate of Apprenticeship.

Name	Kenneth Rodway GIBBS.
Date of Birth	21st January, 1930.
Period of Apprenticeship	Five years from 21st January, 1946.
Where Employed	Swindon Locomotive Works.
Trade	Fitting, Turning and Erecting.

Work on which Employed:

General Fitting and Machine Shops	–	Turning	19½ months
		Fitting	12 "
Boilermounting Shop	–	Turning	3 "
		Fitting	4½ "
Millwrights' Shop	–	Fitting	7 "
Erecting Shop	–	Erecting	14 "
			60 months

Kenneth Rodway Gibbs has served an
apprenticeship in this Department as shown above.   He
bears a good character, possesses good ability as a workman,
and has conducted himself in a satisfactory manner.

Cook.

Some men, particularly those qualified as fitter, turner and erector, opted to do their
National Service with the Merchant Navy (even though they had to sign on for a five-year
period), where they were always welcomed because of the Works' reputation. They started as
junior engineers and on much better money than they would have had in the other services.
They would sign up at the end of their apprenticeships, but before their call-up papers arrived.
An interesting story regarding this is in respect of one Mr X, who was offered a post with
a shipping company in 1953 which he happily accepted. Unfortunately for him he hadn't
realised that he was required to 'join ship' before the completion of 'his time'. What to do? His

father went to see 'the man in the office', a Mr Aubrey Proudler, whose response was 'not a problem' and that he would provide 'the necessary papers' when required. On examining the papers, however, Mr X found that it did not mention that he had completed his apprenticeship, but rather that because he had 'left early' he was classed as 'resigned'. He then challenged Mr Proudler about this and was told that it was normal procedure and that as far as Proudler knew no one from the Works had ever been refused a job because of this 'different paperwork'. On telephoning the shipping company, Mr X was informed that this was not unusual, and that they got many prospective applicants with similar papers, as long as the 'unfinished time' 'was just a matter of weeks, it made no difference'. Having left the Merchant Navy in 1958, Mr X went on to work for several different firms in Swindon and Chippenham who, to his relief, 'all accepted the paper that I had without any query'.

On 1 January 1948, the nationalisation of the railways brought a number of changes not only to the railways of Britain but also to railway apprenticeship. The 'language' of apprenticeship had subtly changed not least in the way the agreement was worded. No longer was there talk of a master, and gone was 'Great Western Railway Company herein after called "the Company"' from the documents and agreements, now, instead, came 'British Transport Commission [BTC] herein after called "the Commission"'. One is suddenly very much aware of the state. The tone of the document is somewhat less authoritarian than previously, although if you were a new apprentice, just signing up, it would probably not appear that way as there were still the numerous terms and conditions and consequences. Close inspection of BTC's Clause 4

National Service had to be factored in to the training obligations and production needs of each shop. In this entry from the notebook of probably the shop clerk, name, date and their individual 'check' numbers are recorded.

BRITISH TRANSPORT COMMISSION

BRITISH   RAILWAYS

APPRENTICESHIP   AGREEMENT

This Agreement made the........................day of
....19..... BETWEEN ....
....
on behalf of the BRITISH TRANSPORT COMMISSION (hereinafter called
"the Commission") of 222, Marylebone Road, St. Marylebone in the County
of London of the first part, and..
.... of
....
in the County of...(hereinafter called "the Guardian")
of the second part, and...
....of ....
....in the County of.................................
(hereinafter called "the Apprentice") of the third part.

       WHEREAS—

1. The Apprentice has completed a period of probation from the
....day of...19........ to the
....day of...19........ and has
attained the age of 15 years.

2. The Commission are willing to accept the Apprentice to be taught
and instructed in the craft of...

3. The Guardian having enquired into the nature of the business
conducted by the Commission desires that the Apprentice shall learn the
craft of...in the service of the
Commission.

       Now it is hereby AGREED as follows:—

(1) The Apprentice, of his own free will and with the consent of the
Guardian, hereby binds himself as Apprentice to the Commission in the craft
of...on the conditions
hereinafter appearing.

On many levels this document represents not only the end of an era and long traditions, but also the beginning of a brave new world, with bright, new hopes and aspirations.

(a–d) shows how much the new agreement reflects the same conditions that Matthew Dickson signed up to in 1872. Ironically, overall, the 'new document for the new age' lays down almost the same conditions as the old indentures and application agreements during the 'old times'; it's just the phraseology and the 'look' of the document that differs. One notable difference is that now all apprenticeships are free – no more premiums.

A mere handful of years later and yet another 'step-change' period bursts on the scene – that of the 1960s. Having stumbled, staggered and slumbered through the 1930s, '40s and '50s, societal attitudes were then bombarded by revolution – cultural and sexual – and suffered huge shocks as outlooks and expectations shifted, aspirations soared and the old order of things (at least for the young) was turned on its head. The Industrial Training Act 1964 and the numerous industrial training boards (twenty-nine) were (or were supposed to be) part of this 'new order', bringing in sweeping and dramatic initiatives set to revolutionise training and modernise apprenticeships. The debate on 'did' or 'didn't' is fiercely argued on both sides by academics, whilst, in the main, being held in disdain by 'old hands' and quiet satisfaction by 'new entrants'. One sweeping change, however, was not enough, and it was followed with a Victorian reforming zeal by many others, until, some complained, 'apprenticeship' was no longer a recognisable entity. 'De-skilling' was the accusation levied at the new policy makers. Even more disastrously, 'apprenticeship' became 'un-cool' for both employers and employees, and with rising unemployment in the mid-1970s, why bear the cost of training when there was a ready pool of skilled labour to chose from? This changing nature of Britain's thrust in world markets from manufacturing to 'service industries' further reduced people's interest in traditional or even 'modern' apprenticeship schemes. Despite numerous Government interventions and training initiatives to 'get boys off the dole', apprenticeships in whatever guise began to disappear from view, sidelined by the more modern National Vocational Qualifications – the new cheaper, quicker, mode of training. By this time Swindon Works had closed, so no need for apprenticeships (or NVQs) of any kind.

As we can see, apprenticeship came with a lot of history and, therefore, a lot of baggage too; so what made apprenticeship of those times so desired – so required?

Notes

1 Website.
2 *Journee* is French for 'day'.
3 Washington State Dept of Labor and Histories Website.
4 Leunig.
5 Quotations from the Elizabethan Statute of Artificers, 1563.
6 Ibid.
7 Leunig.
8 STEAM cuttings 002a/1 Dr B. Carter.
9 *Journal of Social History*, Vol. 13 No. 1 (Autumn 1979), pp. 67–81.
10 Childs.
11 See detailed explanation of this in Matheson, *Railway Voices Inside Swindon Works*.
12 Minns & Wallis.
13 Smith, S.R. 'The London Apprentice as a 17th Century Adolescent', *Past & Present* 61, 1973, pp. 149–61.
14 Deakin.
15 *Steam World*, July 1992.
16 My italics in document.
17 Matheson, *Railway Voices*.
18 *Swindon Advertiser*, 23 March 1874.
19 Letters at STEAM Museum.

2

How it all Began

Today, in the twenty-first century, we tend to think of technology as a modern-day affair or at least a twentieth-century invention, but we would be wrong. Strange as it may seem, technology came long before this, probably as early as the invention of the wheel (*c.*3500 BC), possibly the most important mechanical invention ever. Interestingly, American historian and philosopher of technology and science Lewis Mumford (1895–1960) proposed that the Industrial Revolution had its origins in the early Middle Ages. He argued that the printing press had led the way for 'standardised mass production' – a central feature of the industrial movement; but mass-production skills were in use well before the Middle Ages. Findings of many Neolithic axe heads show just how skilful these people were in producing Stone Age tools to facilitate their lives in a difficult world. These were often used as barter and, therefore, had to be re-made again and again. These natural or organic-based tools gave way to an industrial use of natural materials with the discovery of copper and bronze. These materials in turn gave rise to new tools such as swords, which became commercial products, i.e. to be bought and sold, not kept for use by oneself, so were, therefore, mass production. To produce these on the scale required by military forces, e.g. an invading army such as those of the Greek or Roman empires, it was essential that such skills required in their making be continuously passed on. In the beginning this was probably from father to son, but later, as demand for the products grew, from master to brought in help, i.e. the apprentice.

Whilst 'revolution' appears to imply a sharp and abrupt interruption of the norm, or introduction of the new, the Industrial Revolution in Britain (some may say in typical British fashion) introduced itself in stages over decades. One of the seminal influences and practical inventions that made such revolution possible was Thomas Newcomen's steam engine (the outcome of years of trial and error and practical development) working as a mine pump draining the coal mines of water, making it possible to keep increasing coal production. It is, however, generally held that the beginnings of this Industrial Revolution were closely linked to a number of technological innovations brought about in the second half of the eighteenth century: Richard Arkwright's Water Frame (*c.*1769), James Hargreave's Spinning Jenny (*c.*1764) and Samuel Crompton's Spinning Mule (*c.*1779), which 'revolutionised' textile production, generating an eruption of cotton mills on the northern landscape and an extra-ordinary growth in the cotton industry and the general economy. James Watts' improvements to the stationary steam engine (taking Newcomen's as his basic, instructional model and making it a low-pressure, double action, rotary motion engine) took steam power from its birthplace, the coalfields, into factories where it was then applied to powering production machines. This greatly assisted the development and growth of manufacturing by allowing factories to be built in places where no waterpower was available – something not previously possible. Later the introduction of coke into iron founding 'revolutionised' its production by creating even more possibilities for useful 'outcomes'. Together these key technological innovations brought about a massive scale of production previously unknown and unseen in the country, which in turn gave rise to a new category of labourer also previously unknown: the factory worker.

The 'second wave' of the Industrial Revolution arrived early in the nineteenth century, along with the birth of another 'new age' – the age of the railways. With this new age came another new breed of worker, one that would create and build amazing machines to change the world. The history of engineering is one of huge excitement, being linked to radical thinking, breaking boundaries and even 'revolution' – as in revolutionising the transport systems. The railways heralded an age of experiment and philosophical enquiry leading to technological and scientific advancement. It was an exciting time for innovative men, particularly 'mechanical men'[1] willing to explore such avenues, to find the places to learn the new technology and understand the scientific thinking.

The concept of 'engineering' had been around since ancient times, but it was not until the eighteenth century that it was established as a profession, particularly in France, when civil engineering became separate from that of military engineering. Although the name James Brindley is most famously connected with canals, it was as a straightforward millwright that he had previously made his living. In this 'simple trade' he performed many jobs that would later be described as 'engineering'; from 'constructional' to 'mechanical' to 'civil engineering'.[2] It is, however, John Smeaton (1724–92) who is held as the first English civil engineer and is feted as 'the Father of Civil Engineering'. Smeaton was seen as a different calibre of engineer than Brindley, being highly educated and from an 'establishment' background. He played a major role in making engineering 'respectable', advancing it from an 'upstart trade' to a 'profession'. The role of the mechanical engineer, essential for development of the railways, had yet to emerge. Henry Maudsley, the originator of modern machine tools, and his screw-cutting lathe would lead the way in respect of tool machinery, but it is the genius Richard Trevithick, with his pioneering novel experiments using steam at high pressure to provide tractive power on the roads or on rails, who would play what L.T.C. Rolt called a 'John the Baptist' role in revealing the direction for other railway mechanical engineers to follow. Whilst it is this new emerging breed of 'artisans' that the coming of the railway is identified with, it is interesting to note that Isambard Kingdom Brunel, the man whose name is inextricably linked with the GWR, was in fact a civil engineer by trade and a mechanical engineer (albeit an unsuccessful one, as highlighted by his dreadfully inadequate engines) by endeavour. Still, Brunel would, I believe, have been happy to bask in the definition of a civil engineer to be found on one civil engineering website: 'the most creative inventor after God';[3] as well as his own definition: a 'melodramatic artist in iron'.[4]

Amongst all this frisson of energy and activity it became evident that there was a need to establish a common language, an agreed vocabulary of technical terms and standardised pictorial images, in order to communicate on a wider scale. What was required was a systemised division of knowledge and practice, where theories and concepts could be set to paper, allowing experimentation, analysis, developmental production and, if they didn't work, facilitate technical problem-solving. Even as late as 1869 this communicating of ideas and practices could be very hit-and-miss if not on a face-to-face basis, as illustrated in a letter sent to the *English Mechanic and Mirror of Science* in January 1869 (a medium for sharing scientific ideas). The correspondent informs the reader with regard to the working of a Gifford injector that 'getting my tobacco underway' and hearing several different kinds of 'peculiar noises' are indications of whether things are working well. Whilst there was not a widespread 'in-house language' there were also not many established, recognised pathways either, so ways had to be found and quickly as the need for a skilled workforce was desperate and ever growing. The need for a workforce that could understand and work with mechanisms – one that could then develop and enhance such mechanisms, and then pass on this knowledge – became increasingly urgent. The pot of men with these skills and knowledge was irksomely small, but the hunger to learn and live in this brave, new world became progressively more demanding. This then was the fertile ground for the beginnings of the Mechanics' Institute, which was to play a major role, for several decades, in the educational aspects of the training of early apprentices at Swindon Works, when Swindon's own Mechanics' Institute came into being.

'The Mechanics' was shorthand for the building and the Mechanics' Institute it housed. Formally opened in May 1855 (modified and enlarged in 1892 and 1930), the Mechanics was where it all happened. It had lecture and reading rooms, a dining hall, bathing facilities and, initially, an adjoining market. It was the physical focus and heart of the railway town.

Daniel Gooch was a man much taken with the good works of the Mechanics' Institutes, and wrote in his diary of his time at the Dundee foundry in 1835: 'There was a very good Mechanics Institution here, of which I was a member and attended the lectures regularly. The library was also a good one for such purposes.'

This experience would later bear fruit for the mechanics of Swindon Works when Gooch supported the setting up of its own institute and a library; albeit with the money from fines imposed upon the men. Trevor Cockbill, who was in his lifetime the local Swindon Mechanics' Institute 'expert', maintains that Swindon's Institute was 'unique amongst Mechanics' Institutions'. This was not least because whilst others became mediums of 'fashion', hosting 'popular and ever-more eccentric lectures', it came to be: 'The place where the respectable and socially aspiring could be, *and needed to be*, seen.' Swindon's Institute grew in size, presence and stature, stamping its mark on the educational and cultural development of New Swindon's inhabitants, until, finally, it helped lay the foundations and beginning of Swindon's new technical college and training, some four decades later[5].

The original route to becoming a mechanical engineer, or mechanician, had been by way of 'the art of intuition and experimentation'. Not all who led the way were educated men (look at George Stephenson) but they were men prepared to think outside the box and apply logic and practical application to intuitive thinking, and 'give it a go'. Men such as Newcomen, Watts, Trevithick, now famous and iconic, would, in their early days, have definitely been considered eccentrics, as the introduction in Robert Scott Burns' book *Mechanics and Mechanism: Elementary Essay and Examples* (*c*.1850) shows. He explains how:

An official photograph of the main Reading Room in the 1893 extension. From just a handful of members and a few books at its beginning in September 1843, the Mechanics' library grew at an astonishing rate, such was the thirst for knowledge and self-improvement.

A work, like the present, treating exclusively on 'Mechanics and Mechanism,' ... would, at a period not very far remote in our social history, have been looked upon as an innovation and considered to be, upon the whole, as useless as it appeared strange and uncalled for. And this view, singular as it may now appear, would have been founded upon a comparatively correct estimate of the importance of the subject. Mechanism then occupied but a very subordinate position in the ranks of our social powers, and mechanicians were as few in numbers and unimportant in influence as were their works and labours. Now, however, the position of affairs is singularly changed ... 'Mechanicians' and mechanisms, the emanations of their genius ... occupy an important position in our social and commercial system. It is now scarcely, if at all an exaggeration to affirm that, to the improvements recently affected in various branches of the mechanical arts we owe our present position as a Nation.

Britain, as a nation, had now entered what Carlyle called 'the age of the machine' and Burns was, as can be assumed from the manner of his writing and the subjects of his books, like many Victorians, obviously fascinated with them. He was also aware of the potential (and commercial benefits) of their development, and by the fourth edition of his book the emphasis has subtly changed to focusing on what he calls 'the rising generation'. He informs his reader that:

Nothing to the accomplished mechanician comes amiss, constructing the simple mechanism which effects a single purpose with ease, he as freely masters that which is imitative of operations, which, apparently, nothing less that human skill could execute or human brains dictate ... Seeing then the important part played in all our social movements by the mechanic, using the term in its widest acceptance, we think that it is scarcely necessary to dilate as to

J.C. Bourne, iconic lithograph of the engine house at Swindon in 1846. A 'Firefly' class locomotive stands on the traverser receiving attention from 'the mechanicals' or 'mechanicians'.

the expediency of imparting knowledge of the elements of mechanics and mechanism to the rising generation.

The world of engineering was gathering momentum so that it 'grew to embrace all appliances designed to ease and accelerate performance of the tasks involved in mining, manufacture and transport'. The civil engineers had established themselves with canals and bridges, but 'with the development of the railways, the mechanics came into their kingdom',[6] and in 1847 they established their own professional body, the Institution of Mechanical Engineers. It was to be some time before they were followed by others. Later came the Society of Telegraph Engineer (formed in 1871) and, with the arrival of that awesome yet barely understandable scientific discovery – electricity – came the need for yet another branch of engineering. Alessandro Volta (from whom we get the words 'volt' and 'voltage'), Michael Faraday (electromagnetism) and, of course, Thomas Edison are names we know linked to this amazing world. In 1887 the telegraph engineers and electrical engineers joined to become the Institution of Electrical Engineers. These two new types of engineers – mechanical and electrical – would have a particular resonance for Swindon Works when, in 1950, K.J. Cook became the first mechanical and electrical engineer of the Locomotive Works; and eventually in 1956 the 'man at the top' Robert Alfred Smeddle was given the accolade 'Chief Mechanical and Electrical Engineer'.

Yet even with the coming of all these engineers there was still a gap in the market, and with the growing influence and presence of the railways there grew a need for a specialised locomotive engineer. Harold Holcroft wrote in his paper, 'History of the Locomotive Engineer', that:

Until the early 'nineties' of the last century [nineteenth] there was a very limited means of circulating information on locomotives, or rolling stock or on railway in general other than an occasional Paper read at the Institution of Mechanical Engineers, or even more rarely at the Institution of Civil Engineers ... Text books and works of reference were few and a copy of Pettigrew's 'Locomotive Engineering' was considered indispensable to a young man entering on a railway career.

The Institution of Locomotive Engineers was founded in 1911 for: 'Dissemination of information concerning Locomotive Engineering and its allied sciences by the reading, discussion and publication of papers.' Eventually they integrated with the Institute of Mechanical Engineers (1969) as their railway division. Interestingly, Robert Smeddle's obituary was printed in the *Journal of the Institution of Locomotive Engineers* upon his death in 1964.

Such was the long and formative history that came to influence and shape apprenticeship and training in the railway world, and in particular Swindon Works. When Swindon Works fully opened its doors for business as a locomotive repairing shop on 2 January 1843 it was on a greenfield site, seemingly in the middle of nowhere in Wiltshire, yet it was a factory at the cutting edge of the new technology; it was a place that inspired great excitement and interest amongst mechanically and scientifically minded men, and particularly engineers; it was a place that drew such men from all over the country. By 1843 the Works employed 423 men, of which it is purported that seventy-two were 'highly skilled engineers' – a fact that any company, especially a railway company, would be proud to boast of. A document held in the PRO known as the Fawcett List[7] identifies the 'categories' of these first railwaymen, and from this we can surmise the breakdown of these 'engineers' (most likely those in bold):

Foremen	6
Clerks (Time Office and Stores)	14
Enginemen	48
Firemen	50
Stationary Enginemen	3
Cleaners, Coke men, Labourers etc	65
Fitters & Erectors	**55**
Turners	**10**
Men at Machines	**7**
Contractors	60
Carpenters and plumbers	6
Coppersmiths	2
Brass Foundryman	1
Blacksmiths	14
Springmakers	2
Strikers	14
Boilermakers & Wheelmakers	4
Painters	2
General Labourers	25
Boys	35

The pool of industrial skills needed in its workshops could not have been supplied from within its agricultural vicinity, but had to be imported from those areas that had previously developed and used steam machines, e.g. the coal mining industry. An examination of where the first inhabitants of New Swindon migrated from supports this fact. Cattel and Falkner, in their excellent book *Swindon: The Legacy of a Railway Town*, identify twenty-two different birthplaces outside of Wiltshire, plus a non-specific 'other' category; whilst the 1851 census returns for Taunton Street alone identifies migrants from Scotland, Cumberland, Durham and

Robert Alfred Smeddle was the one and only
man to hold the exalted title of 'Chief Mechanical
and Electrical Engineer', although not just of
Swindon but of British Rail's western region
(1956–62), and, as such, he was based at
Swindon Works.

Northumberland. Interestingly, the returns of Oxford Street of this year shows that of the
occupants of the twenty-one houses, only one, a Robert Berry, smith's labourer, aged 37 years,
hails from Swindon. These were the men brought in for their knowledge and skills – men who
would be required to pass on those skills to the next generation. This then was the beginning of
a tradition of apprenticeship that was to last over 150 years, and a factory that would produce
men with worldwide reputations that placed them amongst the elite in the hierarchy of labour,
not just in the railway world but in all aspects of crafts and engineering. What was held as
certain for a Swindon Works' apprentice was, at the completion of his apprenticeship, the
end product would be a skilled tradesman or engineer, who believed and held himself to be
amongst the aristocracy of railway workers.[8]

Notes

1   This was the description used by the *Mechanics' Magazine*, October 1829, to describe those who
    would be attracted to the Grand Mechanical Competition Rail-Road Race now more commonly
    talked of as the Rainhill Trials.
2   Rolt, *The Mechanicals*, p.4.
3   Civil Engineering Portal website.
4   Website ud.edu/engineers/epi17.
5   Cockbill, *This is Our Heritage*.
6   Simmons, 1995.
7   As cited in Peck's book.
8   Matheson, PhD thesis.

3

Boys

Undoubtedly this is a male orientated book and this chapter could have been called 'Boys Only' or, as in the community Welsh choir, 'Only Boys Allowed'. Although women, i.e. young girls, were in the Works in the Sewing and Trimming Shop from 1874 (see *The Fair Sex: Women and The Great Western Railway*) doing skilled artisan's work such as 'French polishing', they certainly do not figure in the GWR or the BR Works' apprenticeship story.

The only other times women have had a significant appearance in the workshops in the Works was during the war periods, but, once again, 'apprenticeship' was not part of the vocabulary used in connection with their employment. If one looks at the bigger picture of these critical times there are several obvious reasons for this. Firstly, the country was at war and all its resources and energies were focused on defending its people and territory; its thoughts were on immediacy and not long term. Secondly, there was no female apprenticeship structure for the women to step into as there was for the boys, and there was not the time, money or, it has to be said, inclination by 'the powers that be' to set it up. Thirdly, women's employment in the workshops at this time was thought of as short term, i.e. for the duration of the war, and nobody thought that would be for long, especially the first time around. Lastly, and perhaps most importantly, was the fact that the unions and the men did not want women 'skilled up' to take over men's jobs, and the employers and Government concurred – the currency of skill was not to be made available to women, no matter how dire the country's need for them. As one woman, who worked for the LMS during the Second World War, said to me: 'Years later my son went into the same Works where I had been. He worked in the same workshops, on the same machines, for almost the same amount of time, but he came out a qualified tradesman and I came out the same as I went in.' The debate on 'skill' is a fascinating one. What is 'skill'? Who defines it? What is its value? Who should have it? All such questions have taxed academics and historians for a goodly number of years, but here is not the place for that debate.[1] Even after the wars, when women had proven their abilities – physically and mentally – in performing men's jobs, both skilled and unskilled, the intention was to 'get them back into their rightful place', i.e. in the home or doing 'women's work'. This claiming of 'the workplace' as male territory and masculine property carried serious consequences and implications for women, not only in terms of lost work opportunities and wages, but also in terms of worker culture and identity. Such ownership translated into the thinking behind training and apprenticeship, making the discourse of this book that of apprenticeship and *boys*.

Boys were employed in the Works right from the beginning. The Fawcett list (1843) cites thirty-five boys, which was 8.27 per cent of the workforce at that time, a ratio of 1 in 12. They outnumbered all but the enginemen (forty-eight), firemen (fifty), fitters and erectors (fifty-five) and contractors (sixty). Initially the boys employed 'Inside' Swindon Works would have been the sons of the contractors and skilled workmen who specifically came to New Swindon to work in the new workshops, as well as some local lads who had abandoned agriculture in the hope of better wages and job prospects. In actuality there was little else for them to do as New Swindon offered few other possibilities, apart from that of shop keeping of one sort or another.

We definitely know that boys as young as 12 were employed in the Works. Catell and Faulkner cite 12-year-old messenger boy Thomas Keefe of Bath Street, and the Dyer family history has it that Richard Llewellyn Dyer, who lived at 122 Exeter Street with his widower father William, a labourer in the Works, started in the Works in 1851, aged 12. He was apprenticed to boiler-making, or 'The Art of plating and riveting', as expressed on his indentures, in 1854. A record of a fatal accident of one lad who probably started when even a little younger also verifies such. In 1862 William Morris wrote in the local press:

> The fearful death of a lad named Leech occurred in the Swindon Railway Works, in consequence of his entanglement in the driving straps connecting some powerful machinery. This lad, *although but twelve years of age, had for sometime* been engaged in the good work of earning his own livelihood by honest labour. He was a good lad and a great favourite with the men in the shop on which he worked.[2]

Census records for 1871 also confirm this. It shows that William Watts (aged 42), who was a 'Guard GWR' had two sons, William (14), described as a 'Railway Clerk', and Frederick (12), identified as an 'office boy'. Frederick was not alone as the census also identifies George Jeffries (12), working as a 'Laborer' whose father Charles (39) was a 'Gas Man', brother John (17), an

This photograph of the men of the Rail (Rolling) Mills was taken at the turn of the century a few years before the First World War. It could have been taken by William Hooper who was active with his camera in the Works at this time and was a neighbour to the Dawes family, to whom the photograph belongs. The young lads in front could have been as young as ten! They certainly look of 'tender' years, yet they have a stoic stance.

apprentice boilermaker, and brother Daniel (14) a 'Laborer' too. Even more surprisingly in the 1861 Census is it recorded that one Benjamin Holmes, an 'Iron Factory Laborer', who resided at Westcott Place, also had his two sons working with him as 'Iron Factory Laborers', Joseph (aged 15) and John, just 10 years old. Whilst one must bear in mind that there were by this time other foundries situated in Old Swindon, such as William Affleck's Prospect Works, I believe that the 'Iron Factory' refers to the iron foundry within the engine manufactory (a term also used in the same census). At other times the Works is referred to as the 'Locomotive Factories' as in Astills' *Swindon Local Guide* (1878). The 'Iron Factory' could possibly refer to the rail mills which had been erected in 1860, but the workers here were Welshmen brought up from the valleys by Mr Thomas Ellis, who is believed to have constructed and then managed the mills; whereas Mr Holmes came originally from Leeds and the boys were born in Swindon, which means Mr Holmes was a very early migrant worker to the new railway town. The Welsh émigrés would have then been living communally in the so-called 'barracks', Brunel's model hostel, originally built for single men. Only later did they move into Cambrai Place, in the cottages which were erected by Mr Ellis' new building company. Also, it must be borne in mind that at this time it was the practice for the foremen to hire and fire, and so management would have had little interest in the employment of boys – not until the raft of education and factory acts began to hit them. These were not the only young lads around to be already apprenticed at the age of 10 or 11. Records show that Richard Botely (10) of 9 Eastcott Hill was an apprentice cordwainer, whilst Henry Baker at No. 12, and Henry Vickery and George Allen, residing at No. 20 Eastcott Hill, were all aged 11 years and were bootmakers' and shoemakers' apprentices. Both censuses show a number of boys aged 13 years at the Works employed in various capacities from 'office boy' to 'laborer' or merely 'boy at Works'.

Employment at such an age was not uncommon; indeed, it would have been the expectation. Children of even younger years had been employed in the Worcestershire needle trade a good deal earlier. Olive Jocelyn writes how 'children were apprenticed at seven years old, according to Rev'd Treadwell Nash, [who wrote about Worcestershire] around 1799, thirty years before machinery had begun to change the conditions of work in the trade'. Young children were also notable by their numbers in the textile mills from the beginning of industrialisation. The Health and Morals of Apprentices Act 1802 – the first of many acts that some now regard as heralding a new age and new thinking in respect of the rights of children – applied to those very young children who were already working in the mills. Jocelyn also cites that even as late as 1864 boys of 8 years old were employed in the metal trades, blast furnaces, mills and forges, where conditions of work showed no improvement upon those of 1842. The 1802 Act had prohibited the apprenticeship of any child less than 9 years old in the mills and limited their working day to twelve hours and no night work. Not until the 1867 Factory Act were other workplaces engaged in manufacture brought under the factory acts, and then only if they employed more than fifty persons. Those workshops with less than fifty persons were not allowed to employ children under 8 years old, whilst children aged 8 to 13 were restricted to 'half-time' working. Michael Childs claims that 'half-timers' 'were largely defined by geography … being mainly confined to the textiles areas', and certainly I have found no reference to them anywhere, whether official records or anecdotal legend, in respect of the GWR. 'Young persons' under this act were restricted to a twelve-hour day. Not until the Factories Act of 1874 was the minimum age of employment *raised* to 9 years and the working week reduced to fifty-six and a half hours; however, children employed in workshops and non-textile factories could still be as young as 8. Sir Francis Head, author of *Stokers and Pokers*, makes mention of a 'fine little boy' reclaiming material, with the help of a magnet, from shavings and the sweepings in the iron foundry of the London and North Western Railway *c*.1849; such a description suggests a rather young lad.

How barbaric it all sounds now, yet 'childhood' as we know it is a relatively modern concept. Interpreted in this context of the period it is apparent that society, in general, viewed working-class children not as children but rather a rich source of cheap labour. Indeed, many Victorians

B2 Shop built by Brunel in 1842 must have seemed an awesome place to a young lad even at the turn of the century (when this photograph was taken by William Hooper). The young lad on the left also seems overwhelmed by the fact that he is having his photograph taken. *Paul Williams' Hooper Collection*

also thought that 'working' and 'earning one's keep' was the best training for children, especially working-class children. It is a harsh fact that the lives of children of these times (eighteenth to mid-nineteenth century), not of the landed gentry, the professional or the bourgeoisie classes, or of the higher skilled trades, was very hard. Child labour was a fact of life at the time the Works opened, whether it was down the mines, in the collieries, in the factories, in the boot, bottle and rag trades, selling matches on the street or being sent up chimneys as sweeps, even on England's green and fertile fields. In these and many other ways children were employed at very tender ages, and their condition was spiralling downwards until the arrival of a few zealously reforming Victorians and being 'rescued by the school', as E.J. Thompson so eruditely puts it. Child workers were seen as essential by factory owners for the continued profitable development not only of their personal investments but also that of industrial Britain. Child wages allowed exports to be cheap. We must also admit to the fact that, because of their dire situations, most working-class families also saw their children's employment as essential; indeed, it would have been imperative for the children to be useful and 'earn their keep' as soon as possible to help the family to survive. Even on the railways, and even with skilled craftsmen, a child's employment could make all the difference and become essential, as Drummond highlights:

When wage-levels detailed in the LNWR's Crewe Works employee registers during the period 1871–74 are compared with Seebohm Rowntree's indices for estimating 'primary poverty', price inflation being factored into the calculations, it can be seen that even families of those employed there could fall into poverty once their children arrived.[3] For labourers, blacksmiths' strikers and machinists this happened with the arrival of their first child; clerks after two and even the fitters, the most highly skilled craftsmen of the Works, once they had more than three children.[4]

Education, on the other hand, was not thought of as essential, especially when one had to pay for the privilege. Many, if not most, families, especially large families – which the majority then were – could ill afford schooling so a great many children received none at all and large numbers of the population, children and adults, were unable to read or write. Added to this was that up to this time education was thought of as a privilege, and for the privileged few. Even daughters of the privileged received limited education. It was held that education could lead to free thinking and it did not pay to let women or the masses think too much; it could lead to restlessness, uprising and revolution – such as in France. By such means were 'the masses', i.e. the working classes, kept in their place. It was a situation that could not persist if Britain was to maintain and improve her position as the world's leading industrialist nation. This fast-changing world of arts, science and new technology required a better educated workforce, or one that could at least read enough to follow instructions and could understand enough basic arithmetic to be able to take and make measurements. Phillip Bagwell writes in his work on the NUR that 'most [railway] companies thought it desirable to employ only literate men'. Those seeking employment on the Great Western Railway in 1837 were required to write these words: 'Zealously strive to excel. Industry is commendable. Perseverance deserves success. Quietude of mind is a treasure.'

Thanks to the enlightened view and efforts of the factory workmen and the GWR Company, the village school arrived a short time after the Works was opened, built just behind St Mark's church, seemingly in the middle of nowhere. This is a section of the Edward Snell 1849 drawing. Behind the church can be seen the school and children playing in the playground. *David Hyde Collection*

The Elementary Education Act of 1870 (also known as Forster's Education Act) sought to improve the poor situation. This act introduced the concept and became the foundation of the English system of national compulsory education. Before this date education provision could only be described as patchy, although not in New Swindon. The mechanics of Swindon Works and the GWR were more enlightened and a school for the employees' children had been completed in 1844, just a short time after the building of New Swindon had begun. Its intention was 'to sustain and improve the conduct and character and the future welfare of the Company's servants'.[5] It was a fee-paying school with a varied rate for 'juveniles' and 'infants', but those after the fourth child in the family attended free. The school would have been well attended, as a company population table for the village in January 1844 showed that there were 366 children living there, thirty-six of whom had been born in the new settlement.[6]

The 1876 Education Act made school attendance compulsory for all children up to the age of 10, increasing the pressure on the over-stretched school facilities in Swindon. By 1877 there was a desperate need for more schools in Swindon as, it was claimed, 'some 700 to 800 Swindon children were not being taught owing to lack of space' – this despite the fact the GWR Drill Hall had already been pressed into service as such. A School Board was formed and in 1880 four more schools had been made available, just in time to comply with compulsory education for all elementary children.[7]

The Education and Factory Acts gave the GWR a constant headache in respect of the employment of boys, and its circulars return again and again to this issue during the period from the late 1860s to the turn of the twentieth century. The raft of acts brought in from the late 1860s to protect young children in employment had, when acknowledged and applied, a direct practical effect on the running of the factory, as can be seen from the many memorandums sent out by the Works' managers:

Circular: 11 March 1869 Factory Act Regulations (Holidays)

Please note that no boys under 16 years of age can be allowed to work during the standard holidays specified on Notice at the gates.

Sent to all the Foremen. Signed S Carlton

These protectionist acts were not always welcome by those they sought to protect, as they would have had a huge impact on working-class families' earnings potential and whether it was bread with no butter or bread with butter (and sometimes jam). Reform, however, was the socially aware Victorians' mantra and the acts came thick and fast. Once set on the road to universal education, the Government was also intent on raising educational standards. In 1872 a revised code of regulations defining 'Six Standards of Education' in the '3 Rs' (reading, writing and arithmetic) was introduced. These regulations were very specific in their requirements, giving clear directions for levels to be attained. The 'standard' referred to in the following circular required:

STANDARD III

Reading:	A short paragraph from a more advanced reading book.
Writing:	A sentence slowly dictated once by a few words at a time, from the same book.
Arithmetic:	Long division and compound rules (money).[8]

Whilst Standard VI requires a little more:

STANDARD VI

Reading:	To read with fluency and expression.
Writing:	A short theme or letter, or an easy paraphrase.
Arithmetic:	Proportion and fractions (vulgar and decimal).

The circular also shows how these standards governed if and when a boy could leave school and start employment with the GWR:

Circular: 22 January 1879 Factory Act 1875
Attached I have a list of boys who are employed in you shop under fourteen years of age and who must not continue in this Company's service after Saturday 25th inst unless they produce by that date a certificate showing they have passed at least the 3rd Standard. The certificate must in each case be of proper form, either a school book or a Certificate of Proficiency.
Sent to Messrs: Robinson, Veness, Willis, Hogarth, Bremner, Leyser Brittain, Pamison, Morgan, Oakley, Sigh, Laxon, Stewart, Wasson, [crossed out Hall, Loe] Chivers.
Signed per E.C. Riley for S. Carlton

Whilst certificates and not age were the primary concern here, it was the age requirements that caused most vexation to the GWR in trying to comply with lawful requirements and it was not unknown for them to sometimes fall, or very nearly fall, on the wrong side.

Circular No. 569 18 May 1883
With regard to 'Employment of boys in Swindon Works'
I find that for some time past a large proportion of the boys who have been employed here have been under 13½ years of age. I shall be glad if you will give instructions for the following rule to be observed in the future:
    The usual age for the employment of boys to be 14 years, but provided they have obtained the required Labour Certificate there is no objection to their commencing work a few months before their 14th birthday. No boy should however be taken on younger than 13 years 6 months, unless in a special case which you think is desirable that an exception should be made.

Sent to S. Carlton, W. Ellis, John Armstrong, G.J. Churchward by William Dean

In March 1883 a similar circular was sent out again and then, some two years later in November 1885, Dean returns yet again, now somewhat exasperated, to this subject: it was now imperative that the situation be understood in order for the company to stay on the right side of the law.

Circular No. 669
It does not appear to be generally understood that the full time employment of any Boy under 14 years of age is prohibited by law, unless he has passed the examination of Standard 1V or some higher St, at a public elementary school in all three subjects of reading, writing & arithmetic. A boy under 14 years of age who has not been educated at a public elementary school cannot be employed unless he is first presented for examination to the Inspector of Schools for the district and awarded a Certificate of Proficiency.
    The Clerk of the Local Educational authority (i.e. a School Board in places where a School Board has been formed and in other districts the School Attendance Committee) will furnish, on application, a 'Labour Certificate' authorising the employment of any boy under 14 who is duly qualified.
    The regulations for the employment of boys under 14 in this Department are as under:
    No boy under 14 must be allowed to commence work until he has obtained a Labour Certificate from the Local Educational authority, and no boy must in any circumstances be employed who is under 13 years of age. As a general rule 13½ years should be the minimum limit for employment but in exceptional cases boys between 13 and 13½ may be taken on; but in no case should they start work until the authority of the Superintendent has been obtained.
    These regulations apply to all boys whether employed in Engine-Sheds, Factories or Offices.

I shall be glad if you will instruct all persons concerned in your district, so that these Regulations may be strictly carried out in future.

Sent to S. Carlton, Signed W. Dean. For WHS. (W Stanier)

This problematic age situation did not abate, but continued for sometime. Examination of a GWR record book entitled *Manager's Register of Wages of Factory Staff* shows that even after the turn of the century, boys under 14 were being taken on, some just meeting the 13½ statutory requirement, but, presumably, with the appropriate documentation:

Surname, Christian	Occupation	DOB	Date of entering service	Rate on entering service
Thomas, William Edwards	Time off, boy	21.5.83	9.11.96	5/- pwk
Gibbs, George Ernest	Office boy	00.3.90	5.10.03	5/- pwk
Richmond, Charles Henry	"	8.2.88	26.8.91	5/- pwk
Holder, William Henry	"	00.1.90	5.10.03	5/- pwk

Meet 'the gang'. Men of the steamhammer. Alfred Williams was Swindon's iconic 'hammerman' and young Tom Hamblin (second from right) was known to him. Tom belonged to Swindon Amateur Bicycle Club in 1907.

Swindon Works and 'the Institute' had a reputation for making music that went back to the earliest of times and continued through the decades. This rather splendid picture, posed probably outside the north entrance of the Mechanics, has two rather young gentlemen, one stood between the two bandsmen seated right, the other tucked in behind the bandmaster's right shoulder. Two other apprentice-age boys can also be seen.

Even up to the First World War, boys were still starting in the Works at barely 14. Mr A. Kibblewhite, boiler-smith, appeared in an *Evening Advertiser* feature in February 1962, aged 65. He told how he had left school aged 13 and entered the Works in 1911 'barely fourteen years old'.

In 1894 there had been a very real danger that the company would be prosecuted as they had apparently again over-stepped the line in respect of employment law and boys and they were looking for 'wriggle-room' within the definition of the acts to escape, as this communiqué of June that year highlights:

> The Chief Inspector of Factories in relation to proceedings which have been threatened against the Company in consequence of the employment by them of persons under the age of 18 years during the night in the Steam Hammer Works. & Rolling Mills of the Co., at Swindon. He explained that the Factory & Workshops Act 1878 forbids the employment of persons under this age … after the hours of 7 o'clock in the evening but makes the exception in the case of Iron Mills … and the question in the present case is whether the process carried out at the Works … brought them within the definition of 'Iron Mills' as given in the Act. [regarding] one of the processes [which] was the conversion of Scrap Steel.

One is intrigued to know the outcome of this particular instance!

Although the Fawcett List gives us information about boys, it is not specific as to what they did, so we do not know for sure if any were actually apprentices, although some of them

Opposite: This very detailed document is a rare treasure. It shows not only the actual numbers of apprentices and boys in the Locomotive Works in June 1872, but also where they worked and what they earned too. *STEAM Museum Railway Collection*

June 1892.   10.04 hrs   GREAT WESTERN RAILWAY

Statement shewing the number of Men employed at Locomotive Factory, Swindon, & their Rates of Wages.

Class	Shop	3/-	2/11	2/10	2/9	2/8	2/6	2/4	2/3	2/2	2/-	1/10	1/9	1/8	1/6	1/4	1/3	1/2	1/-	10	Total No.	Average Rate	Grand Totals	Rema
Erectors	B	7	6			6	7	4	1	3		2			2				10		48	2/0.0	136	
	C		2			2	3	1	2	1		1	5		3			1			21		70	
Fitters	D		1										1				1				3		8	
	G															1		2			3	1/6.9	14	
	N																						4	
	C		4			1	1		1	1		3		2		4					17		66	
	R		2			4	4	2		4		7				9	10				42		99	
	S					2	1										4				7		15	
Turners	D						1					2	1		1		8				13		16	
	C											2	1		2		4				4	1/2.2	5	
	N							1	2			1	2		2		4				13		19	
	Q		1	1		1			2			6			29		18				58		101	
Machinemen	D						6		9										15		15		19	
	C					1	1	3		1	2		2	1	2	1					15	1/6.1	47	
	N																						7	
	P					1			1			1			1	6	11				11		81	
Grinders	R					13		3	1	3	1	11	5	7	1	16					61	1/6.3	158	
Forgemen																							1	
Smiths	B					2	5		2	5	6		9	8	1		1	2	2		43		89	
	N							1						2					2		5		19	
	G					1		2	1			2	3	1	3	1	2				16	1/7.8	54	
	Q														1				2		2		15	
Spring Smiths	F								1							1					1		106	
Wheel & Tyre Smiths	S					1															1		23	
Carriage "	B																						1	
Strikers	B																						40	
	F																						30	
	Q																						61	
	R																						2	
Spring Strikers	F					1			4	1				3					9		9	1/9.1	12	
Copper Smiths	K																						29	
Masons		7		1		3	5		6	3	2	5		3	1	10					46		42	
Boilersmiths & Assistants	B						1	4	1						1	2	7				17	1/6.9	153	
	C					4	5	3	5	3		3	2		6	3	21				55		73	
	Q					1	1		2	1					3		3				11	1/6.1	146	
	H					1	1															2/3.0	82	
Carpenters	R					4	1		1	1		1	1	1	1	5					18		7	
Saddlers	J								1			1			2	4					8		58	
Moulders Iron	J																					1/5.4	17	
Brass																							6	
Dressers Iron Fdy.	J																						5	
" Brass Fdy	J					1	1						1				3				3	2/0.0	18	
Brass Finishers	R								1				1	3	5						5	1/11.2	6	
Gas fitters	J																						15	
Lock Smiths	J					1										1					1	2/6.0	39	
Painters	L							1								1					1	2/2.0	14	
Gasmakers																								
Laborers															1		1				1		14	
Hauliers																							37	
Erectors	B					1				2							1				1		20	
'	C																				4		12	
	D					4	3		2						1	2	10				10		14	
	F						1	1		1						2	5				5		35	
Coppersmiths	K																1				1	1/5.1	12	2/5.8
Painters	I					1											1				1		31	
Carpenters	H															1	1				1		27	
	N					2	2	2								1	7				7		56	
	Q															1	6	8			8		15	
	R											2					2				2		7	
	S					1	1					1			1		4				4		123	
	J																11				11		82	
Masons																								
General		14	16			28	42	28	29	39	39	7	29	67	13	11	74	42	151		629	1/6.6	2544	Gen. Av.

probably were. The first official document that I have found that identifies apprentices is one entitled: 'Statement showing the number of: Men employed at Locomotive Factory Swindon, & their Rate of Wages' for June 1872. There are two sub-headings: 'Mechanics etc.' and 'Apprentices and Boys'. By its nature it is a detailed document stating the class of mechanic, the shop they are in and how many men/apprentices/boys in each, at each individual rate of pay. The total number of men is given as 1,915 (including labourers). The numbers of boy labourers is 56, whilst that of apprentices is 573, making their total 629, and a grand total of 2,544.[9]

A more succinct and standardised document giving numbers and wages in which apprentices appear is the obligatory documentation that had to be made available to the Board of Trade for the years 1886 and 1891. Here 'Trade Apprentices' have a special section of their own:

Return to be submitted to the Board of Trade
Weekly Rate of Wages and Hours of Workpeople employed by Great Western Railway Company for the first complete week in October 1886 and 1891

Departments Grade & Rates of pay per week	Number employed		Normal weekly hours of labour	
Locomotive and Carriage & Wagon	1886	1891	1886	1891
Foremen & Inspectors	10	15	54 exclusive	54 exclusive
Over 70/ and up to 80/–	27	48	"	"
60/– 70/–	55	53	"	"
50/– 60/–	54	47	"	"
40/– 30/–	44	38	"	"
30/– 40/–	9 (199)	2 (213)	"	"
from 26/– 30/–				
Labourers (Mechanics)★			"	"
Men over 30/– and up to 35/–	1	3		
25/– 30/–	68	86		
20/– 25/–	479	604		
18/– 20/–	781	1,076		
14/– 18/–	2,169	3,049		
Lads over 10/– 15/–	304	350		
5/– 10/–	387 (4,189)	499 (5,667)		
Stationary Enginemen	1	10		
Over 30/– and up to 32/–	31	21		
25/– 30/–	51	61		
20/– 25/–	65 (148)	67 (159)		
7/– 20/–				
Mechanics (Metals)			54	54

Over 45/- and up to 55/-	8	9		
40/- 45/-	31	29		
35/- 40/-	255	293		
30/- 35/-	850	1,113		
25/- 30/-	665	748		
19/- 25/-	207 (2,016)	327 (2,510)	*Very rarely on a Sunday*	*Very rarely on a Sunday*
(Wood) –				
Over 35/- 38/-	37	62		
30/- 35/-	123	172		
25/- 30/-	322	583		
20/- 25/-	180 (662)	183 (1,000)		
Bricklayers Stone Masons and Slaters			54 exclusive	54 exclusive
Over 35/- and up to 36/-	2	1		
30/- 35/-	6	6		
25/- 30/-	52	63		
18/- 25/-	20 (81)	12 (82)		
Painters Polishers Plumbers & Carriage Trimmers	26	22	54 hours	54 hours
Over 30/- and up to 38/-	87	147		
25/- 30/-	88	149		
20/- 25/-	54 (25)	84 (402)		
15/- 20/-				
Machinist (Iron & Wood) and Turners			"	"
Over 25/- and up to 35/-	48	63		
20/- 25/-	152	213		
5/- 20/-	213 (413)	288 (564)		
Trade Apprentices				
Lads over 15/- and up to 21/-	266	328		
12/- 15/-	186	232		
10/- 12/-	226	238		
From 5/- 10/-	550 (1,228)	877 (1,675)		

Note: ★ *Figures and comments in italics are handwritten; all others are printed on the form.*
Also included in submission but not included in this table: engine drivers, firemen, engine cleaners; wagon shunters; carriage & wagon examiners, greasers; carriage cleaners & lampmen; female employees; paddlers & strapmakers; rollers & roughers, labourers (shed); shop clerks & storekeepers; crews of ferry steamers.

All boys wishing for employment in the factory, even those whose fathers worked there, had to meet certain employment requirements. Obviously there were those that related to their age; another, as we have seen, was being able to provide a 'Certificate of Proficiency' or the 'Labour Certificate'; yet another was producing a good 'character' (or 'reference' in modern terminology) either from the school or from one's previous employers. On leaving school, whether at 13, 14 or 15 (the school leaving age was raised to 15 in 1947), young boys at this time would have a 'fill-in' time before they started their apprenticeships. This was usually inside the Works but could also be 'outside' as an errand boy. Boys who stayed on to do Higher Certificate would go immediately into their apprenticeships.

The last employment requirement was that of having good eyesight and being in good health. 'Good health' was a flexible concept, depending on who was doing the defining. It is unsettling to see in the early record books that the reason for several boys not completing their apprenticeship was due to being 'deceased'. Examples of such recorded deaths are of 'Charles Randall, Fitter, died 1890', 'Elijah Proctor, Locksmith serving 7 years – deceased 3 December 1894' and 'George Ingram – boilermaker – serving 7 years – deceased 6 September 1896'. In one record book of apprentices a casual glance through yielded over ten recorded deaths. Although some of these deaths were likely to have been due to fatal accidents in the factory, as with young Leech and the young lad buried in St Mark's churchyard who had been blown up by a boiler, for the rest it would have been because of ill health.

Conditions in many parts of the Works, such as the Bolt Shop, known as 'the Devil's Den' – a place that filled young apprentices with dread – were deplorable and very challenging for those not constitutionally sound, even in the first half of the twentieth century. Whilst being medically sound was always a requirement: 'It is particularly requested that no application be made on behalf of any youth who is not of sound constitution and of good bodily health and strength as otherwise he would not be able to carry out satisfactorily obligations specified in this Memorandum.' (This requirement and exact wording appears on documents for the 1890s, the 1920s and 1930s, and even throughout the time of British Rail Western Region.) Despite a 'medical certificate of his suitability for employment' being required, there were still times when this appeared to be somewhat generously overlooked, especially, it would seem, if they were paying apprentices, as can be seen from Sidney Leopold Fisher Tibbles' first six-month record accompanying the request for his second premium instalment. It shows that already he has lost a great deal of time through illness. Other correspondence on his file informs that he suffered chills and influenza.

Six months ended 1928	HOURS						
28 MAY	Works open	Worked	LOST				
			Special Leave	Illness	Without Leave	Total
	1,158	663¾	26	468¼	----	494¼

We can see that but for a mere eighty-five hours, Sidney Tibbles would have lost half of the time available to work. Not a good or even adequate attendance record. Undoubtedly Sidney was physically unsuited for the harsh regime in the workshops, this despite having been considered 'fit' to start in the first place. Eventually, in November that year, Mrs Tibbles (with whom all the correspondence had been conducted, despite his father, a greengrocer in Cheltenham, signing the contract) is forced to write asking C.B. Collett to release Sidney from the apprenticeship contract on the grounds of his continuing ill health and that the nature of the work he was doing being 'not suited to him'. Tibbles signs off from his apprenticeship on 9 November 1928. After the Company returning his birth certificate to him in 1933, his mother wrote to acknowledge its receipt, informing them that her 'son died last year'.[10]

After the Factory Act 1937 all boys under 18 years of age had to be entered in the Factory Act Register kept at each factory, and all boys under the age of 16 had to be recorded as having been examined by the 'Certifying Surgeon'. The surgeon had to certify that he had 'personally examined the person named in Cols 1 and 2' and found 'such person to be fit for employment in the factory for which this register relates'. It is not surprising that such matters were getting stricter and being enforced, as Dr Paul Ryan writes of his study of apprentices in British engineering between 1925 and 1965: 'modern estimates suggest around 10% of apprentices died, even more must have experienced serious illness and disability.' That the GWR were abiding by the rules is shown by at least one entry in company record book, 'Allotment of Apprenticeships and Vacancies 1932–1943', which shows that A.L.W. Compton, son of J.R. Compton, boilermaker in L2 Shop for fourteen years, had tried to follow in his father's footsteps and applied for an apprenticeship in boiler-making but 'failed the medical exam'.[11] Boilermen were a hardy lot, and needed to be, but if one were being cynical and looking at the wider context, one might wonder and call to mind Alfred William's remarks: 'their ranks were often over crowded and when trade is slack [as was this period] the services of many are often dispensed with.' As to the extent of the 'physical examination', John 'Jack' Fleetwood sums up his, which also happened around this time: 'cough, drop your trousers, cough – I was passed' – obviously very extensive!

This medical certificate carried sparse information. A sight test was also carried out, certainly in the GWR days. One amusing tale is that both father and son, Sidney and Ken Gibbs, underwent the same eye-sight test when having their medicals – both read the same piece of text from the same tatty note. The time between the tests? Approximately thirty years!

The nature of the first boys who fetched up in the factory workshops to become apprentices is interesting to consider. In the earliest days of the Works the pool of available boys would have been confined to sons of the Works' employees. Old Swindon, situated up on the hill, made up of a few shops, taverns and markets, served the agricultural community within its surrounding area. A village blacksmith would have been the nearest trade to be relevant to a railway workshop. New Swindon, down the hill, was a purpose-built 'dormitory settlement to service the workshops'[12] of the GWR Company. As the Works grew so did the numbers employed and gradually the village and new town housed more families with sons to follow their fathers into the Works, as well as single men.

By 1900, however, Old Swindon and New Swindon had grown and become one – Swindon – and in 1901 the number employed in the Works had reached 11,500, just over a quarter of the population. The inhabitants in the town had also increased, producing young lads keen to take their chance with the GWR. Transport was now available to outlying villages and so the pool of possible apprentices had grown. Alfred Williams, who found these youngsters worthy of consideration and comment, referring to and discussing them often throughout his book (1915), highlights this fact in his description of young apprentices in the Lathe Shop:

> The boys come from all parts, from town and country alike, immediately after leaving school … They are all sorts and sizes, of many grades and walks in life. There is the country labourer's lad who formerly worked on the land amid the horses and cattle; the town labourer's lad who has been errand boy or sold newspapers on the street corner; the small shopkeeper's lad; the fitter's lad, tall and pale in clean blue overalls and the engine-driver's lad, fresh from school whose one ambition is to emulate his father and like him drive an engine. There are tall and short boys, boys fat and lean, pale and robust-looking, ragged and well kept, with sad and merry faces.

Originally, statutory apprenticeships were for a minimum period of seven years; however, later, the length of time actually served varied according to the age of the person undertaking the apprenticeship. The major factor is that the apprenticeship had to be completed by time the boy (a minor) reached the age of 21 (then the age of majority), when he would have to be paid 'a man's' rate. A study of many of the GWR Apprentices Register bears witness to this fact. Examples of apprenticeships undertaken at the Works illustrating this are:

Alfred Edward Morgan	dated 1864	aged 16 years	for 5 years to be 'an Engine fitter'.
William Reynolds	dated 1868	aged 15 years	for 6 years to be 'a Smith'.
Henry Marten Hill	dated 1872	aged 14½ years	for 6½ years in 'Coach Bodymaking'.
Matthew Dickson	dated 1872	aged 15 years	for 6 years for 'Carriage Finishing'.
Frederick J. Pottinger	dated 1881	aged 14 years	for 7 years for 'Coach Painting and Writing'.
George W. Dickson	dated 1883	aged 15 years	for 6 years to be 'an Erector'.
Wm E.F. Dickson	dated 1902	aged 14½ years	for 6½ years for 'Coach Bodymaking'.

This 'norm' was not set in stone, however, as it would also appear from other GWR records that internal pressures and external critical times could change this drastically. The records for the late 1890s show that apprenticeships started then could take the boy to way beyond attaining his majority:

Name	Present occupation	Present wage	In Service	Present age	To learn	To be bound	Date of advice from Mr Dean
Herbert, A.E.	Office boy	1/2d	May '97	15 8/12	Carpentering	7	June '99
Stinton, J.W.	Mach. boy	1/6d	Dec '96	16	Fitting & Turning	7	June '99
Poole, W.	CBM boy	1/10d	June '96	17	Coach Bdy Making	6¾	Aug 31st '99
Stanley, W.G.C.	Painters boy	1/2d	Dec '96	17	Coach Painting	6½	Aug 31st '99

These records are intriguing to decode. They show that the lads had been in the GWR's employ as 'boy' for a number of years, so why was their apprenticeship so delayed? What we do know is that there was the prolonged Great Depression between the late 1870s and the mid-1890s, which badly hit industry and commerce all around the country and created a lack of confidence in investments, especially with the railways. The GWR, like other companies, would have felt the impact of this; yet D.E.C. Eversley argues Swindon weathered the storm whilst the rest of the GWR system felt the heavy hand of layoffs.[13] During the early 1890s there had been great expansion in the Works and many extra hands had been taken on to deal with the problems of the gauge conversion and demolition of rolling stock, which had put the Works under severe strain. The heavy concentration on these activities may have meant that the usual production practices were severely disrupted or limited, so the need for new apprentices was low. This is only a suggestion but I can find no documentation that satisfactorily explains this 'blip'. Whilst extremely unusual, it was not a completely unknown phenomenon. Family legend has it that William Hooper, the famous social commentator-photographer, having moved from the countryside to Swindon with his family in 1882 when he was 18, was offered an apprenticeship as a mechanic's assistant in B shed.

Yet other GWR record books for early 1920s described another such blip. The book shows that whilst the majority of those commencing their time were of usual ages, i.e. 14–16, there were also a goodly number who were 17, 18, 19 and even one of 20, and these are all registered for five years. Here there is a much more obvious explanation as it would appear something of the knock-on effect of the First World War, which had finished barely fifteen months previously, after which there was a serious shortage of manpower and of young men too. Once again the records are intriguing and not straightforward – take that of 20-year-old Tom Bigley, born 5 July 1899, who joined the Works in October 1913. At the time of his apprenticeship registration he was working as a 'player's helper' in 13 Shop at a rate of 9/1d. Tom was registered for five years from February 1920 (when he would have been 21 years old) 'to learn wagon riveting'. His father George Bigley, who was a frame builder and had served the Company for twenty-three years was 'deceased' so obviously had not applied on his son's behalf as was usual.[14] I can find no record of Tom having served in the war (but that does not mean he didn't) so it may be only be internal reasons that delayed his apprenticeship.

What is apparent from the records is that a number of these late apprenticeships are for those whose father's jobs would not normally qualify them for a skilled apprenticeship – people such as labourers or strikers – but because of the shortages of young men and skilled men, they were offered second-class trades.

In the early days of regulated apprenticeship all indentured apprentices had to be registered with their guilds. In early GWR days, having signed up, apprentices were entered on a register with a registry (or folio) number – such as William Edwin Frederick Dickson who was registered No. 748 on 29 July 1902 in coach body-making for six and a half years. Signing up, making it through the month's probationary period and on to the register book did not,

The men and boys in this photograph outside a workshop in the carriage department (c.1900) do not conjure up the image of the high-status 'white apron' men that latterly went with carriage building and fitting. They could, of course, have been wagon builders, fitters or labourers. What is of interest here, however, are the young lads in the front row.

however, guarantee that one would make it through to the end. As we have seen from the indentures, 'misconduct' and 'failure to attend' were amongst the reasons for an apprenticeship to be withdrawn. Looking through GWR's record book shows that amongst the most common reasons for not completing one's time are: 'Discharged – convicted of stealing' or 'Discharged – losing time', such as:

    D.J. Williams   Boilersmith 6½ years   discharged losing time 21.11.92

More unusual reasons appear for entries in 1889 and the 1890s, including:

W. Case	Moulder 6½ years	Absconded 10/9/90
Wm Jefferies	Moulder 6½ years	app. cancelled – assaulting Watchman 10/8/95
A.S. Potbury	Millwright 6½ years	joined Army 5/11/91
Arthur Pearce	Fitter 6½ years	Discharged damaging Company bridge over Wotton Bassett Rd. 24/9/95
A. Hicks	Bricklaying 7 years	Absconded. 12/9/1895
J. Williams	Moulding 6½ years	Joined the Navy 27/1/1897

Another reason that recurs over the years at the more difficult economic times is that of 'Discharged – shortening hands', which meant that hands, i.e. workmen, were being laid off.

The men who worked in the Trimming Shop were skilled and respected 'white apron' craftsmen. Their skills were as necessary as a fitter's or turner's. This photograph shows a number of young lads at the workbenches – in 'white aprons' – learning their trade, one rather young-looking one centre-left.

An entry in 1905 which raises one's sympathy is that of William Hobbs. It seems hard on poor William four years into his apprenticeship to pay such a harsh price for the economic downturn. What this also shows is that William was not an indentured apprentice, because if he had been, he could not possibly have been laid off. One wonders if, when things improved and hands were taken on again, he was allowed back to re-commence and finish out his time, or if the company used the laying off as an opportunity to get rid of him because of his lack of ability or suitability.

Numbers of apprentices in the Works in the early decades are hard to ascertain. Some of the company registers record apprentices as being 'given up'. This table shows how many apprentices were 'given up', i.e. let go, over the enormously tough years of the Great Depression. As the Depression deepens, the numbers increase. Whilst it doesn't tell us how many apprentices were actually there, it gives us an indication. Also we do not know if these were usual numbers or whether more apprentices had been taken on during the Depression to replace laid-off hands, thereby increasing the numbers 'given up' at the later time. Nevertheless, they make intriguing reading:

Menial, repetitive, low-skilled jobs were the lot of the pre-apprentice lad and young apprentices alike. Chopping wood and putting them in bundles for use in the factory fires, and chopping up recycled wood for selling on to employees came within this.

Apprentices in Swindon Loco Workshops 'Given Up' 1878–1903

Year	Jan	Feb	Mar	Apr	May	Jun	Jul	Aug	Sep	Oct	Nov	Dec	Total
1878	6	6	3	1	1	3	3	6	3	4	2	3	41
1879	5	5	1	3	1	3	3	4	5	3	11	5	49
1880	6	6	4	3	7	2	1	3	3	3	8	7	53
1881	7	4	7	7	2	7	4	1	4	5	6	3	57
1882	8	7	7	2	10	7	4	2	8	14	10	8	87
1883	4	9	12	7	14	8	13	8	19	12	7	7	120
1884	10	11	13	6	5	4	6	7	11	12	8	5	98
1885	10	9	9	10	9	8	13	9	4	6	6	4	97
1886	3	11	11	6	7	9	8	8	9	8	4	3	87
1887	8	12	5	10	9	16	8	8	9	9	9	12	115
1888	7	9	11	13	12	18	16	16	10	15	13	14	154
1889	17	17	12	8	13	23	16	19	16	14	11	17	183
1890	16	18	15	15	14	14	7	12	10	10	15	11	130
1891	13	1	19	10	11	10	8	12	10	10	15	11	130
1892	7	13	14	12	11	7	3	3	2	0	1	3	76
1893	13	12	7	8	12	11	14	14	6	8	9	5	119

Young boys and older lads join 'the Works' Mad Rush' out of the main tunnel in London Street, making their way home for the dinner break (or maybe at the end of the day). Locals knew to stay out of the way so as not to be caught in the crush.

Whilst indentured apprentices had a guarantee of a job for the period of their apprenticeship and certificated apprentices had an expectation of a job for the period of theirs, as long as they did not 'blot their copy books', neither had a guaranteed job on finishing it. Rather the expectation was to have to continue the long-established tradition and 'go on the tramp' to look for work and experience elsewhere. When this happened the one good thing in their favour was that Swindon Works' reputation travelled with them, no matter how far round the world they went.

Notes

1 'Skill' is covered a little in the railway workshop context in Matheson, *Railway Voices.*
2 Matheson, *Railway Voices*; author's italics.
3 Using TNA RAIL410/1946 Crewe Works' Wages Book, 1871–74.
4 Drummond, *Victorian Childhoods.*
5 Warnes, 1985.
6 Cattel & Faulkner, p. 63.
7 Wells, *Studies in the History of Swindon* p.112–113.
8 Wikipedia.
9 Private Collection.
10 STEAM archive.
11 Ibid.
12 Drummond.
13 For further information see Matheson, *Railway Voices*, 'Insiders'.
14 STEAM archive.

4

What was a Railway Apprenticeship?

T he fundamental basis of apprenticeship was the tried and tested 'learning on the job' approach. Apprenticeship in the workshops was the first step in this process and getting one's hands dirty was an early initiation to it.

Getting Dirtied

Details of what type of apprenticeship and what was involved in early railway apprenticeships are hard to come by, however, the Institute of Mechanical Engineers holds records that give some indication of what would have happened in general. For instance, their records show that a George Reynolds of Liverpool was indentured to Robert Stephenson as an apprentice 'millwright and engine builder' in July 1832, whilst Joseph Matthew, also indentured to Robert Stephenson but in 1849, was apprenticed 'for managing a lathe, drilling machine and planing machine, erecting machinery and vice work for a period of seven years'.[1] Knowing what kind of work apprentices 'dirtied their hands' on in the early days of Swindon Works' workshops has not been straightforwardly documented or written up, but insightful information can be gleaned and assumptions made by reading around the subject in respect of first-hand personal recollections and reflections of those who worked in similar situations, as well as from those whose interest in railways drove them to make visits to and studies of these workplaces.

J.B. Snell's *Mechanical Engineering: Railways*, gives what Snell calls 'an instructive insight into workshop practices in the early railway age'. One enlightening titbit is when he tells how Sir Joseph Whitworth (1803–87), famous maker of precision machine tools and advocate of a 'Standard Decimal Measure for Mechanical Engineering Works', complained bitterly of his early career: 'What exact notion can a man have of such a size as a "bare sixteenth" or a "full thirty-second" and what inconvenient results may ensue from the different notions of different workmen as to these terms?' – such exasperation showing just how inexact standards of general manufacture were in those early times. (It is intriguing and incredibly surprising to find that even in the twentieth century such terms were still be used as instructions to the craftsmen in Swindon Works workshops.)[2] If the manufacturing of precision tools was difficult, the manufacture of locomotives, especially interpreting other people's vague ideas and designs, was also difficult and a very inexact practice, particularly when one is given instructions such as Brunel's: 'The following *are a few conditions which must be complied* with' (my italics). The rest, according to Brunel's own report to the Board of August 1838, he 'left the form of construction and the proportions entirely to the manufacturers, stipulating merely that they should submit detailed drawings to me for my approval' (this with the GWR Board's sanction),[3] thereby leaving the rest open to the 'engine maker and engine inventor's' own mechanical gut feeling and intuitive thinking. These early engines were invention-cum-ingenuity-cum-trial-by-error creations, and McDermott aptly summed up the products of such an arrangement, saying: 'It may be safely stated, without exaggeration, that in the whole history of British railways, there has never existed such an extraordinary collection of freak locomotives as those which were built for the Great Western and delivered during a period of about eighteen months from November 1837.' I find it highly amusing then to read a letter from Daniel Gooch to George Saunders of the GWR Board, in January 1839, demanding and using extreme precision. Reporting on the 'evil' of the Mather & Dixons' engines, *Ariel* and *Premier*, in respect of the valves and valve gear (which he believed were a defect in the design), he writes:

> in the first place the valves are much too large or rather there are two of them when one would do as well, causing a very great increase of friction and strain upon the gear which works it … after an engine has worked a few weeks there is a degree of straining in the levers, etc, driving them and when we set them with 5/16ths to 3/8ths of an inch lead we do not get more than half this when running. Therefore, if instead of having 3/8ths when no strain is on the gear we have 1/16th the other way (or what we call lap) how will the valve be placed when working with the full pressure on, particularly when the valves are very heavy as in this case?

When Gooch finally took responsibility for the design of GWR's locomotives, all manufacturers (or locomotive builders as they were called then) were provided with very precise instructions and information – all drawings were lithographed, specifications printed out and sheet-iron templates provided for those parts which were to be interchangeable.[4]

The reality of the situation was that in the infancy of the railways, and even in its more mature years, precision was difficult. Writing of GWR workshop practices up to the late 1920s, McDermott states:

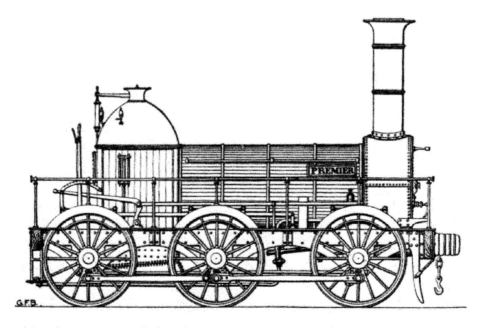

Daniel Gooch was very critical of Mather & Dixon's *Premier*, one of the early 'freaks' delivered to the GWR. It had already been withdrawn by the time the goods engine *Premier*, illustrated above, was built at Swindon in 1846. The goods engine *Premier* was the first locomotive constructed in the new workshop, but with boiler provided by an outside firm, probably Robert Stephenson's company.

It goes without saying that frames should be truly 'square' and that the centre lines of the cylinders should be exactly parallel to them. In engineering construction however, the terms 'square' and 'parallel' can be relative, and practical tolerances have to be laid down, permitting slight deviations from the mathematically precise values.

Little wonder then that infancy practices relied so heavily on the skill and judgement of the craftsmen. Sir George Bruce, speaking in 1887 as the President of the Institute of Civil Engineers, recalled when he was apprenticed to railwayman extraordinaire, Robert Stephenson, in 1837:

> In 1837 there were no small planing or shaping machine; there was only one slotting machine, the use of which was very, very restricted. Wheels were driven onto their axles by sledge hammers, wielded by strong arms alone. Steam hammers were, of course, unknown, and only hand labour was available for the ordinary work of a smith's shop and boiler yard, with the exception of the punching and shearing machinery. Riveting by machinery was unknown. It is scarcely credible but it is a fact that there was not a single crane in Robert Stephenson's shop in 1837. There were sheer-legs in the yard by which a boiler could be lifted in the shop, by the skilled manipulation of which, at no little risk to life and limb, wonders were done in the way of transmitting heavy loads from one part of the shop to another.

Summing up the early railway workshop of the 1830s and 1840s, Snell informs us that apart from hand tools the only machines one would find would be:

> the lathe (which produced accurate round surfaces, even complicated ones, including male screw threads), the planing machine (which produced accurate flat surface), the boring machine (which can be regarded as a specialised lathe producing a concave curved surface and which was soon modified so that it was a cutting tool which moved, and not the workpieces) small drilling machines and the slotting machine.

The situation in Swindon Works, a brand new factory, can be ascertained by artistic depictions of the new workshops. One of the earliest of these was by the artist John Cooke Bourne. Bourne's lithograph of the Engine House (c.1846) gives us some idea of what the inside of this magnificent shed looked like. A series of depictions, purportedly drawn by one of the employees, show men in various trades at work on a variety of machines. These illustrations appeared in *The Illustrated Exhibitor* in 1852; they show that such machines had been incorporated into the workshops, including Nasymth's majestic controlled steamhammer. Gooch liked to make use of modern technology and use the new machinery of the day, state Crittall et al.:

> The minute books reveal a growing complexity of machinery, and the frequent addition of new shops to house these or the rolling stock. Gooch knew the leading engineers of his day and liked to install the latest developments at Swindon. Thus, in 1842, he was in touch with James Nasmyth of Patricroft (Lancs.) who supplied steam-hammers. These are shown in a shop on the north side of the works in the plan of 1846. D. Napier of Lambeth supplied hydraulic presses and an overhead crane for 'C' shed in 1844 which was still at work in 1911.

Strangely, perhaps even surprisingly, in view of the speed of changes brought about in the design of engines and carriages over these years, over fifty years later when Harold Holcroft was doing his apprenticeship at GWR's Stafford Road, Wolverhampton, in the late 1890s, it would appear that very little had changed in terms of working practice. He recalls that:

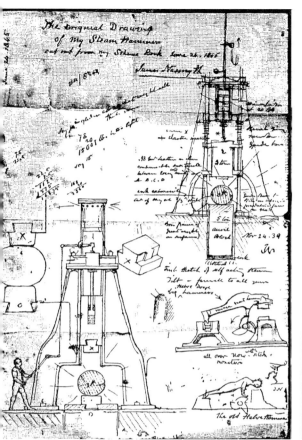

Scottish born James Hall Nasmyth (1808–90) was an engineer and inventor. Seen here demonstrating his steam power-assisted hammer at Patricroft foundry, Nasmyth went on to create other important machine tools such as 'the shaper' machine. *Ken Gibbs Collection*

There being no pneumatic or electric appliances, everything was done by hand. Copper stays had to be drilled out at each end by ratchet braces and drills. Rivet heads were knocked off by means of a sledgehammer and chisel held by a hazel wand. Tubes were expanded by rotating the expanders with ratchet levers. After stay holes had been re-tapped to a larger size, copper stays were run in with a cranked driver and then the heads were riveted over by three men, a holder-up and two others raining light blows alternately, the head was completed by snap and heavy hammer. Rivets in the foundation ring were driven out by sledgehammer and punch after the head had been cut off.

This contrasts with the experience of A.H. Malan who took 'A Look Round Swindon Works' in 1891 and wrote of the experience in the *English Illustrated Magazine*.[5] Malan was very taken with the amount and modernity of the machinery he saw in each department, particularly their aspects of 'duplication of work', i.e. cutting through a 'pile of frame-plates … thereby producing plates absolutely identical'. He enthused about machines with 'multiple drills [that] bore all the holes needed' and 'large saws fastened side by side so as to be actuated simultaneously'. Obviously Swindon Works, being the 'premier' workshop, was way ahead in technology. A memorandum dated 21 January 1890 makes interesting reading as it further highlights the situation regarding the exact machinery in the workshops at this time:

Machinery for Swindon Works
Authority is required for the purchase of the following
Machinery for Swindon Works:-

Wagon Works	Estimated Cost £
1 1 Milling Machine	300
2 2 Double Radial Drilling Machines	520
3 1 Duplex Hydraulic Wheel Press	500
4 1 Machine for drawing off spring buckles	260
5 3 Hydraulic Riveters	400
6 1 Flattening & Straightening Machine	220
	2,200
Carriage Works	
7 1 Radial Drilling Machine	160
8 2 Emery Tool Grinders	120
9 1 Slotting Machine	150
10 1 Punching & Shearing Machine	160
11 1 Screwing Machine	100
12 1 Planing Machine	130
13 1 Shaping Machine	160
	1,000
	£3.200

The boiler house as depicted (purportedly) by one of the Works' employees and produced in the *The Illustrated Exhibitor* (1852) was one place where rivets were definitely needed. The young lad at the front (a rivet-hotter) tends his brazier which had to be maintained at a certain heat, this was done by using bellows and careful feeding of extra coke.

Rivet-hotting is mainly thought of in connection with the Loco Department, but there was also a call for it on the C&W side, in the wagon shop, as can be seen in this picture with two young lads busy at work.

It was not, however, these marvellous machines that the new loco-side apprentices would start on, but on the most basic of jobs – 'rivet-hotting'. This was one of the earliest and most long-standing jobs that young lads were put to – even before their apprenticeship began. It was one of the dirtiest, messiest, most unpleasant jobs they would do and would certainly make sure that they got their hands dirtied. If we look at those early depictions of the Works, namely that of the boiler house, we can see front left what looks like a young lad working over his brazier fire, probably rivet-hotting – rivets were an essential ingredient in the make up of boilers as can be seen from looking behind him.

Alfred William describes this 'character' at his time during the early 1900s:

A feature of the frame shed is the rivet boy. It is his duty to hot the rivets in the forge for his mate and to perform sundry other small offices such as fetching water from the tap in the shed, or holding a nail bag in front of the rivet which is being cut away, in order to keep it from flying and causing any injury to the workmen. The forges for hotting the rivets are fixtures [no longer the braziers] and are supplied with air through pipes beneath the ground from the fan under the wall. Several boys usually work from one fire, and there often is a scramble for the most advantageous position on the coals. An iron plate is used to facilitate the heating. This has been perforated with holes at the punch to allow its receiving as many rivets as are required. It is then placed over the whitehot coke in the forge and the rivets inserted. Each boy has a certain number of holes allotted to him and he must not trespass on his mates.

Yet another dirty introductory job was that of nut-scragging in the scraggery (part of R Shop); it was an introduction to machining metal. It was dirty, boring and repetitive – a job all the boys hated. Roy Henry Taylor went in the factory in May 1938. He recalls:

I went in on tapping nuts and screwing bolts in the scraggery. It was very repetitive work, you had to do hundreds a day. Had to do a binful which was weighed, that's how you got paid, by the weight. It was queer because I was told to come in clean clothes and then I got put into the scraggery where it was filthy.

Those bound for 'white-apron' jobs (i.e. woodworkers or 'the sandpaper kids', as apprentices here were known, because whether working or not it was always good to have a piece of sandpaper in hand to make it look like you were working) would start on something different. John Attwell, recalling his start on the carriage side (and the sandpapering) in the 1940s, remembers:

> There were 26 shops in the Carriage side … and I worked in No. 7 shop – coach finishing. There were about 100 workers in the shop, skilled finishers and upholsters, with a few labourers for carrying materials. There were four apprentices in the shop. The body shop built wooden teak frames for the coaches and then they would be brought into our shop where we would produce and fit all the interior woodwork. At any one time there would be 12 coaches in the shop.
>
> Apprentices always started on No. 1 gang, which was a light job based in a siding outside the shop where we had to refurbish drop light windows. This meant removing the drop lights and the mouldings, which would be repaired inside, and then re-glazing the windows prior to fitting them back in the coach. When we were working on the drop lights we would spend a whole day just sand papering – and then often the chargehand would make us do them all again. Time was not a problem – the question was quality. After three months we were moved to a gang that undertook more complex work. The work got a little more complex with each move.

The tradition of what had become the 'process' of apprenticeship in the Works was a matter of 'those in the know' knowing what you needed to know and where they needed you to be for production purposes. William Bullock writes that during his process in the 1930s he was 'passed on from shop to shop, from foreman to foreman, from chargehand to chargehand, to fitter to machinist, the poor apprentice was always the general dogsbody'. Graham Attwel summarises the process that his father and others with him experienced during the 1940s:

> 'The Works had at that time a quite astonishing intake of apprentices' and with such a large 'apprentice labour force, training had to be related to an actual usable something, produced for use in an existing system'.
>
> There was no written curriculum or even a list of skills or tasks that had to be learnt. There were no written plans or procedures – learning was from the practice of doing the work. Whilst there was no curriculum framework, tasks were graded and progressive, both through an ordering of progression and movement from one gang to another, and through a progression from simple (and often repetitive) tasks to gradually more complex work. Apprentices were moved around between the gangs, usually spending about three months with a particular gang before the foreman would move them on.

Six months Ending	Shop	No	Total Hours Worked	Hours Works Open	Hours Lost				Work on which Employed	Report on Ability	Report on Character	Report on Attention to Duty
					Special Leave	Illness	Without eave	Total				
July 19 1919	W.G.+C.O.		894	1080½	—	—	—	18½	V.g.d. Turning	V. good.	V. good.	V. good.
Jan 17 1920	H.I. K.J.		752	887½	—	—	.	135½	Pattern making Smithing Erg. Fitd. Welding	good	good	good.
July 14 1921	U.O.A.C. AE.G.		895	1162	—	—	—	204	Erecting Hydraulics	"	"	"
Jan 15	F. V.A.		443½	1004	—	—	—	260½	Smithing Boiler Mtg	"	"	"
July 16	Test Ho Rug Sh		414	1156½	.			139½	Shunting Driving	"	"	"

Bullock W.O.B.

1932												
May 7	R	1504	825¼	1071½	3¾	242½	.	246¼	Turning	good	good	good
Nov 5	R	1504	820½	1033	36	176½	.	212½	"	"	"	"
1933 May 6	R.	1504							"	"	"	"
	am	99							"	"	"	"
	R.	1712	997	1067	10½	59½	. .	70	"	"	"	"
Nov 4	R.	1712	.						"	"	"	"
1934 May 5	G	3315	861	1033	95½	72	4½	172	"	"	"	"
	G								"	"	"	"
	R	1614	856¾	1071	9	205½	.	214¼	Fitting	"	"	"
Nov 3	R	1614							"	"	"	"
1935 May 4	am	208	929½	1033	52½	51	.	103½	"	"	"	"
	AM	208	898¾	1071½	45¼	127½	.	173¾	"	.	.	.
Nov 2 1935	G. G O	3432 3432 3055	1062½	1123	56	—	4½	60½	breaking	"	"	"
1936 May 2	BL AL AL O	1128 1128 0698 0698 2055	1042¼ 753	1179½ 871¼	67¼ .	47 .	— . .	114¼ 118¼	Fitting	"	"	"
Sept 19										.	.	.

Each apprentice had a 'Work Record', which followed him from shop to shop. This is the 'Apprentice Training Record' of premium apprentice William Bullock. Note the comments regarding 'Ability', 'Character' and 'Attention to Duty'! *David Hyde Collection*

Every apprentice had an 'Apprentices Training Record' card which travelled with him from shop to shop. This recorded the date of each shop transfer and the nature of the work undertaken there.

Time spent in 'working' or 'not-working' was also recorded. In the nineteenth century and early twentieth century this was also laid out in detail on one's final 'Apprenticeship Certificate', as we can see on that of Raymond Edward Reece, dated 1 June 1899, who did a five-year apprenticeship in 'Railway Carriage Building' from 14 May 1894 to 13 May 1899:

YEAR ENDED	HOURS WORKS OPEN	HOURS WORKED	TIME LOST (HOURS)			
			SPECIAL LEAVE	ILLNESS	WITHOUT LEAVE	TOTAL
May 1895	2,561¾	2,491½	1	41½	27¾	70¼
" 1896	2,540	2,487¼	–	27	25¾	52¾
" 1897	2,635½	2,337	9¾	257½	31¼	298½
" 1898	2,681½	2,484¼	17¼	122½	57½	197¼
" 1899	2,400	2,324¼	45¼	3½	27	75¾
TOTALS	12,818¾	12,124¼	73¼	452	169¼	694½

Note: For this and the subsequent similar tables, the 'Hours Works Open' does not include the Works' holiday (averaging about twenty days per annum); 'Special Leave' represents time lost for holidays in addition to the usual Works' holidays (includes 50 hours overtime).

It is rather amusing to see the detail of the fractions of hours, but this highlights how time conscious the GWR were and how time controlled the men were too. It is interesting to do the maths here and work out the actual days worked and lost, remembering at this time it would have been a ten-hour day. (Harry Holcroft records his very precisely: 'A 54-hour week was worked on three shifts per day, 6 a.m. to 8.15 a.m., 9 a.m. to 1 p.m., and 2 p.m. to 5.30 p.m., a total of 9¾ hours per day. On Saturdays work stopped on the second shift at 12 noon.') We can see that Reece has a significant amount of time lost to illness, but also rather a hefty amount of time lost 'without leave' and a rather surprising total time lost of 694½ hours. I find this all rather unexpected as the GWR had a reputation of being almost despotic about timekeeping and attendance, yet here we see blatantly poor attendance. Presumably Reece would be one of the completed apprentices 'let go' as his attendance record was so poor.

It is interesting to compare such tables with other eras where documentation is available. Almost a quarter of a century later John Douglas Dawson started his five-year apprenticeship to be a 'Fitter Turner and Erector' in the Locomotive Works on 21 October 1918 at the closing of the First World War. The work on which he was employed was divided thus:

General Fitting and Machine Shop	Turning	3 months
Millwrighting Shop	General Turning	15 months
	General Fitting	16 months
Erecting Shop	Erecting	26 months
	Total	**60 months**

His hourly record raises some interesting questions too:

YEAR ENDED	HOURS WORKS OPEN	HOURS WORKED	TIME LOST (HOURS)			
			SPECIAL LEAVE	ILLNESS	WITHOUT LEAVE	TOTAL
Oct. 1919	2,344¾	2,079¼	3	262½	-	265½
" 1920	2,354½	2,259¼	95¼	-	-	95½
" 1921	2,263	2,083	115½	64½	-	180
" 1922	2,141½	2,064½	64	13	-	77
" 1923	2,354	2,134½	91½	128	-	219½
TOTALS	11,457¾	10,620½	369¼	468	-	837¼

Looking at these figures Dawson's total time lost – 837¼ – makes Reece's loss of time – 694½ – appear almost insignificant. What is also startling is the 369¼ hours of 'Special Leave'. Why was so much taken and, even more intriguingly, why was so much given? Had, one wonders, John Dawson been a fighting man in the recent war? Was this why he had been so ill during the first year of his apprenticeship? Was this a patriotic management showing tolerance and support, despite their own troubles? It seems incredible to be having so much time off, but Circular No. 1145 of February 1904 shows that long absences were not totally unknown and tolerated for surprising lengths of time: 'Absence from duty 26 weeks. When any of your men have been absent from duty for 26 weeks (excepting in cases of injury sustained in the works) a leaving Voucher must at once be sent to this office showing cause of absence, and marked Circular No. 1145.'

It is all intriguing stuff but very frustrating to have such limited records to work with.

Just two years after Dawson had finished, Thomas George Jones started his five-year apprenticeship in the Carriage Department on Coach Bodymaking (New Work and Repairs) on 22 December 1925. His certificate also details his hours worked and lost:

YEAR ENDED	HOURS WORKS OPEN	HOURS WORKED	TIME LOST (HOURS)			
			SPECIAL LEAVE	ILLNESS	WITHOUT LEAVE	TOTAL
Dec. 1926	1,892	1,886½	-	5½	-	5½
" 1927	2,278½	2,277	1½	-	-	1½
" 1928	2,303½	2,287	16	-	½	16½
" 1929	2,307½	2,254¼	44¾	8½	-	53¼
" 1930	2,138½	2,128½★	10	17½	½	22
TOTALS	10,920	10,833¼	72¼	31½	1	104¾

Note: ★ *includes 18 hours overtime*

Looking at Jones' record it is immediately apparent from the hours the Works was open that this period had been a difficult one for the Works. The hours were significantly reduced in comparison to the prevous two periods, with 1,898 hours fewer than the 1890s period. We know that there was a deal of 'short-time' working over this period, which would account for some of this. It is also immediately apparent that something significant happened in the year 1926 – the General Strike. What is also noticeable is that Jones, in the first year of his apprenticeship, did not lose time because of the General Strike.

'Time lost' of course, had a particular significance for apprentices because in order to gain a full apprenticeship one was supposed to serve the full allotted time – whether eighty-four months or later, sixty months. Not for nothing had Collett warned the premium apprentices wanting extra time off for Christmas holidays that it would appear on their certificates.[6] Obviously, with so much time lost, there would be 'gaps' in one's knowledge and experience, which would be apparent to future employers; however, how much real weight this all carried is open to discussion – it does not appear to have stopped these three men from getting their completion certificates, although decades later, as we saw with Mr X (Chapter 1) and his National Service experience, it did have a significance. What would be enlightening here in regard to these three boys would be to know the human story behind these figures, but nothing on the certificate gives any indication or insight. All three have the standard, formal commentary which varies little over the decades, apart from mention of 'the foremen' who thereafter disappear from the text. Reece's is handwritten, as relevant to the time; the two others are typed:

> **RAYMOND E REECE** has completed a term of five years apprenticeship at these works as shown by the above table. He has borne a good character in the workshops for diligent attention to duty and the foremen under whom he has been employed report that he is a good workman. Signed W Dean.

> **JOHN DOUGLAS DAWSON** has completed a term of five years as shown above; he bears a good character, has been attentive to his duties, and the foremen under whom he has been employed report that he possess good ability as a mechanic. Signed C B Collet.

> **THOMAS GEORGE JONES** has completed an apprenticeship in this department as shown above.
>
> He was successful in obtaining a three years free Day Studentship awarded by this Company at the College Swindon during sessions 1926–1929.
>
> Jones bears a good character, possesses good ability as a workman, and has conducted himself in a satisfactory manner. Signed C B Collett.

What we can surmise is that Jones was very academically able, having achieved the full three sessions of day-studentship, but without full personal records or personal testimony we can never know the full story.

Book Learning

Pupillage, in respect of apprenticeship, suggests some taught elements, and for the small band of privileged and special pupil apprentices it did, but a traditional apprenticeship, i.e. pre-1964 Industrial Training Act, was learning by doing, although, obviously it had to have an element of showing. As Ken Gibbs points out 'the Works was not an academic training establishment [and] any operator had to make a genuine contribution to the functioning and production of the Works'. Whilst he is correct in highlighting that the essence of a traditional apprenticeship had always been hands-on, there always had been an educational element to apprenticeship, particularly in the Works. As many men said to me in interviews: 'On the floor we learnt the "how" and in the class we learnt the "why".' Learning the why or 'the book learning', as the men put it, generally came through night school. For apprentices in the Works, the early book learning came through the Mechanics' Institute.

The Mechanics' Institute had led the way around the country in the introduction of technical instruction. Swindon's own Mechanics' Institute, or 'the Institute', as it was affectionately known locally, had come into being in New Swindon through the efforts of a few of the workmen employed by the GWR. Meetings were originally held in a large room in the Works, and from these humble beginnings it quickly grew and flourished. The Institute's own building (later referred to as 'the Mechanics') was formally opened in May 1855. It rapidly became the physical and social focus of New Swindon – the place where it all happened for the GWR workmen and their families. Practising its philosophy of 'disseminating useful knowledge', educational courses in a variety of subjects were available under its umbrella, not just for apprentices but for men, boys and young women. These were popular and well attended. The *Swindon Advertiser and Monthly Recorder* reported in 1868 that the numbers attending 'education classes' had grown, as had the numbers taking the RSA (Royal Society of Arts) examinations. The Institute was fully aware of the importance and its responsibility of imparting scientific knowledge to the next generation of engineers, mechanics and tradesmen, as another report in the now *Swindon Advertiser* of November 1874 shows. At the meeting to distribute the Institutes' prizes for students in their science and art classes, Sir Daniel Gooch, the then chairman of the Institute, took the opportunity to:

> Urge upon those young mechanics of the Works … the importance and necessity not only of making themselves acquainted with the mere mechanical work of their profession, but of attaining a knowledge of the sciences of their profession by which they would be enabled to demonstrate to others, on paper, any theory or invention which had presented itself to their minds.
>
> They would be enable to do this if they devoted a few of the now long evenings of the week to those classes which had been organised for that purpose, and he could not do better than earnestly *invite* them to do so.

In order to encourage higher attainment in study, Gooch, as chairman of the company, had introduced the GWR Chairman's Prize for Engineering Students in 1891. The prize was the princely sum of £10, a veritable fortune to any young man of those times. T.C. Davison claimed the prize in 1891 and notable names such as Charles E. Stanier (1898) and Frederick William Hawkesworth, who went on to be the last Chief Mechanical Engineer (CME) of Swindon Works under the GWR (1904), laid claim to it down the years. In 1909 the prize was taken by Alfred Lawrence, who then went on to win the Whitworth Exhibition Prize, value £50, in 1910 and followed up with a Free Studentship for 'Mechanic' tenable at Imperial College, South Kensington in 1911 – obviously a very capable scholar.

The message that education was important to aspiring engineering and craftsmen was repeated again and again by the Institute, as its *Report of Science & Art and Other Educational Classes Session 1887–8* highlights:

> The necessity for supplementing the practical experience of the Workshop with exact knowledge of technical science is becoming year by year of greater importance and one of the principle objects of the committee in providing the course of instruction set forth … is to afford the younger members of the Mechanics' Institution the opportunity of obtaining such knowledge.

The report shows that in 1886–87 those boys attending night classes were studying scientific subjects such as 'Practical Plane and Solid Geometry, Building Construction, Theoretical Mechanics, Magnetism and Electricity, Arithmetic and Mensuration, Inorganic Chemistry, Carriage Building and Steam and Steam Engine', along with, perhaps surprisingly, 'Art Drawing, Shorthand and French'. The 'List of Certificates & Prizes awarded by the Science & Art Department' includes seventy-four apprentices among the prize winners, whilst those

This Form must be forwarded, properly filled in and certified, so as to reach the Secretary, Board of Education, South Kensington, London, S.W., not later than the 15th of June.

BOARD OF EDUCATION, SOUTH KENSINGTON,
LONDON, S.W.

(Telegraphic address. "Instruction, London.")

WHITWORTH SCHOLARSHIPS AND EXHIBITIONS.
PARTICULARS OF CANDIDATE'S WORKSHOP EMPLOYMENT

(See section 2 of Prospectus of Whitworth Scholarships, &c.)

The Candidate is requested to state below :—

Name and Address in full) *Frederick William Hawkesworth*
121 Manchester Rd. Swindon, Wilts

2. Age last birthday _22_

3. Where he commenced work, and when; whether he was apprenticed, and if so, to whom; and what workshop or workshops he has been employed in up to the present time. (The length of time spent in each workshop should be stated, exact dates being given as far as possible.)

Commenced work April 10th 1899 in Great Western Railway Co. works at Swindon.
Apprenticed to G.W.R. Co.

Worked in	From	To
Tool shop	*April 10th 1899*	*June 1st 1902*
Loco. boiler mounting shop	*June 2nd 1902*	*Oct. 19th 1902*
Loco. erecting shop	*Oct 20th 1902*	*May 4th 1903*
Testing Dept.	*May 5th 1903*	*April 11th 1904*
Drawing Office	*April 12th 1904*	*to date*

Sir Joseph Whitworth was an extraordinarily successful engineer and in 1868 he left a legacy to provide scholarship to assist apprentices in pursuing an academic engineering degree. These scholarships were hard fought for and only awarded to those with the highest academic abilities. If we look at the details of Hawkesworth's 'Shop' experience, we find that despite serving his apprenticeship as a 'Fitter and Turner' he did a considerable time in the Erecting shop too. The details show he was an apprentice of high calibre as he was also in the Tool shop and Testing Dept., eventually arriving in the Drawing Office.

taking 'Prizes and Certificates awarded by the City and Guilds of London Institute' numbered ten. Here gas manufacture apprentice Charles E. Botley achieved a first class certificate, the first prize of £3, as well as the silver medal. There were many monetary inducements by way of prizes to encourage attendance – some offered by the Institution, others by its president and also by Sir Daniel Gooch; his for mechanical drawing being £4, £3, £2 and £1. It was a way for the students to reclaim their expenses as all classes had to be paid for, with fees ranging from 6d each class; and for the session up to 3s for non-members. Further inducement to sit the examination in May was that those not intending to do so were penalised and made to pay a hefty 10s. The report indicates that the Institute's Council believed that such classes were highly desirable and the way of the future, as it states: 'The provision of a Science and Art School with proper class rooms, would add greatly to the success of the Education work of the Institution, and the Council trust that at no distant date such accommodation may be provided.' This is the first indication of the intention of bringing a technical college to New Swindon, way before the Technical Instruction Act of 1889. An article in *The GWR Magazine* of November 1890 regarding 'Distribution of Prizes' for the Institute offers up some interesting figures and thinking regarding the students attending 'Educational Classes' and the nature of some of the subjects they studied, i.e. art drawing. We are told by Viscount Cobham (in the chair giving the address) 'that in 1856 only 1,869 men were employed in the Works; in 1876 the number had risen to 5,188 and in the present year to 9,471'. He went on to say the total numbers of students in 1876 was 440, but in 1890 had risen to 1,015 (one should remember that a few of these would have been girls and young women who would have studied 'Arithmetic, Dictation, Reading and Needlework'.) As to the subject of 'Art', well he could understand why 'some people might be tempted to ask "What have railways to do with art; railways are strictly utilitarian things"'. Not according to the GWR way of thinking. Viscount Cobham replied that when building railways, bridges, locomotives and carriages it was: 'the duty of their manufacturers and handicraftsmen; if they could do so without any sacrifice of economy, strength or durability; to make things as beautiful as they possibly could.'

Despite this seeming fervour for education, the educational evening classes were not yet a compulsory requirement of the apprenticeship agreement, as Conrad Knowles Dumas, who entered GWR's service as a premium apprentice in April 1893, later wrote in his personal memorial:

> In 1893 apprentices *were not bound* to go to Evening Classes, though, if I remember rightly, they were recommended to. No official advice was given as to what to take up and apprentices just decided for themselves, with such advice as they could get from their friends, what classes to attend.[7]

In consideration of this and the fact there was no technical school until the late 1890s, it is strange to see No. 14 Condition as laid out in the 'Application for Apprenticeship' in 1892: 'No. 14. Every Apprentice is required to become a Member of the Science and Art Classes in connection with the Technical Schools at Swindon and to attend the Winter Sessions the course of theoretical instruction which may be prescribed for him.' However, this was also a modified document and this compulsion was probably added in 1908.

In 1889 the Technical Instruction Act placed technical instruction outside secondary schools and passed responsibility to the new County Council and County Boroughs and their Technical Instruction Committees. A new level of education was formalised and technical schools/colleges were introduced. In 1891 a Technical Education Committee was formed in Swindon representing the Local Boards, the School Board, the Mechanics' Institute and the Wiltshire County Council. An open town's meeting was held and it was agreed to raise a loan in aid of the erection of suitable buildings for the accommodation of the 'Swindon and North Wilts Technical School'. The Mechanics' Institute Council then reported: 'The Council of the Institution have transferred to this Technical Institution Committee, the management of the Classes, which have for many years past been carried on by the Mechanics' Institution.'

SCIENCE CLASSES, 1887-8.

SUBJECT.	TEACHER.	No. of Students in Class	Average Attendance 1887-8.	Average Attendance Previous Year.	Number Examined 1888.	Number Examined Previous Year.	Advanced First Class	Advanced Second Class	Elementary First Class	Elementary Second Class	Total 1888.	Total Previous Year.
Practical Plane and Solid Geometry ...	Mr. J. T. Newman ...	11	8	7	5	6	—	—	—	—	2	2	3
Machine Construction and Drawing, Elementary ...	" E. C. Riley, " J. F. Tonkin, " W. Hawksworth	60	34	49	41	50	—	—	—	9	23	32	32
Ditto Advanced ...	" T. O. Hogarth, " H. C. King	28	15	18	22	24	—	1	15	—	—	16	18
Building Construction ...	" J. J. Smith ...	14	9	—	10	—	—	—	—	2	3	5	—
Arithmetic and Mensuration	" G. Pressey, " H. Brighton	59	35	31	29	34	—	—	—	—	—	—	—
Mathematics, 1st Stage ...	" G. Walters	30	20	12	20	11	—	—	1st Stage} 6	1st Stage} 7		13	7
Ditto, 1st, 2nd and 3rd Stages ...	N " R. J. Chirgwi ...	55	35	34	41	41	1st Class 3rdStage} 1	2nd Class 3rd Stage} 3, 2ndStage} 5	1st Stage} 1	1st Stage} 8	18	24
Theoretical Mechanics ...	"	16	11	12	13	13	—	—	3	2	5	10	12
Applied Mechanics... ...	" F. Apted ...	21	14	12	15	13	—	—	1	3	6	10	9
Steam	"	30	19	16	21	18	—	1	—	3	11	15	13
Magnetism and Electricity...	" F. W. Harris ...	25	16	7	17	8	—	—	1	2	13	16	4
Inorganic Chemistry ...	"	27	19	16	19	19	—	1	1	2	8	12	14
Carriage Building (City and Guilds of London Institute)	" Marillier ...	22	14	15	19	17	Honours Grade —	1	Ordinary Grade. 2	Ordinary Grade 3	6	4
TOTAL ...		398	249	229	272	254	1	7	26	32	89	155	140
Total Attendances ... 11523	Individual Students...	230			184	181						

67 Students submitted Works in Machine Drawing in April last for examination at South Kensington, upon which the Government payment is £25. The Works of GEORGE E. ANDREW, obtained the full payment.

A National Book Prize has been awarded by the Science and Art Department to GEORGE E. ANDREW, in Stage 23A, for measured drawing of a Locomotive with condensing gear.

A 3rd grade prize for 2 drawings in Stage 1B, Machine Drawing has been awarded by the Science and Art Department to ERNEST J. EVANS, and 2nd grade prizes for works in Stage 1B, Machine Drawing to HERBERT E. COLLINS, JOHN O. FORD, ALBERT E. KINNEIR, HENRY WESTON, and FREDERICK W. R. WILLIAMS.

ART CLASSES, 1887-8.

SUBJECT.	TEACHERS.	No. of Students in Class.	Average Attendance 1887-8.	Previous Year.	Number Examined Students	Papers	Freehand 1888. 1st Class	Freehand 1888. 2nd Class	Freehand 1888. Passed	Freehand 1887	Model 1888. 1st Class	Model 1888. 2nd Class	Model 1888. Passed	Model 1887	Geometry 1888. 1st Class	Geometry 1888. 2nd Class	Geometry 1888. Passed	Geometry 1887	Perspective 1888. 1st Class	Perspective 1888. 2nd Class	Perspective 1888. Passed	Perspective 1887
Second Grade Freehand and Model Drawing Geometry, and Perspective	Mr. W. Broad, (of the Stroud School of Art), Mr. R. S. McHardy, Mr. W. J. Read, Mr. J. F. Tonkin, and Mr. G. N. Gilchrist	189	122	111	118 (Number successful, 77)	127 (Number successful, 84)	5	40	33		3	19	11		1	13	3		1	2	3	
Geometry	Mr. J. T. Newman and Mr. W. J. Read	61	41	28	33	—	—	—	—	-	—	—	-	—	—	-	13	5	—	—	—	-
Total Attendances 9014		250																				

HENRY HARVIE passed "Excellent" in Freehand and Model Drawing, and ARTHUR W. STOTE passed "Excellent" in Perspective, and obtained 2nd Grade Prizes.

WALTER W. HILLIER passed in the 3rd Grade Examination, Stage 5a, Shading from Models.

45 Students submitted 101 Drawings in April last for examination at South Kensington, upon which the Government Grant is £1 6s.

Attendance numbers were good and rising and there are familiar names amongst the teachers who would have come from the Works.

The Swindon and North Wilts Technical Institute was erected on a site in Victoria Road, presented by W.V. Rolleston and was made possible by grants from the Department of Science and Art and the County Council. It was formally opened on Wednesday 27 January 1896/1897, 'a red-letter day' claimed *The GWR Magazine*, which reported on the event. It related how Lord Herschell presided over the opening and went on to deliver an eloquent address 'on the subject of technical education. He dwelt principally on the subject of foreign competition in the technical arts remarking that we [Britain] were falling behind our German neighbours because they had devoted care, attention, money and energy to technical and scientific education.' He went on to say that whilst many in industry complained that they did not see 'immediate results' for all this technical training, there could be no doubt 'that training of the eye and hand and reasoning process which came from technical and scientific teaching was of incalculable importance to those who were going to fight the industrial battle of the world'. His words were enthusiastically received and in responding, Lord Emlyn Fitzmaurice moved 'that this meeting … expresses its satisfaction at the completion of the new technical school and the progress made towards the establishment of a complete system of technical instruction for the town and district'. It was indeed a momentous and significant moment in the progress of the town's educational system, as well as in the provision of training for apprentices who were now being prepared for not the nineteenth, but the twentieth century.

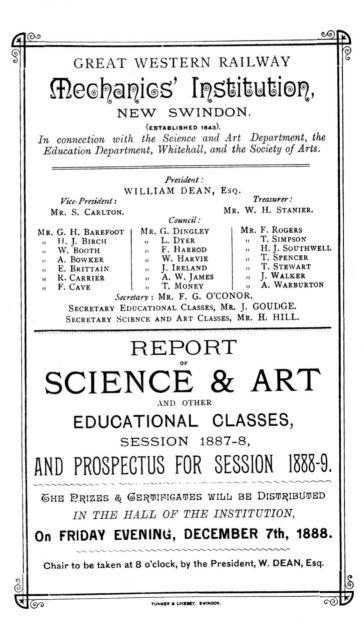

Science and art were common bedfellows at this period, much more so than today. Educational classes offered included reading, geography, writing, French, shorthand and elementary singing.

Being the North Wilts Technical Institute, it was open to a certain number of pupils outside Swindon. Straight away day and more importantly to the Works' apprentices, evening classes, were available. Indeed, the Technical Institute got off to a 'flying start', according to Mechanics' Institute historian Trevor Cockbill, not least, he claims, because of the 'complete package' they were handed by the Mechanics' Institute Council, which included:

> the better part of a thousand part-time students, a great variety of instruction courses each with its own proven and successful syllabus, a considerable quantity of apparatus and, by no means the least important, a small army of part-time lecturers, trained by the Institute itself and mostly certificated by examination to the satisfaction of the Department of Science and Arts at South Kensington … Furthermore to ensure a smooth transfer of all of this to the new college the County Council was please to appoint all serving members of the Institute Council's Education Committee as the first governors of the new establishment.[8]

Some package indeed. It speaks volumes about the character and nature of the Mechanics' Institute Council and the men who had run it over all those years. In 1926 the Technical Institute was reorganised as a college of further education and the following year was renamed 'the College', and as such was talked about and figured in later generations of apprentices' 'night school' education.

Undoubtedly the men and management of those early decades in which Swindon Works was formed and grew into a community were men of insight and vision in respect of the role that education would play in the future of the workforce, the company and the country. These early Victorians robustly believed in 'self-improvement' and applied such belief vigorously and consistently over the years in the widest ways possible. The Company school, the Mechanics' Institute and now the Technical Institute, were dedicated milestones of their commitment to progress through education. They did not, however, limit themselves to formal education boundaries but extended learning possibilities in other ways too, one of which was in the setting up of the GWR Mechanics' Institution, New Swindon, Junior Engineering Society. This society held its 'First Annual Conversazione' (doesn't that title just encapsulate the whole ethos of the movement?) on 23 January 1894. The purpose of the society was, as assessed by its first Speaker, Mr N. Story Maskelyne, MA, FRS, FIC, FGS, to be:

> something more than a debating club or mutual improvement society, and that while embodying what is good in such associations [to] aspire to higher office – that of gathering from every source, whatever is important and fresh in every department of engineering and putting it in its most practical form before your members.

He went on to deliver a paper on 'Science and Practical Engineering' and in particular to address the question 'What is electricity?' – something rather exciting and exhilarating at that time – taxing them with the problem of 'finding the means of producing only the rays we want without the prodigious waste [we produce now in order to achieve] an electric light of any intensity'. This society, whilst junior in the age of its membership, was by no means junior in its intellectual scope or aspirations.[9]

In 1903 George Jackson Churchward introduced the Day Studentship Award, which released apprentices for further academic studies with fees and wages paid. These awards were competitive places given on the results of examinations taken at night school and were, therefore, only awarded to the most academically able. All were able to compete for them but it was not a level playing field, for those that had left school at 14 or 15 with only the basic elementary education had to then go up against those who had attended until they were 16. Also those in lower trades would not have been deemed suitable. Like everything set up by the GWR, it was carefully regulated and controlled. The conditions and requirements for these awards were laid out in the Technical Institute's Annual Reports. That of 1911 states:

Day Studentships for Apprentices at Swindon

The number of free Studentships will be limited to 30 at any one time, generally in groups as follows – For a three years Course-

1st year's Course	15 students
2nd " "	9 students
3rd " "	6 students

For each year's Course there will be a competitive Examination, successful Students passing on from one year's Course to the next.

The course of Study for each year will consist of:

PRACTICAL MATHEMATICES
PRACTICAL MECHANICS INCLUDING HEAT ENGINES
GEOMETRICAL AND MACHINE DRAWING
HEAT, ELECTRICITY AND CHEMISTRY

Candidates must be registered apprentices between 17 and 18 years of age on the 1st June in the year of entry upon the Course.

They must have spent at least six months in the Factory and must have attended for at least one session the prescribed Evening Classes at the Technical School.

They must produce evidence of good conduct and attention to their work in the Factory and at the Technical School and only those who attain a minimum qualification at the Examinations will be successful.

Successful Students will attend Day Classes at the Technical School on two half days per week for 26 weeks from October to April.

Those attending the Classes will have their wages paid as if at work in the Factory and the GWR Co., will pay their school Fees.

Students who distinguish themselves will be allowed to spend part of their last year in the Drawing Office or Chemical Laboratory.

The Entrance Examination will be held at the Technical School at the close of the Evening School Session.

Forms of Application may be obtained from the Works Manager early in May.

At the end of the third year the apprentice in the No. 1 position with highest marks was awarded the GWR Chairman's Prize of £10. Alan Peck, now a well-known name because of his popular book on the GWR Works, was one of those who won a Day Studentship for the session 1937–39. Ernest Raymond Radway, who was apprenticed in Fitting and Turning in the late 1920s, remembers Day Studentships well and has good reason to as he was one of the very few who achieved all three Day Studentships, his for sessions 1928–29, 1929–30 and 1930–31. He was one of those who, despite his father being a first-class tradesman, had to leave school early because of financial circumstances, and was always having to play catch-up with the level of knowledge of most of the others contenders. 'It was,' he writes in his memoir *Craftsmen and Engineers the 'Swindon Way'*, 'a cut-throat situation … [and] the competition was fierce'. Despite this and through sheer hard work, he also took the Chairman's Prize in his third year. The pass mark for the entry examinations taken at night school was not preset, but was judged by the highest marks attained at each examination session, so that in the examinations of 1929–30 (to be awarded for the 1930–31 sessions) the highest mark was 79 per cent and the cut-off mark for the fifteenth place awarded was just 59 per cent, whilst in the examinations for the 1934–35 session the highest mark was 85 per cent and the cut-off mark for the then just thirteen studentships awarded was 70 per cent. A register detailing examination results and awards made for the period during the 1930s records:

Results of Examinations of Apprentices who made application for Day Studentships at the College – Session 1929–30
These applicants were awarded a free Day Studentship during Session 1930–31

Position	Name	Maths	Mechs Drawing	Heat Elec Chem	Av Mrk %	
1	Fortescue P	1	1	1	1	79
2	Cocks E C	1	1	1	2	78
	Fisher J K	1	1	1	1	78
4	Tarrant J G	1	1	1	1	74
5	Pimm S	1	1	1	1	72
	Radway H G★	1	1	1	2	72
7	Peasey W H	1	1	F	1	66
8	Dashfield E D	1	1	1	2	65
	Adams H A	1	1	1	2	65
10	Hobbs A J	1	1	1	2	63
11	Gleman A	1	1	1	2	62
	Kidmar H R C	1	1	1	1	62
13	Smith B H	1	1	1	2	61
14	Buckland F J	1	1	F	2	59
	Gee J R	1	2	1	2	59

1 is First Class pass; 2 is 2nd Class pass; F is Failure; A is absent from examination.
The average marks per cent column is based on the number of examinations attended.
Note: ★ *This Radway, in his first free session, was no relation to Ernest Radway, just finishing his third year.*

These handful were the successful ones but there were fifty other applicants who were not. Their average marks ranged from 58 per cent down to 16 per cent, with one achieving only 5 per cent because he had been absent from some exams and failed the others. Over the years the number of places awarded and the number of years attending varied as 'Correspondence 6202 August 1933' informs: 'First year students will be reduced to 12 for the next Session.' Further information adds: 'This year the scheme will be re-arranged to cover 4 sessions with 12 students in each session. For Session 1933–1934 however it was only possible to include seven students in the 4th year.'[10] The scheme was surprisingly generous, including, as it did, pay for the time away from work, but this latter point was open to interpretation depending upon the current circumstances and the staff clerk administering it, as Ernest Radway found out to his own financial cost when the Works was placed on short-time working. He writes:

> The day for short time working was to be Monday, and that was the day that was to be my day at College. In the mean manner of those days, some staff clerk interpreting the Day Studentship Rule that one could only be paid if the recipient was at work literally, although probably not intended for those circumstances, said no wages would be paid for the day at school.

Such support was not, however, Radway argues, purely philanthropy, as by such a means did the GWR ensure a continuous supply of 'high quality, dedicated men for the many technician posts, cost clerks, inspectors, foremen and engineers. They knew that any apprentice who had won a place in the final year was a man of the highest calibre and that the one who won the

Chairman's Prize was outstanding!' Such a summation, I would suggest, is probably correct. The students were expected to give time each evening to private study 'devoting themselves to the prescribed courses so as to attain a thorough knowledge of a few of the most important subjects rather than a smattering of a greater number'. During their second year of attendance they were encouraged to join the Institute of Mechanical Engineers as student members. Unfortunately, those who had left school early (like Radway) found that they were required then to pass both the English and foreign language papers before proceeding to the second stage of their professional examinations. This, radway points out, placed an extra burden of study on them than those who had 'stayed on for a Higher Elementary Education and studied both subjects could claim exemption from'.

A limited number of other apprentices were also allowed to attend the day classes to study the same courses, but for these less fortunate lads it was a double whammy, as they had to pay their own tuition fees and were not paid for time spent out of the factory. Such a situation took a lot of commitment and belief in their future prospects. In the 1931–32 session, an S.R. Radway (yet another Radway and no relation to Ernest Radway), a fee-paying day

---

GREAT WESTERN RAILWAY COMPANY'S AWARDS.

Session 1927-28.

G.W.R. CHAIRMAN'S PRIZES.

I. £10 to *Engineering Apprentices*

II. £5 to *Clerks*

WINNERS OF G.W.R. DAY STUDENTSHIPS.

(In Order of Merit in each Section).

THIRD YEAR.

(These Students are now in their Final Year).

Wanklyn, P. W. B.	....	Engine Fitting, Turning and Erecting.
Hillier, R.	....	Fitting and Turning.
Arkell, O. H.	....	Engine Fitting, Turning and Erecting.
Sutton, C. L.	....	" " " "
{ Sly, A. C. L.	....	
{ Jones, T. G.	....	Coach Bodymaking.

SECOND YEAR.

Griffiths, W. N.	....	Engine Fitting, Turning and Erecting.
{ Hilliard, A. E.	....	" " " "
{ Mutter, J. F.	....	Coach Bodymaking.
{ Thorburn, D. A.	....	Engine Fitting, Turning and Erecting.
Smith, S. A. S.	....	" " " "
Martin, F.	....	" " " "
{ Daniels, L. T.	....	" " " "
{ Morse, A. E.	....	" " " "
Slatter, W. C.	....	" " " "

FIRST YEAR.

Palphramand, G. E.	....	Engine Fitting, Turning and Erecting.
Woolfrey, P. H. J.	....	" " " "
Ellison, J. W. W.	....	" " " "
Bellinger, H. C. J.	....	" " " "
Davis, C. E.	....	Coach Trimming.
Lewis, T.	....	Engine Fitting, Turning and Erecting.
Olden, J. M.	....	Coach Bodymaking.
Johnson, W. T.	....	Moulding.
James, R. T.	....	Engine Fitting, Turning and Erecting.
Radway, E. R.	....	Fitting and Turning.
Bryant, R. H.	....	Engine Fitting, Turning and Erecting.
Nash, S. A.	....	" " " "
Hartley, J. H. A.	....	" " " "
{ Heath, R. G.	....	Wood Wagon Building.
{ Knight, J. E. G.	....	Engine Fitting, Turning and Erecting.

GREAT WESTERN RAILWAY COMPANY'S AWARDS.

SESSION 1931-32.

G.W.R. Chairman's Prizes.

1.	£10 to Engineering Students	...	...	...	E. R. H...
2.	£5 to Clerks	...	...	...	J. E. B...

Winners of G.W.R. Day Studentships.

(In order of Merit in each Section).

THIRD YEAR.

(These Students are now in their Final Year).

Fisher, J. K.	...	Engine Fitting, Turning and Erecting.
Cocks, E. C.	...	" " " "
Fortescue, P.	...	" " " "
Tarrant, T. J.	...	" " " "
Coleman, A.	...	Fitting and Turning.
Smith, B. H.	...	Engine Fitting, Turning and Erecting.

SECOND YEAR.

Ford, H.	...	Engine Fitting, Turning and Erecting.
Selwood, J. L. B.	...	" " " "
{ Cox, H. R.	...	" " " "
{ Hayward, A. E.	...	" " " "
Wood, R. A.	...	" " " "
Mountford, C. E.	...	Coach Bodymaking.
{ Bellinger, R.	...	Engine Fitting, Turning and Erecting.
{ Harris, W. C.	..	Coach Bodymaking.
Hookham, H. K.	...	Engine Fitting, Turning and Erecting.

FIRST YEAR.

Richards, J. A.	...	Fitting and Turning.
Robinson, G. R. H.	...	Coach Bodymaking.
Toogood, G. D.	...	Engine Fitting, Turning and Erecting.
Elliott, G. L.	...	" " " "
Clarke, L. V. P.	...	" " " "
Harbert G. M.	...	" " " "
Bradfield, H. C	...	Fitting and Turning.
Edmonds, W. A. H.	...	Engine Fitting, Turning and Erecting.
Warren, R. H.	...	Fitting and Turning.
{ Law, A. E.	...	Engine Fitting, Turning and Erecting.
{ Rushen, E. J.	...	Wheelwrighting.
Hodey, A. H.	...	Coach Bodymaking.
{ King, D. G.	...	Engine Fitting, Turning and Erecting.
{ Maisey, G. L.	...	" " " "
{ King, P.	...	Pattern Making.
{ Jarman, J. V.	...	Fitting and Turning.

Day studentships, i.e. paid study, were highly prized. It is interesting to see a solitary 'moulder' (First Year 1927-28) and 'wheelwright' (First Year 1931-32) amongst the usual FTs and FTEs and Coach builders.

student, won the Chairman's Prize with an average mark of 86 per cent; with such a high percentage one wonders why he hadn't made it into the free chosen few.

Relatively few apprentices went to day school, however most went to night school or evening classes. Once established, night school was a continuing requirement of the apprenticeship agreement and the company did all it could to encourage and support it, even, amazingly, to bending its rigorous timekeeping rules, as this statement printed in the Technical Institute's Annual Report for 1911 shows:

—❦❦❦—

GREAT WESTERN RAILWAY
TECHNICAL INSTRUCTION FOR
APPRENTICES AT SWINDON

In order to encourage good work at the Evening Classes, it has been decided that when Apprentices attend the Engineering Classes regularly three Evenings per week, and give evidence of industry and perseverance, their absence from the Factory before 9 o'clock on the Three Mornings immediately before or immediately after the Classes will not be recorded against them.

A continuance of this privilege will depend upon individual results.

G J Churchward
Locomotive & Carriage Department
Engineer's Office
Swindon
September 1911

—❦❦❦—

The Technical Institute provided a range of evening classes. The syllabus for 1911 shows these included 'Preparatory' classes for 'Engineering and Trade Students under 16 years of age'. These covered '*simple Machine Details, including the making of dimensioned Hand Sketches and Working Drawings; Technical Description and Calculation and Elementary Practical Mechanics*'. There was also a 'General Engineers' Course', where the syllabus of the first- and second-year classes had an emphasis on the practical, i.e. '*Practical Mathematics; Practical Geometry and Technical Drawing and Practical Mechanics and Heat Engines*'. In the third, fourth and fifth years students were encouraged to study '*Machine Construction – stage 11 or 111, Advanced Physics; Advanced Chemistry; Geometry and Graphics stage 11 or 111; or Applied Mechanics and Practical Mathematics stages 11 or 111*'. These all had to be paid for out of one's own pocket and the course fee at this time for three of the above subjects was 5s per session.

Whilst Radway says of some of his contemporaries in the late 1920s that 'some of the apprentices were not interested in fulfilling their obligation to attend night school, preferring to go out dancing until the early hours of the morning, then come into work boasting of their success with the females of the species', Gordon Ing, who started his five-year apprenticeship in 1935, remembers he '*had* to go to night school three times a week after work. It was go or get out – even though that was when we were doing a forty-eight-hour week.' He still has his night school exercise book for the years between 1935 and 1937. It records that in October 1935 he had to explain the practicalities of 'Seams and Joints'. He wrote:

There are really only five ways of joining metals together namely – soldering, brazing, grooving, riveting and welding, each of them being used specifically for its different requirements. When deciding on which form of joint should be used the thickness of the material, the kind of metal, also whether the joint is to be subjected to different pressures of working, must all be taken into consideration.

Left table — THE COLLEGE, SWINDON. PRIZE LIST, SESSION 1931-2.

CLASS or COURSE	PRIZE	NAME
Engineering & Science—		
Mathematics V.	Prize	James, Timothy
„ IV.	First	Adams, Herbert A.
„ „	Second	Potter, Richard H.
„ III.	First	Richards, John A.
„ „	Second	Harbert, Geoffrey M.
		Parker, Alex L.
Mechanics & Heat Engines—V.	First	James, Timothy
„ „	Second	Reeves, Frederick S.
„ IV.	First	Slatter, Christopher C. A.
„ „	Second	Potter, Richard H.
„ III.	First	Richards, John A.
„ „	Second	Parker, Alex L.
Machine Design—V.	First	Smith, Selborne A.
„ „	Second	Woolfrey, Phillip H.
Machine Drawing IV.	First	Rodda, Horace J.
„ „	Second	Cocks, Edward C.
		Tarrant, Thomas J.
„ III.	First	Ford, Hugh
„ „	Second	Ferguson, Ronald S.
		Hayward, Allan E.
Special Engineering—III.	First	Wakefield, Albert E.
„ „	Second	Thompson, Horace S.
Engineering—II.	First	Eagle, Joseph W.
„ „	Second	Clarke, Leslie V. P.
		Spinks, Beresford G. P.
		Vince, Donald A.
Engineering—I., A	First	Toogood, George D.
„ „	Second	Elliot, George L.
		Ricks, Alan W.
I., B, C, D, E	First	Bradfield, Herbert C.
„ „	Second	Furkins, Frederick E.
		Gale, Gordon W.
		Lovegrove, Eric E.
Electrical Installation Work—III.	Prize	Prichard, Oliver E.
„ „ II.	Prize	Powers, Graham G. L.
„ „ I.	First	Ing, Howard J.
	Second	Bullock, Leslie W. M.
Boilermakers' Work—III.	Prize	Ashton, Henry R. H.
„ Course II.	Prize	Mulcock, Harry
„ Course I.	First	Lewis, Walter H. J.
	Second	Parker, Gordon W.
Rail Carriage Drawing—IV.	First	Hayward, Frederick J.
„ „	Second	Mann, Norman A.
„ III.	First	Baugh, Leslie J.
„ „	Second	Myers, John A.
„ Materials—IV.	Prize	Mann, Norman A.
„ III.	First	Hurcom, Godfrey S.
	Second	Pearcy, William H.
„ Mechanics IV.	Prize	Robinson, George T.
„ Work II.	First	Hodey, Albert H.
	Second	Trueman, Donald E.
„ I.	First	Robinson, Geoffrey R.
	Second	Hext, Thomas W.
		Probert, Guy B.
Coach Trimmers' Course—III.	Prize	Jennings, Reginald C.
„ II.	Prize	Windridge, Horace G.
„ I.	No Prize	
Heavy Motor Body Course—II.	Prize	Rushen, Edgar J.

Right table — THE COLLEGE, SWINDON. PRIZE LIST SESSION 1927-28.

CLASS OR COURSE	PRIZE	NAME
Science and Technology.—		
Mathematics V.	Prize	Norman C. Haigh
„ IV.	First	John H. Rodda
	Second	David J. G. Bowen
„ III. A.	First	Sidney J. Jones
	Second	Leslie C. Hancock
„ B.	Prize	John P. Hampton
„ C.	Prize	Joe Scott
Mechanics & Heat Engines V.	First	Norman C. Haigh
	Second	Reginald A. Brookman
„ IV.	First	David J. G. Bowen
	Second	John F. Dendle
„ III.	First	Joe Scott
	Second	Reginald G. Townsend
Heat Engines III.	First	Frank A. Bailey
	Second	Robert N. Clanchy
Machine Design V.	First	Henry J. Fortune
	Second	Charles T. Roberts
Machine Drawing IV. A.	First	Harold A. Stafford
	Second	Alfred C. Jackson
„ IV. B.	First	John H. Rodda
	Second	Leslie R. Giles
„ III. A.	First	Selborne A. Smith
	Second	Donald A. Thorburn
„ III. B.	First	Edward M. Jarvis
	Second	Joe Scott
Special Engineering III.	Prize	Stanley T. Jones
Engineering Course II. A.	First	Philip H. Woolfrey
	Second	William T. Johnson
„ II. B.	Prize	George W. A. Davage
„ I. A.	First	George E. Palphramand
	Second	Frederick T. Barwell
„ I. B.	First	Norman H. Cooke
	Second	Edward G. Witcomb
„ I. C.	First	George Kilminster
	Second	Lewis G. Sondermann
„ I. D.	First	Sydney G. Herrington
	Second	Leslie N. Whatley
„ I. E.	Prize	Richard W. Harvey
RailCarriageWorkDrawing IV.	Prize	Wilfred H. Scribbins
„ Materials IV.	Prize	Wilfred H. Scribbins
„ Mechanics IV.	Prize	Harold J. Ridout
„ Drawing III.	First	Thomas G. Jones
	Second	Victor H. Gardiner
„ Materials III.	First	Thomas G. Jones
	Second	James A. Dixon
„ Course II.	First	Cyril E. Davis
	Second	Clarence Howell
„ I.	First	Leslie T. Gough
	Second	Raymond A. Jarvis
		John M. Olden
Boilermakers' Course I.	Prize	Donald C. Perrett
Metal Plate Course III.	Prize	Evelyn A. Angell
„ II.	Prize	Francis J. Purnell
„ I.	Prize	Stanley G. Ayres
Building Trades Course II.	Prize	Lionel D. Bradley
„ I.	Prize	Ronald S. Smith

Prizes were offered in order to encourage both attendance and attainment. Those who 'won' were acknowledged in, initially, the Institute's reports and latterly those of the College.

One of the subjects he studied at evening classes was practical mathematics (just as in the syllabus for 1911). On 17 March 1936 the task set was to explain 'How to bend a 2 inch pipe', and in March 1937 the more challenging calculation: 'A hot water tank holds 20 Galls. it is 24" in dia. and has a centre flue 3" in dia. Calculate the sizes of the various pieces of plate required to make it.' In September 1937 he was tackling: 'Calculate the number of galls a cylindrical tank will hold whose dia. is 21" perpendicular, height 3'6" making allowance for a hemispherical insertion in each end'. Knowledge of the properties of chemicals and metals was considered essential for his learning, as was the working out of numerous tables of their capabilities, e.g. 'approximate weight per square foot of copper: brass: iron:' and 'equivalent gauges and weights for sheets 4ft. x 2ft'.

The exercise book makes fascinating reading, particularly in the light of the debate today regarding the standards of education. One wonders how many young mechanics nowadays would be expected to not only know all the formulae for working out the area of a circle, square, rectangle, triangle, elipse, sphere, cylinder, cone, pyramid, frustsom of cone and annular ring, but also to be able to do it without the aid of a calculator! No wonder Gordon Ing feels able to say, 'I come from Swindon Works, I can do anything.'

Night class had so long been an accepted and expected part of the apprenticeship that even a war was no excuse to miss it, as remembered by Roy Taylor of the Second World War:

I went to night classes. If you missed, they would know. The Inspector in my shop was one of the teachers and first thing in the morning the Foreman would ask him 'anyone missing last

Gordon Ing.   March 11ᵗʰ

A hot water boiler holds 20 Galls. It is 2½" in dia. and has a centre flue 3" in dia..
Calculate the sizes of the various pieces of plate required to make it.

Specification.

2 Grooved seams on body (¼"). Flue to penetrate above lid 6". Knocked-up bottom. Wired top edge (no. 10 wire). Flue grooved seam – flanged & rivetted bottom.

$$\text{Height} = \frac{20 \times 277.25}{\text{Area of base}} = \frac{20 \times 277.25}{2½^2 - 3^2 \times .7864}$$

$$= 5545 \div 445.3218$$

$$= 12.4 \text{ ins.}$$

2 sheets for body, 12.4 + ⅝ × circum
each = 12.4 + ⅝ × 3.835 ...

1 sheet for flue = 19.4 × 9.4
2 sheets for bottom = 2.5 square

Allowance for wiring.

Gordon Ing.   Nov. 19ᵗʰ 1935.

Test

1. Find the square route of 14402.2001.
2. ⓐ How many ways are there of joining metals together.
    ⓑ Name them.
3. Find the area of an irregular triangle whose sides are 6", 7" and 8".
4. What is a flux. ⓐ give the names of 8.
                    ⓑ say when you would use 3.
5. What diameter main pipe would it take to carry away water from three branch pipes whose diam are 4, 5·5 and 6.
6. What weight of water would a cylindrical bore whose diam of base = 7·5 and 16·5 perp. height.

Gordon Ing is rightly proud of his notebook recording his 'book work' at night school in the 1930s. It makes fascinating reading and conjecture in the light of current debates of standards in schools.

With such a thorough description of brazing copper, anyone should be able to do it!

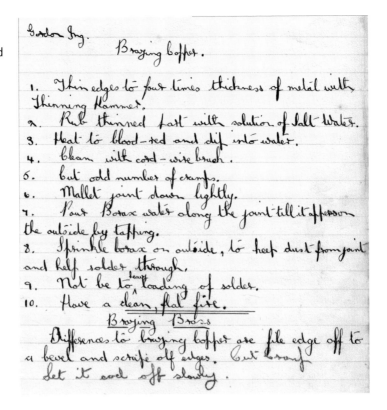

night' and you'd get told off if you hadn't been there. During the war you had to work 8 am to 8 at night. You did a 12 day run then 2 days off. You could only get time off in an evening to go to night class. The only class we (coppersmiths) could do was sheet metal work. I made a pair of brass vases at that night school. You did the theory side two nights a week and on the third night or Saturday afternoon you did practical. We took the City Guild Certificate and had to pass the exams. You had to make a model for your exam piece. During the war, 1941, because of the bombing in London, they came down to Swindon and looked at the pieces. I got a First Class Pass. I was 17 when I did that.

Such was the rule, but as we know, a great many lads of such ages (of any era) perhaps less academically inclined have other things of interest on their minds – such as football, running (very popular in Swindon), being in a band or, that inevitable distraction, girls – and such lads would, when the opportunity arose, bunk-off, as Peter Withers confesses he did: 'We were supposed to go to night school, but because of the war [Second World War] they didn't bother so much and I didn't go' (obviously it depended on whose shop one was in). Bob Townsend, who was more into running than books, remembers being hauled in front of his foreman many times and being given a 'dressing down' because of his poor night school attendance. He would start to go again, and then get lax again and be hauled up again for another strict talk. This pattern repeated itself until eventually it became easier for everyone – foreman, college, Townsend – to just 'forget about it'; obviously where there was a will there was a way, for those who went and those who didn't. Night school also offered opportunities for wider advancement. Those that went could have studied for and achieved the National Certificate in Mechanical Engineering. This offered the possibility on completion of apprenticeship to transfer to the drawing office. For those with ambitions in other directions there were other opportunities too, such as the C&G Machine Shop Engineering course, which was more

CITY & GUILDS OF LONDON INSTITUTE
INCORPORATED BY ROYAL CHARTER

DEPARTMENT OF TECHNOLOGY

This is to certify that *Kenneth Rodway Gibbs*

after satisfactory attendance at a Course of Instruction covering two years

at *The College, Swindon*

and satisfactory completion of the specified Practical Work, passed in the

Second Class in the year 1951   the INTERMEDIATE Examination

in MACHINE SHOP ENGINEERING (Machinists', Turners', and Fitters' Work)

Chairman of the Technology Committee

Principal

Director, Department of Technology

Signature of the holder of this Certificate

City & Guilds courses were the 'standard bearers' of work-based training and education. Achieving a 'Certificate' was looked on as a singular accomplishment.

practical, including the use of machine tools, such as milling, shaping drilling, available in the college's own Machine Shop. Ken Gibbs, who undertook this course, remembers it also included other engineering aspects such as blacksmithing and foundry operations, including pattern making.

This approach of educating apprentices in 'book learning' continued until the sweeping changes of the 1960s, when the initial learning, both book and practical, were combined and taken out of the factory and college, to be delivered as one package through the Apprentice Training School. It was the beginning of a new era – and the end of a long tradition.

Notes

1   Institute Mechanical Engineers Website, Record 14 of 68.
2   Ken Gibbs remembers this exactly from his time working there.
3   Nokes (Nokes was actually Sekon, the editor of *The GWR Magazine*).
4   Macdermott.
5   His transcript was reproduced in a Wild Swan Publication 1985 – *Special GWR Edition No. 2*.
6   GWR records.
7   Can be found at Newton Abbot Railway Centre.
8   Cockbill, *This is Our Heritage*.
9   Pamphlet, Swindon Central Library.
10   Information from National Archive RAIL 264/295.

The Way In

The primary route into apprenticeship had traditionally been through the father's trade, often in his place of work, so that a shoemaker's son would become a shoemaker and a brewer's son a brewer, thereby carrying on the family tradition and family business. For those who came from outside such arrangements, entry was by payment.

Generally speaking, for those whose fathers worked for the GWR, there were two routes into apprenticeship, but, as in all realms of life, there were always the exceptions. One of those exceptions, and notably so, was that of Ken Gibbs' grandfather. The Gibbs' family legend is that great-grandfather William started working as a platelayer with the GWR as a 13-year-old boy in 1849 and was involved in constructing a culvert into a large pond behind the provender store at Didcot. Years later when the GWR were in dispute over some boundaries to certain properties in that area, because of his earlier work, William was able to help the GWR to establish the situation to their advantage; the reward for this help was to have one son apprenticed in Swindon Works. This was to be grandfather George, who started his apprenticeship in 1875. As Ken Gibbs, his great-grandson, explains: 'great-grandfather's occupation is confirmed as "platelayer" on my grandfather's birth certificate, so something exceptional must have occurred to allow a platelayer to apprentice a son to the premier trade of fitter, turner and loco erector without having to pay!' Another unusual exception was the case of Albert White. Albert lost an eye whilst working in the Spring Shop. He received no money but in compensation the company promised to apprentice his sons. Albert had six sons and four were able to benefit from this arrangement. At this time it was most unusual for a labourer's sons to be apprenticed and his fourth son, Harold Victor White, apprenticed as a bricklayer (1920–26), was often embarrassed by one particular man who never failed to taunt him about it in front of others. Another White, Ken White, well-known Swindon artist and muralist, was incredibly fortunate in how he fell into his apprenticeship by the intercession and help of an older colleague, Ernie Painter. In 1958, aged 15 and straight from school, Ken somewhat reluctantly followed his brother Mike into the Works. Ken loathed the work he was doing – rivet-hotting. His passion was art and he talked to Ernie about it and showed him what was doing at art evening classes. Ernie was impressed and thought Ken's talents could be put to better use than rivet-hotting, so he spoke to the 'powers that be' and Ken was transferred into the Sign-writing Department in the Carriage & Wagon Works and became an apprentice sign-writer. He remembers it well:

I was the first apprentice they'd had for years. Fifteen or twenty. I was something of a novelty. It was a bit overwhelming, being seventeen and all the other blokes being so much older. First thing was to make my own palette. I was given some plywood. I enjoyed that. Made it real artistic like. Not just a square with a whole in. I was proud of that. Still got it in fact. In my studio. I started on stencilling. They provided the stencilling brushes. They were named after birds. Still are. Depending on their size. Goose. Swan. Duck. They had to be cleaned and laid in a dish of oil every night to keep them in good condition. Every morning we would go up

Sign-writers were a small select group. Their work required a creative flair and many, such as Ken White, were artists in their own right. The notice on the board the young man is holding reads: 'Klondyke Writers 1902'. Their names are given from back to front as: A. Jeramed, G. Turner, F. Cavill, W. Wakefield, C. Dowley, A. Andrews, I. Norton, P. Collins, E. Raleigh, H. Wakefield, S. Pearce, S. Hobbs, A. Stanley.

'the Bank' and do touch-up of old work. Go over the work already done to bring it back up. Do whole letters. I did that for about a year.[1]

The lads whose fathers worked in the GWR workshops in the early years would have, in the traditional manner, 'followed in their fathers' footsteps', if not in actual trade then certainly into the Works, after all most had come to Swindon to specifically do so. Perusal of the 1861 and 1871 censuses shows that the influx into New Swindon was still growing. The migrant workers were a motley lot with a range of skills, or even none at all, still coming from all around the country. Despite some retrenchment hiccups and development foot-dragging, the Works had greatly expanded. After the initial engine establishment there came the 'puddling furnaces and rail mills' in 1860, followed by the Carriage Works by 1868, and so the need for tradesmen kept growing. This was a period of opportunity for the young men of these times. No limit appeared to be placed on what was available to them, as was the case in later years. John Broughton (48), coach painter from London, had four sons all in the Works: John (23), coach maker; James (19), carriage fitter; William (17), coach maker's apprentice; Valentine (14), coach maker's apprentice. There is an interesting conundrum in the census of both these decades. It is possibly, and most probably, because of sloppy enumeration. Whilst some young men are identified as 'apprentices' many others are just attributed an occupation, e.g. James Broughton (19), carriage fitter. Thomas Brittain (19) and Edwin Brittain (18), both sons of Edwin Brittain (41), engine fitter from London[2] residing at 18 Wellington Street, are also classified as engine fitter. We know from the Brittain family records that both these boys were indentured and did full apprenticeships in the Works, so at this time they were obviously both apprentices.[3] The sons of engine fitter, Thomas Turbull (47), George (21), Thomas (17), David (15), are all identified as engine fitters (all these in 1871). In 1861 the sons of William Hogarth (50) (probably the William Hogarth identified in the Fawcett List as 'Second Contractor for New Engine Wheels'), described in the census as an 'engine smith', add to this perplexity. William (17) is identified as an 'engine fitter', whilst Robert (15) is described as 'apprenticed to engine fitter'. The problem with all this is that we know that the GWR was very strong on apprenticeships. We also know that apprenticeships were usually of a six- or seven-year period. They did not start until the lad was at least 14, so someone of 17, 18 or 19 could not possibly be working as a journeyman and, therefore, must be an apprentice.

For those who came decades later, the nature of the apprenticeship given depended on one thing: the craft status of your father – skilled, semi-skilled, unskilled labourer. The craft status of one's father was a double-edged sword for many entering the Works, especially those wishing to be something other than his father was, particularly if his father was not fortunate enough to be a 'first-class tradesman', whether on the Locomotive or the Carriage & Wagon side. Over time, trades had been classified 'first' or 'second' according to complexity, custom and practice and in negotiations with and between the different guilds and then the trade unions. On the Locomotive side, fitters, turners and erectors were top of the pile, patternmakers were also 'first class', whereas moulders and painters were second. On the Carriage & Wagon side, fitters, turners, coach finishers, coach body-makers and painters were first class; electricians, wagon-builders, plumbers and coppersmiths were all second class. First-class trades received higher wage rates but the bigger difference was in status.[4]

Over time a hierarchical structure had been built up that was to be maintained at all costs. The GWR became incredibly inflexible upon this point. In the twentieth century, as in March 1920, they even had very clear and exact explanatory information sheets laid out in columns of who could have what and how long their father had worked for to get it.

Mr E.A. Loveday, who had been in the company service for twenty-six years (six over the required period), was a salaried warehouseman when he applied in 1925 for an apprenticeship for his son Edward in the coach body-making trade. However, management were very quick to spot his subtle manoeuvre and C.B. Collett responded firmly stating:

> I have made enquiries into this case and find that had Warehouseman Loveday not been transferred to the Stores Department he would have been offered a secondary trade for his son, if he wishes to do anything in this direction I shall be pleased to make the necessary arrangements. If he wants apprenticeship to a primary trade I am afraid it will be necessary for us to ask him to pay the usual premium.

This protocol stretched across the decades, so that even during interviews in 2010 those who started apprenticeships in the 1930s and '40s could still recite it by heart. It was a bitter pill for any lad to have to swallow and many resented it immensely. Hugh Freebury writes of his experiences in the 1930s:

> My father, Harry Freebury … was only a second-grade machine-man … [they] looked up my father's status and finally decided they could accept me as an apprentice to boilermaking … I found myself earmarked for the mediocre apprenticeship … which many scoffed was 'more of a disease than a trade!' … even a labourer's first son could go as a boilermaker.

So incensed by this practice were local teachers, in 1945 (no doubt emboldened by having just lived through a war and nursing high hopes of a brighter future) Mr John May, honorary secretary of the Swindon Association, NUT, wrote a strong letter to the CME to express the Association's dismay that apt pupils and good grades went unacknowledged and carried no weight in allowing a boy a choice of trade:

Dear Sir,

The teachers of Swindon do not lose interest in the youths of the town when they leave school, but are concerned with what becomes of them when they enter the world of commerce and industry.

For some time past they have felt that some of their best pupils, who have entered your Swindon Factory, have, in their opinion, not been given the opportunities warranted by their abilities.

Some, who have been outstanding at school, have found vacancies only in the lower grade trades or as labourers, whilst others, who, to say the best, have been only average in their ability, have been granted free apprenticeships at such things as fitting and turning and other first grade trades.

We feel that for some reason the right boys are not always being given the best chance. Since in the near future it seems that the competition for youths entering industry is likely to be keener than before, it behoves both you and us, as far as we can, to see that the best possible use is made of the material available, from your point of view, that you will be better able to fight the competition and also for the good of the country as a whole whose future prosperity will, to a large extent, depend upon the skill of its workmen, which will alone compensate the numeric superiority of other countries.

For these reasons, therefore, I should be extremely obliged if you would be kind enough to inform me of the conditions governing the award of free apprenticeships in your Works, so that we as teachers, may be in a better position to advise the lads leaving our schools.

F.W. Hawkesworth, the CME of the time, replied succinctly:

… our present practice is as follows:

1   Generally the sons of men in primary trades with ten years service are accepted to primary trades up to two in number free, plus a third son to a secondary trade free.
2   Men in secondary trades with ten years service can apprentice two sons in a secondary trade free.
3   Semi-skilled men and laborers, after 20 years service, can apprentice two sons to a secondary trade free.
4   A reduced premium is payable where the service of the father is between 5½ and 10 years.
5   Boys granted free apprenticeships are normally required to have reached the top standard in an Elementary school.
6   Where a boy has shown outstanding ability at his school, the above regulations are relaxed in his favour.

This is not the only time that the sentiment expressed in item No. 6 had been stated. An official document back in January 1926 entitled 'Regulations Governing Apprenticeships in the Locomotive and Carriage Departments' outlined the requirements and stated that:

QUALIFICATIONS FOR ADMISSION	grade and service of father or guardian to conform to our present apprenticeship practice. Boys must be of good character. They must have passed the 6th Standard examination to qualify for a primary trade, while boys not having passed the 5th grade, cannot be considered for apprenticeship.
SPECIAL SCHOLASTIC QUALIFICATIONS	boys who have done specially well at Secondary Schools (and would normally be taken to secondary trades) will be considered for Engine Fitting, Turning and Erecting as opportunities occur.

Whilst the sentiment may have been there, obviously the 'opportunities' did not seem to occur, or did so extremely rarely, as I have not met anyone or been aware of anyone who was offered an apprenticeship out of their category because of their scholastic abilities. Indeed, Mr Harry

Freebury actively argued his son's scholastic ability to get him a better trade, but to no avail, as Hugh Freebury remembers:

> My father produced my School Leaving Report. Could they not offer him on my behalf at least the apprenticeship of a machine-man like himself. 'No,' was the emphatic reply, 'You are only on the 40 shilling rate. If you were on the top grade we might consider it. Sorry.'
>
> So that two extra shillings a week made all the difference.

The type of apprenticeship given to Swindon Works' 'Insiders', i.e. 'free' or 'premium', depended on three things: the skill level of their father; how far down the sibling chain they were born; and whether there were any vacancies available in their preferred trade.

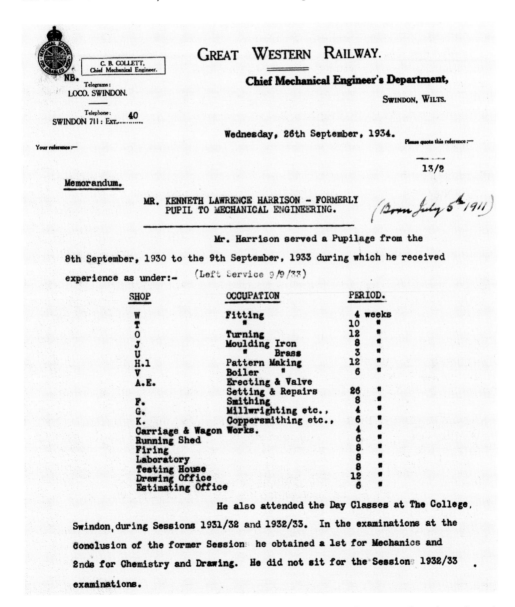

Note that there is no talk of 'apprenticeship' here, just an explanation of study and work undertaken. *STEAM Museum Railway Collection*

For those without family connections to the GWR, the only route in was the fee-paying one, whereby one paid for the privilege of the apprenticeship. There were two categories of fee payers: 'pupil' and 'premium'. From the earliest times of the GWR it was common practice for Works' superintendents and managers to take on pupils. It is known that Daniel Gooch, the first Locomotive Superintendent at Swindon Works, had several pupils 'who gained experience working in the shops, on the engines and in the drawing office'. These were an extra source of direct income for Gooch. He, having decided on this practice, was advised by his brother Tom Gooch to inform Brunel in order that Brunel would not get annoyed finding out indirectly. Tom suggested that Gooch should 'have £400' – a not inconsiderable sum it must be said; however, these pupils usually made good careers because of his patronage and went on to make their own fortunes.[5] 'Pupillage' came with 'patronage', i.e. a special relationship with their master that ordinary trade apprentices would not have had. Such a relationship would help an apprentice comes to terms with the fact that, despite the hefty fee, there was absolutely no pay. Pupillage also came with special attention to their interests and little, if any, stints on boring, repetitive jobs. Pupils came from not just around the country but also further afield, from overseas, as can be seen in the 1861 and 1871 censuses. In 1861 Henry Martineau (17), described as 'Engineer Rail', boarded with John Holmes, the railway District Superintendent, in the superintendent's house in the village, along with Sidney Sorby (18), also 'Engineer Rail', who came from Yorkshire. Martineau's place of origin is given as 'America, British Subject Overseas'. He is not alone in coming from so far away. Later, in 1871, an Edward Chandler (14), 'Apprentice Fitter', is found to be boarding with Thomas Nash (48), machinist, and his son Henry (16), 'Engine Fitter', and is identified as having come from 'Desse, East Indies, Overseas British Subject'.

Pupillage was still alive in the works in the 1930s, as the record of one K.L. Harrison shows. In a memorandum, which serves as a testimonial, Harrison's pupillage (not apprenticeship) is set out.

Pupil apprentices were not shaped for the workshop but for engineering management, and Harrison's report sheet shows that breadth, rather than depth, was what was required and was undertaken – that and application to one's studies of course. How much say pupils had over their passage through the Works is not clear, but probably a lot more than your average trade apprentice did. Pupillage continued in Swindon Works, whether continuously or not I cannot say, but a letter from Hawkesworth to S.J. Ellis of the Mechanical Engineering Department, of the university at Edgbaston, Birmingham, dated October 1945, shows that pupils were still being taken on at that time. Hawkesworth wrote in response to a request on apprenticeship requirements:

> I shall be glad to know if you have in mind our premium apprentice regulations … if so I will forward particulars … lads for these usually come to us at the age of sixteen and the premium is £100, payable in advance in six-monthly instalments of £10. We also take a very small number of Pupils, the fee in this case is £150 per annum and no wages are paid during Pupillage.

Interestingly, in the early times of the GWR there was yet another layer between pupils and straightforward premium apprentices, as Harold Holcroft points out in his book. He records:

> After I had attained my sixteenth birthday [1898] enquiries were made at Crewe and Swindon as to the prospect of my being taken on as a pupil at one or other. Stafford Road had ceased to take any more pupils after George Armstrong left at the end of 1896. The Great Western replied that they intended to initiate there a new grade of premium apprentice shortly which would be intermediate between the pupil and the former premium apprentice, who was admitted on payment of a relatively small sum, but had to take his chance as to which shop he was placed in and how many moves he got subsequently.

CHIEF MECHANICAL ENGINEER'S DEPARTMENT,

GREAT WESTERN RAILWAY. (4049 C)

Memorandum

OF

Regulations under which APPRENTICES are employed

IN THE

CARRIAGE WORKS, SWINDON.

1.—Apprentices are taken in the Carriage Department, as vacancies arise, to one of the Trades of Carriage Body-making, Finishing or Trimming.

2.—An Apprentice should serve a term of 5 years in order to be considered a fully qualified Journeyman, but the engagement may be terminated on either side at the end of any six-monthly period. In this event the time served cannot be regarded as a complete apprenticeship.

3.—A Premium of £5 is payable in advance for each period of six months. 2s. 6d. Stamp Duty is payable on the registration of the application form.

4.—Apprentices are generally taken at the age of 16 years. As a rule there are many more applicants than can be received, and if no vacancy arises before a candidate is 17 years of age, the application is considered to be cancelled. It is particularly requested that no application be made on behalf of a youth who is not of sound constitution and of good bodily health and strength, as otherwise he would not be able to carry out satisfactorily the obligations specified in this Memorandum.

5.—Before a youth is accepted as an Apprentice he will be employed in the Workshops on probation for one month without wages. During this time he will be required to work the ordinary hours of duty as given in paragraph 11. At the expiration of the probationary period, if his conduct and ability are found to be satisfactory, he will be entered on the Register of Apprentices, and receive wages under the conditions stated in paragraph 10.

6.—Every registered applicant must produce a certificate of registration of birth before commencing the month's probation, also a medical certificate of his suitability for following the employment.

7.—During the month's probation it is desired that the probationer will make himself thoroughly familiar with the significance of these Regulations, and if at the end of the month he is not satisfied with the conditions laid down, or if he has any doubt of his ability to comply strictly with the requirements specified, it is expected that his application to be entered as an Apprentice will be withdrawn.

8.—Apprentices are subject to the Rules and Regulations in force as to the management of the Workshops in which they may be employed. Great importance is attached to regular and punctual attendance. In the absence of a justifiable reason, an Apprentice will be liable to dismissal if he fails to make full time regularly, or if he misconducts himself in any other way.

9.—It must be understood that Apprentices being in receipt of wages for work performed, must necessarily be kept for some considerable time upon work in which they have become tolerably proficient. Variety of work will be given to Apprentices from time to time so far as the general arrangement of the Workshops will permit, but it is impracticable to remove them frequently from one class of work to another.

10.—The following scale of wages represents the maximum rates for the respective years of service, but the advances from year to year will be dependent on good conduct, and if there is any ground for complaint in regard to time keeping or in any other respect, the advances may be withheld, or lower rates given than are specified in the scale :—

First Year (16 years of age)	10/6 per week
Second „ (17 „ „)	12/6 „ „
Third „ (18 „ „)	13/- „ „
Fourth „ (19 „ „)	15/- „ „
Fifth „ (20 „ „)	17/- „ „

11.—A normal working week consists of 47 hours. Payment is made for the number of hours actually worked. All Apprentices are required to commence work punctually, and to make full time.

No Apprentice is allowed to work when the Works are closed, except under special authority.

12.—Apprentices are not bound by Indenture, but those who complete satisfactorily the full term of apprenticeship, will at the end of the term receive a certificate stating the class of work on which they have been employed and their ability and general character. A record of any time that may have been lost during the Apprentice-ship will be entered in the following form :—

YEAR ENDED	HOURS WORKS OPEN	HOURS WORKED	TIME LOST (HOURS)			
			SPECIAL LEAVE	ILLNESS	WITHOUT LEAVE	TOTAL
TOTAL FOR 5 YEARS ...						

13.—The usual holidays are as follows :—

Easter, 3 or 4 days: Annual Works holiday, about July, 7 days: Christmas, from 4 to 7 days. The holidays may be extended by one week at Christmas, and by one week at the Annual Works holiday, provided that written application is previously made by the parents or guardian. No extension beyond this will be allowed unless the circumstances are exceptional.

14 —Every apprentice is required to attend the Engineering Classes at the Technical School during the winter session and to take the course of theoretical instruction which will be prescribed for him.

C. B. COLLETT,

Chief Mechanical Engineer,

Swindon,

NOTE.—It must be distinctly understood that Employment is not guaranteed after completion of Apprenticeship.

Note item No. 12 – 'Apprentices are *not* bound by Indenture' (as discussed in Chapter 1). Note also the wording down the side. With no job guaranteed it was a leap of faith for apprentices that they would find good jobs at the end of it.

This poor 'pupil' did not last long, starting in May 1925 and finishing at his first six-month review. *David Hyde Collection*

In the new grade the premium would be raised considerably, but it would be offset to some extent over the years by the payment of wages, commencing at 5*s* per week with annual increments of 2*s* 6*d*. Practical training would be by moves from one shop to another at intervals under a definite plan, and a programme of technical training would be followed by attending classes at the Technical Institute.

Privileged premium apprentices, such as Thomas Hoddy Pratt, who came from Mary-le-Bone, Middlesex, and 'put himself Apprentice to the Directors of the Great Western Railway Company' in April 1861, or Alexander Lamb, who came from Swansea, Glamorganshire, and was apprenticed to Joseph Armstrong 'to learn the Art of a Fitter' in 1865, would have followed a different pathway through apprenticeship than the usual trade apprentices. Harold Holcroft wrote that he was informed by the Works' Manager, E.E. Lucy, that: 'I was not in the Works to make myself proficient in one or other of the skilled jobs as the trade apprentices had to do, but to familiarise myself with all aspects of locomotive construction and maintenance.' Many of these pupils and privileged premiums went on to higher and greater things, and became known, respected names in the railway world – men such as John George Robinson, who became a pupil of Joseph Armstrong in 1872. Twelve years later he moved to a post on the Waterford & Limerick Railway in Ireland and by 1900 he was the Waterford & Limerick's Locomotive Superintendent.

Premium apprenticeships were notable for, and got their name from, the fee which had to be paid for them. The paying of premiums was a long established practice and there is evidence of such in the reign of James I, Olive Jocelyn writes. She goes on to point out that:

> The payment of premiums was not merely a London and localised custom. From a pamphlet written in 1681, it appears that throughout the country they were paid to men engaged in retail business. 'It will cost a round sum of Money,' says one writer, 'before a child can be settled in any Shop-keeping Trade. First, to breed him at School and to make him fit for the same. Secondly, to place him forth to the said Trade when he is fit: Which will cost in a Country Market-Town not less than fifty or sixty pounds, but in London upwards of an hundred.'

At Swindon Works there were two kinds of premium apprentices. Firstly there were the 'Insiders'. These came in various categories:

Over the decades the Company would have received many letters from parents anxious to secure an apprenticeship for their son(s) and willing to pay the price that bought the good name of the GWR with it.

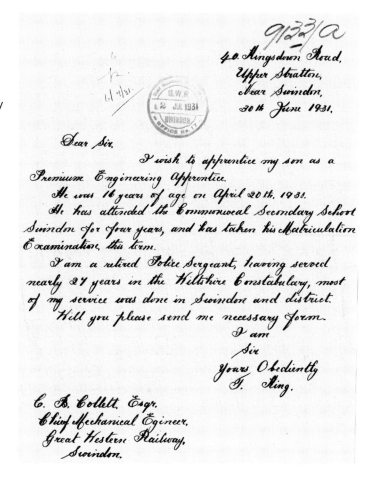

a) those who were not entitled to a free apprenticeship, i.e second, third or sons even further down the line
b) those who were prepared to pay for something different or better than they were entitled to
c) those who paid because it enabled them to get started sooner rather than waiting for a vacancy, which might be a long time coming

One young 'Insider' lad who found it hard to get his apprenticeship started and so chose the premium route was Stanley Joseph Smith. Archives at STEAM Museum show the potted apprenticeship history of Smith, who lived at 12 Exmouth Street. His father, Joseph William Smith, had thirty-five years in the company's service when he ambitiously applied for a coach body-making (an elite trade) apprenticeship for his son in 1923, whilst Joseph was a boiler plater in AB Shop, in the Locomotive Department. The father had originally applied for a free apprenticeship, but it is not shown whether Stanley was too late in the line of siblings to have one. Stanley was already working as a coach body-making boy filling in time until a vacancy arose, but there was not one available, or at least not one available for him. Joseph tried again, this time for an apprenticeship in coach finishing, but once more he received a letter saying there was no vacancy. He was sent a list of trades where vacancies existed, but none matched his hopes for his son; so, after Stanley being in the job for just a few weeks, Joseph applied again, this time for a premium apprenticeship, presumably in order that his son could get on with what he really wanted to do. As Stanley had already been working in the shop he did not have to undertake the usual one-month trial, without wages, to test his suitability for the work; instead a letter was written to Mr E. Evans of the Coach Body-making Shop requesting information as to Stanley's 'conduct and attention to duty'. He obviously passed muster because on 16 February 1923 his father received a letter stating:

> I am pleased to say your son has conducted himself in a satisfactory manner and I am now prepared to accept him as a Premium Apprentice in Coach Bodymaking as from the 9th inst. If you agree I shall be glad to receive your cheque or money order for £5 made payable to the Great Western Railway Company to cover the first instalment. A postal order for 2/6d left blank will also be required.

The 2s 6d was in payment of the Stamp Duty. Stamp Duty had been introduced by the Stamp Act 1709 and came into function from 1710, giving the Government an easy profitable source of revenue. The duty then was sixpence in the pound on sums of £50 or under, and 1s upon sums of over £50.[6]

Having started well, Stanley's commitment wavered over the years, but it is to his father, who was considered responsible for the actions of his son, that a sharp rebuke is written on 24 November 1927:

> I find that during the Month of October, your son attended the Evening Classes for only 17 hours out of a possible 28 hours. This cannot be regarded as a satisfactory commencement, and as you are aware, we have previously drawn your attention to the importance we place upon theoretical training.

Poor Mr Smith had already received a reproach in May that year, highlighting the hope that Stanley's 'absences would not have an adverse effect upon the results of the examinations which he should take next week'. Despite this laxity, Stanley managed to stay the course and in August 1929 his father received acknowledgement from A.C. Dalbertanson, the chief cashier, of his final instalment of £5 which had 'been placed to the credit of PREMIUM APPRENTICE S.J. SMITH SWINDON for the total Premium of £50'. Finally, to testify to his having completed the apprenticeship satisfactorily Stanley's received his Certificate of Apprenticeship.

The problems of 'no vacancies' was a persistent one and not confined to any one era, as the example of David John Robinson in the 1950s shows. Robinson applied unsuccessfully twice, once to be a coach body-builder and then to be a wood wagon-builder; both times there were no vacancies. Finally, he took up a five-year training course in 'iron machining' starting in December 1954.

The second type of premium apprentice was one with no connections to the GWR. In 1861 Edward [?] (46), baker and grocer, living in 7 Alma Street, had a houseful of premium apprentices, all identified as 'Fitter & Turners'. There were both his sons, Jan (18) and Richard (15), as well as lodger William Wesbro (20), who hailed from Bath, Somerset. Some intriguing ones in these early censuses are those where the head of the household is a woman, such as that in 1861 of Ann Fox, residing at 2 Westcott Place but originally from Long Burton, Dorset, whose sons must have been premium apprentices although they are not identified as such. They are John (16), 'Boilersmith' and James (15), 'Fitter & Turner'. Her last son Henry (14) is identified as 'Factory Laborer'. There is also Anna Cooper (59), residing at 21 Regents Street in 1871 but hailing from Exmouth, Devon, whose son Robert (17) is identified as an 'Apprentice Boilersmith'. None of these boys are designated as having been born in New Swindon. Were these women widows of Works' employees or did they come to New Swindon for the sake of their sons and their futures? If so, one wonders how were they able to pay the premium required? It would be intriguing to know all these things. Even in the difficult times of the nineteenth-century Great Depression, records show that young men were willing to take a chance and become premium apprentices. Many decades later John Attwell had to be a premium apprentice in the 1940s. Born in Wales in 1927, his family had immigrated 'up the Great West Road' to England to escape the economic depression which was sweeping the coal-mining valleys and to seek work on the railways. His father managed to secure a job as a storeman. Attwell recalls: 'It was hard to get in as an apprentice. Tradesmen could put their sons in. The only other way in was the way I followed – to become a "premium apprentice". This meant my father had to pay £10 a year for five years – about one week's wage a year.'

Whether through choice or necessity, there were a great many premium apprentices that went through Swindon Works during the GWR era. They would arrive at the Works from all over the country and, as 'Dusty' Durrant, apprenticed just after the Second World War, recalls, even from abroad. Leaving the family home was the first step on their chosen career path. During their apprenticeship they would have to 'go into digs' or lodge with local families. If they were lucky there would be other lads there doing the same as them. Dusty remembers how he was delivered to Swindon by his grandad to an 'attic-bedroom in Mrs Morris' boarding house at the bottom of Rolleston Street'. An early indenture agreed with Works Manager Minard Rea shows that part of the arrangement was the provision of accommodation. By this time, however, apprentices were sorting out their own accommodation.

As probation was unpaid, it was, as Durrant remembers, a particularly tough time for these young lads:

> Social life for a probationer apprentice in lodgings was almost non-existent. On week-days there was a bath and a meal, followed simply by listening to the other lodgers recounting their adventures or complaints. Saturday was laundry day, not included in the lodging tariff. And I patronised OO LEE CHINESE LAUNDRY, a steamy little establishment just around the corner.

Like pupil apprentices, many of those who started as 'outside' premium apprentices went on to great careers. After Nationalisation (1948) there were no premium apprentices – it all came free.

In later decades there was yet another way in – the academic route – as a 'sandwich' apprentice (see Nigel S.C. Macmillan's personal explanation in Chapter 7). The GWR also had 'sandwich' apprentices but the first official mention I have found is not until 1963 and the number of them was rather small – just seven at that time. How popular or successful this scheme was, or became, I do not know.

The final way in to apprenticeship came via the Apprentices' Training School (later known as the Works' Training School), which arrived in 1963. One came straight from school. The trade each boy was apprenticed to depended on the individual's ability, the would-be apprentice's wishes and the technical instructors' recommendations. Most people were lucky enough to get their first choices. This then became the only way into apprenticeship until the Works closed in 1986.

Notes

1   All from Matheson, *Railway Voices.*
2   For fuller details see Matheson, *Railway Voices.*
3   Read the story of Edwin Brittain in Matheson, *Railway Voices.*
4   Attwell, 1997.
5   Platt, *The Life and Times of Daniel Gooch.*
6   Jocelyn.

Two World Wars and In Between

Historian Professor Arthur Marwick called the twentieth century 'the Century of Total War'. Within his concept the First World War was also the first 'total war'. Marwick maintained that 'total war' is when the whole of society is involved and organised in such a way that all resources are utilised in support of the nation's war effort to effect the nation's survival. A good example of this is the use that is made of the railways for the duration of the First World War. Herbert A. Walker, acting chairman of the Railway Executive Committee, explained to the public that: 'The control of the railways has been taken over by the Government for the purpose of ensuring that the railways, locomotives, rolling stock and staff shall be used as one complete unit *in the best interests of the State* for the movement of troops, stores and food supplies'. O.S. Nock fully understood the concept and in his book, *Britain's Railways At War 1939–1945*, entitled his second chapter 'A Weapon For Total War'. Yet another brilliant example, but in the Second World War, is the Battle of Britain, which, as author James Holland asserts in his recent book of the same name, was won not just by the RAF and the magnificent fighter pilots, but 'everyone'. He writes: 'Everyone played their part; the Navy, the Army, the auxiliary services, the Home Guard, the ground crews, the Observer Corps, the civilian repair units … Britain's defiance in the summer of 1940 was a collective effort.'

As we know, the twentieth century had two such total wars. The impact of these two wars on Britain and her people was massive and long lasting. The impact on its institutions was marked and profound. One of the institutions greatly affected was the railways, not least in that it touched all aspects of railway life – production, procedures and practices, especially

The GWR was proud of its war work and articles and pictures appeared in their in-house magazine in 1919, after the war was over and things no longer had to be kept secret. This shows batteries of 6in long-range naval guns built in A Shop. They stand outside A Shop with St Mark's church in the distance.

Part of the GWR's First World War effort, these ambulance coaches were built at Swindon Works.

employment practices. Undoubtedly the railways were affected by total war and the GWR, because of its 'geographical considerations',[2] particularly so.

The immediate effect of the railways being taken over by the War Office was to turn the railway workshops into non-profit-making production factories for the war effort. Their very first order was somewhat mundane yet eerily prophetic – 12,500 ambulance stretchers, of which the GWR were to produce 1,500 at a rate of 200 per week. After this came the order for general service wagons. The GWR adapted a large number of open goods wagons by adding rails to add depth to the wagons, thereby making them suitable for the transportation of horses. Swindon Works war work started with the provision of 'two ambulance trains and a large number of road vehicles for artillery and general transport'.[3]

It was not until later in 1915 that the railways became seriously involved with armament and munitions production, working for and with the Ministry of Munitions, the Woolwich Arsenal, the Admiralty and private firms working for the Government, greatly changing the character of the workshops; the 'pebble-in-the-pond' effect in turn affected the nature of apprenticeship and training.

The GWR as a company were very much behind the war. *The GWR Magazine* brimmed with war information, reports, promotions, bravery awards and death-in-actions, as well as splendid photographs of handsome chaps in uniform and suitably feminine females brought into the railways to do 'their bit for the Country'. The company responded to each Government call for assistance with alacrity and even enthusiasm. There was the GWR company of railway troops of the Royal Engineers, the 116th Railway Construction Co. (June 1915) and the GWR Railway Volunteer Company (formed 15 September 1917 – with uniforms provided from a fund supplied by the directors). The Company's patriotic fervour swept through the Works, so much so that men worried for their jobs if they did not sign up and the management had to send out re-assuring notices:

Circular No. 2414 September 3 1914
Men leaving the Works to join the army.

The rumour which has got about that young men are being discharged from the Works unless they join the Army is absolutely without foundation.

On the other hand all young men willing to join the army will be rendered every assistance in this direction and their places kept open for them. Allowances are also being granted by the Company to all those that are married or have widowed mothers dependent upon them.

Any cases of immediate need or distress that are known should be at once brought to my notice.

Kindly post this notice in your shop.

Sgd C B Collett

GWR men, including apprentices, were also quick to respond to the 'call to arms'. A GWR 'Records of War Interruptions WWI' recod book shows that on 4 August 1914 forty-one apprentices from all over Swindon factory had signed up, with the total number between 4 August 1914 and 14 October 1918 (the last entry) being 251. In the company as a whole 25,479 or 32.6 per cent of the pre-war establishment joined the colours during the course of the war.[4]

Enlistment meant disruption of an apprentice's training. Such time out, known as 'black time', had to be made up. An agreement between Government, employers and unions – the Interrupted Apprenticeship Scheme – enabled this to happen and any relevant Services' experience had to be taken into account to assist this. It was left to each industry to adapt the scheme as suitable, whilst applying its general principles. This made-up time generally occurred after the apprentice had reached the age of 21, when he would normally have been paid a full

Group of G.W.R. Swindon Works men attached to the R.O.D. " somewhere in France."

man's wage, however, because of his time out he was still not a fully trained craftsman so under the terms of the scheme the remaining agreed time was completed on a sub-craft or improvers' wage (despite the fact that he had been fighting for his country). War service interruptions, as they were called, were vigorously recorded to ensure that all apprentices served their 'real' time. An alphabetical register for the First World War lays out precisely the timing element of this interruption in relation to the bound over period and the Government allowance time:

Shop	Check No.	Name	Grade	D.O.B.	Date enlisted	Date resumed work	Time in Army	Time at trade in Army	App'ship years bound for	App' time served	Time to serve	To complete under scheme	Government grant allowed	
													From	To
17	9904	Ackrill L.F.	Wheelwright app.	27.5.97	*4.8.14	29.12.19	5. 4	---	6¼	2. 5	3. 10	2. 7 2. 0	29.12.19	28.12.21
21	6933	Collard C.W.B.	Wagon Bldr app.	15.4.00	15.5.18	17.3.19	0. 10	---	6¾	3. 10	2. 11	0. 6	4.4.21	18.10.21
14	7342	Newman H.V.	Smith's app.	12.9.01	+4.10.18	6.4.20	1. 6	---	6½	2. 7	3. 11	1. 0	12.9.22	18.9.23
21	6851	White W.G.	Wagon Bldr app.	4.12.94	*4.8.14	28.4.19	4. 8	---	5½	2. 8	2. 10	1. 11	28.4.19	2.4.21
7	1401	Woodcock J.L.	Finisher app.	22.3.97	11.1.16	13.8.19	3. 7	3. 7	6	3. 10	2. 2	---	---	---
12	714	Woodley S.	Carp. app.	12.3.97	4.10.15	10.11.19	4. 1	4. 1	6½	4. 1	2. 5	---	---	---

Sample of information taken from Register STAFF RECORDS & AGREEMENTS Part 2. Misc. STEAM MUSEUM
* this is the first date of entry for men signing up.
+ this is the last signing-up date.

Right: All 'lost time' was also meticulously recorded on one's Apprenticeship Certificate at the completion of the apprenticeship.

1171.

Great Western Railway.

Locomotive, Carriage & Wagon Department,
GGW
CHIEF MECHANICAL ENGINEER'S OFFICE,

30309 N.   Swindon, Wilts, November 1st 19 21.

(21-1)

Certificate of Apprenticeship.

I hereby certify that

FRANCIS HARRY HAYES

born on the 8th June 1899 has been employed as an Apprentice in this Department as follows:-

Period of Apprenticeship   6½   years.
from 8/12/1913 to 7/6/1920.
Trade Engine Fitting, Turning & Erecting.
Works at which employed Locomotive Works, Swindon
Hayes joined the Colours in May 1918, and returning here in December 1919, completed his term under the Government Interrupted Apprenticeship Scheme on the 13th July 1921.

CHIEF MECHANICAL ENGINEER.
G.W.R. Loco, Carriage & Wagon Department.

Opposite: A somewhat enigmatic title to a rather sombre-looking photograph, but by such means the GWR were able to publicise and promote their men's efforts without giving away any secrets.

GREAT WESTERN RAILWAY.

LOCOMOTIVE, CARRIAGE & WAGON DEPARTMENT,
ENGINEER'S OFFICE,
SWINDON Tues., November 2nd 1920.

4934/A/N. GW.

Certificate of Apprenticeship.

Name THOMAS JAMES DRAPER.

Period of Apprenticeship Five years from 31st July 1911.

Where employed Locomotive Works, Swindon.

Work on which employed

Erecting Shop.	Erecting	3½ months
General Fitting and Machine Shop.	Turning	15½ "
General Fitting and Machine Shop.	Fitting	17½ "
Military Service from 8/8/1914 to 3/3/1919.		
Engine Erecting Shop.	Erecting	15 "
	At trade	4 years 3½ months.

YEAR ENDED.		HOURS WORKS OPEN	HOURS WORKED	TIME LOST (HOURS). SPECIAL LEAVE.	ILLNESS.	WITHOUT LEAVE.	TOTAL.	
July 20th	1912	2509¼	2426	10½	59¼	13½	83¼	
July 19th	1913	2599	2321½	22½	242	13	277½	
July 18th	1914	2635	2471¾*	175¼	-	16	191¼	*Includes 28 hrs overtime.
July 19th to Aug. 3rd	1914	106¾	106¾	-	-	-	-	
		Military duty from 8/8/1914 to 3/3/1919.						
Mar. 6th	1920	2288½	2178	93½	17	-	110½	
Mar. 8th May 17th	1920 1920	453	444½	-	8½	-	8½	
TOTALS.........		10591½	9948½*	301¾	326¾	42½	671	*Includes 28 hrs Overtime

N.B.—The "Hours Works open" does not include the Works Holiday (averaging about 20 days per annum); "Special leave" represents time lost for Holidays in addition to the usual Works Holidays.

THOMAS JAMES DRAPER, was registered as a premium apprentice, at these Works, to Engine Fitting and Turning for a term of five years as shewn above. He enlisted for Military Duty in August 1914, returned here in March 1919, and completed his term under the Government Interrupted Apprenticeship Scheme on the 17th May 1920. Draper has always borne a good character, has been diligent and attentive to his duties, and the foremen under whom he has been employed report that he possesses good ability as a Mechanic.

This is a delightful certificate, being so complete and giving so much detailed information, including 'War Interruption Service'. Most are more like that of Francis Harry Hayes.

Such interruptions were repeated during the Second World War. Gordon Ing was one who had a somewhat 'modified' apprenticeship because of the war: 'I did four years and then one year working on the war effort in Germany. That was taken as part of my training and so it was accepted as a full apprenticeship'; whilst Eric John Day's Certificate of Apprenticeship states that he served just four years, from August 1943 until August 1947, to learn the motor-fitting trade at Swindon Repair Shop and that the apprenticeship was 'interrupted by service in Forces from 1/1/45/'. Unusually, but appropriately, it is signed by G.S.H. Halliday, Road Motor Engineer.

MINISTRY OF LABOUR.

TRAINING   DEPARTMENT.

SCHEME No. 1

For the Training of Apprentices whose Apprenticeship has been interrupted by-service in H.M. Forces.

Apprentices in the Engineering Industry.

This scheme has been prepared by the Engineering and the National Employers' Federations and the Amalgamated Society of Engineers, Steam Engine Makers' Society, United Machine Workers' Association, Amalgamated Society of Toolmakers, Amalgamated Instrument Makers' Trade Society, United Journeymen Brassfounders, &c., Association of Great Britain and Ireland, Associated Blacksmiths' and Ironworkers' Society of Great Britain and Ireland, United Kingdom Society of Amalgamated Smiths and Strikers, Electrical Trades Union, and National Brass Workers and Metal Mechanics as representing the Associations of Employers and of Workpeople in the Industry and approved by the Minister of Labour.

The scheme shall come into force on and as from the 1st day of January, Nineteen Hundred and Nineteen.

In order to qualify for this Government programme, an agreement form had to be filled in and signed by both parties. It was important to do so in order to make up the 'black time' lost through war service and to gain a full apprenticeship.

Whilst the GWR were wholeheartedly behind the war effort, it gave them many headaches, not least of which was the constant loss of men. Joining the Colours led to a constant haemorrhaging of male workers (as well as apprentices). This meant a depletion of men in all grades and trades which meant that the company was always short of skilled labour. The railway companies had fought to 'retain in their service men who were essential to the working of the railway' and initially this was achieved until, eventually, universal conscription was introduced. Training up skilled labour, as we know, took time, even years. In war periods time is of the essence, things are needed now, not next year or the year after, and this was certainly the case for munitions. It was some eighteen months before new munition factories were ready for production and in that time railway workshops stepped up to fill the demand. A small article in *The GWR Magazine* informs the reader:

With regard to the Locomotive factory, the commencing order from the War Office was for work in connection with the preparation of 4.5. howitzers, viz., gun-carriage and limbers and ammunition wagons and limbers. These proved so successful in the field that the authorities decided to construct ammunition wagons and limbers for 60.pdr guns modelled on similar lines. This being a new departure rendered it necessary to prepare appropriate jigs and tools in Swindon before the detail work could be proceeded with.

This was a small beginning of something that became much larger. Who then were the men achieving this production? At one time so great was the lack of skilled men that the Government had to release 2,650 skilled machinists from the armed forces back to the railway to assist the GWR in the production of some 2,000 6in-high explosive shells every week.[5] The Ministry of Munitions' response to the need for skilled persons quickly was to set up special training schools. Here, with the agreement of the unions, skilled jobs were broken down into smaller parts – that is diluted – and men (and women) were trained up in these smaller tasks. These new employees were known as 'dilutees', i.e. not fully skilled workers, some of whom, much against the men's wishes, were introduced into the Works. A management report to the Board states:

> It is proposed to extend the employment of women in wages grade … and to dilute skilled labour in Swindon Works. These steps are to an extent being opposed by the men and in the case of the mechanics it has been found necessary to arrange a meeting with the Trade Union in order to come to an understanding on the subject.[6]

The role or place, changed or constant, of apprentices in the policies of war practices does not figure in any of the books, war specials or general information related to the railways; neither do their experiences or contributions. Official reports, memorandums and statements do not make mention of them. Perhaps this is not surprising. Apprentices, after all, are but minnows in such grand-scale scenarios, but it is exceedingly frustrating and difficult to trace a history or experience in such barren ground. In times of crisis, such as war, under-represented groups are often fore-fronted in public debates or discourses, but this did not happen here for apprentices, at least not in their working capacity. They were, however, sadly recorded in their deaths (see Appendix).

Whilst the end of the war brought peace, it also brought the end of 'collective endeavour' and ushered in an era of unprecedented industrial unrest in Britain. It is said that 1919 was the year that brought Britain closest to a workers' revolution, such was the strength and persistence of the agitation. All the pent-up grievances from before and during the war – the anger and even desperation to achieve a decent life and a living wage or what was known as a 'family wage', i.e. one that a low-pay man could keep a family on – burst out of a people who now wanted their say and did not want to return to the old order of things. The year 1919 saw millions of working days – 34.969 million according to Office of National Statistics – lost to industrial action; army servicemen mutinied, even the police came out on strike. The National Railway Strike of that year started at midnight on Friday 26 September and lasted nine days. It was, according to the National Union of Railwaymen, action against the Government's intentions to apply wartime pay agreements in such a manner that they would actually bring about significant wage cuts. The press called it 'a Lightning Strike' and even the GWR reported it in their own *Magazine* as 'a great surprise [even] to railwaymen themselves', but Mr F. Evers, JP, addressing a rally in Swindon town organised by Swindon's Trades Council on Monday 29 September, informed the thousands-strong crowd: '1907 was the year that the movement started which has resulted in this strike' – it had been a long slow fuse but now the fire had ignited. He went on to tell them that though 'the call to station has not yet come' for Swindon, when it did they would all be 'wholeheartedly' behind it, and so it proved, as an extract from the General Manager's Labour Report to the Board 7 November 1919 states:

> The majority of the men at Swindon Works went on strike, some thousand employees only presenting themselves for duty on Tuesday morning … but as the majority of them were youths and apprentices it was decided to close the Works at noon that day. Following the settlement of the strike it has been arranged to re-open the works for four days per week only (Tuesday to Friday) until further notice.

The strike did not capture the public's sympathy. Even the *Swindon Advertiser*, usually pro local railway people's issues, appeared to be more on the side of the Government, declaring: 'It is fortunate that the people are supporting the Government so energetically … and the Government's call for volunteers has not been in vain.' Whilst this strike delivered successful outcomes in terms of government agreements for the railwaymen, it was a small victory in an uneasy landscape. It was a victory that did not allay railway people's worries, quite rightly, as more were to follow.

After the war and demobilisation, the numbers of men in the workshops 'were unduly inflated', wrote Kenneth J. Cook in his work *Swindon Steam 1921–1951*, as the GWR, in

Dear Comrades,

At the time of writing we find it impossible to make any definite arrangements as regards to ensuring the 'Daily Herald' being brought to Swindon for to-day's issue. We feel certain that we shall succeed in obtaining a supply for Thursday.

REPORTS FROM STRIKE CENTRES.

Wootton Bassett. Solidarity and good spirits reign here.

Newport. Absolutely solid.

Newton Abbot. Out to a man.

Chippenham. Splendid solidarity, 98% all grades out.

Westbury. Magnificent solidarity.

Cirencester. Astounding success, absolutely solid.

Gloucester. 1310 on strike out of 1325.

Lydney. Only three working.

Telegram received from **Brighton** :—
Every shop worker out here, traffic also, position splendid. Wires from other centres state same position.

RAYNER
Sec. Shop Workers' National Committee.

The following reports were received by 'phone at midnight.—

Welshpool. Confidence not shaken.

Exeter. All standing firm.

Derby. Position excellent. District solid including shopmen.

Plymouth. Top hole. All out.

Our old friend George Brown wiring from **Bristol** states " position splendid

Telegram received from **Brighton** :—
Every shop worker out here, traffic also, position splendid. Wires from other centres state same position.

RAYNER
Sec. Shop Workers' National Committee.

The following reports were received by 'phone at midnight.—

Welshpool. Confidence not shaken.

Exeter. All standing firm.

Derby. Position excellent. District solid including shopmen.

Plymouth. Top hole. All out.

Our old friend George Brown wiring from **Bristol** states " position splendid from Bristol to Weymouth," and the Bristol Secretary wires, " all grades responded magnificently."

SWINDON.

The Strike Committee are satisfied with the magnificent response. If members loyal success is assured, above reports give greatest confidence. **We are bound to win.**

Swindon's Strike Committee published its own bulletin to keep the strikers 'truthfully' informed. On Thursday 2 October it reported: 'All reports from strike centres indicate the men are remaining loyal ... the women are in this fight, an enthusiastic meeting of the Swindon Members was held yesterday.'

true patriotic spirit, reinstated all those men and apprentices who had gone to war, just as they had promised. They even extended the deadline for men to return to company services from 30 June 1920 to 31 July 1920 (as detailed in the Minutes of Board of Directors, 4 November 1920). The Company also exhibited a change of attitude and practice in respect of apprentices, as is demonstrated in the communiqué sent out by C.B. Collet, then Locomotive Works' Manager, on 26 March 1919: 'Should a father have a son killed during the War, who was an apprentice here, if he has another son we will endeavour to apprentice him to the same trade.'

Of the 25,479 men who had enlisted, 20,031 men (78.8 per cent) returned to company services; 2,259 (8.8 per cent) sought employment elsewhere; 137 (0.5 per cent) re-enlisted; and, at the time of meeting, 91 (0.3 per cent) were still expected to return. Sadly, 2,436 men and boys (9.6 per cent) were killed. I say 'boys' because some of this number were apprentices and being such they would have been under the age of 21. Despite these 'non-returners' there were, Cook says, 'double numbers of apprentices coming out of their times'. In normal circumstances, as stated previously, many of these would not have been kept on as journeymen, but the GWR would need a quick pool of skilled, if not experienced, men to replace the thousands it had lost. It was a complicated state of affairs as again the GWR needed to reduce its costs. Its usual way for doing this was to reduce the intake of apprentices (or sometimes to increase the number of apprentices and lose higher paid skilled workers); let more apprentices go; 'shorten hands' or go on 'short-time' working. Short-time working became a feature that was to last through the late 1920s and into the 1930s too. Whilst we talk and write of the 1930s as the 'Great Depression', we like to view the earlier decade as 'the Roaring Twenties', a time of gaiety, frippery, liberated fashion and high living. Such thinking was (and is) a social therapy. People needed it after the trauma of the 'War to End All Wars'. Unfortunately, high living and high-jinks may have been the way for the few, but the reality for the masses was that the 1920s was a very tough period. An extract from a foreman's diary (believed to be of A Shop) highlights the difficulties the GWR were facing. At this time the Chief Mechanical Engineer, C.B. Collett; Locomotive Manager, W.A. Stanier; and Champney, foreman and union representatives would sit down to a 'Round Table' meeting (as identified in the diary). Such a meeting took place in January 1922 and was recorded:

> Mr Collett ably put the situation (bad trade, engine miles down 12,000,000 miles). A saving of 25 per cent on wage bill at Swindon was needed, either in men, time or money. What could be saved on PW would reduce the discharge or shortening of time, men's reps agreed to give their best towards a good situation.[7]

The 1920s was a decade that demanded change, but was plagued by poverty and unemployment, social unease and massive industrial action. Britain was in great difficulties, in-hock to the USA, with its industrial economy in disarray. Despite this, gradually, in the early years, Britain had begun to make a slow recovery, creating new market products to try to replace those old markets it had lost. When, in April 1925, Winston Churchill, in his role as the chancellor in the Conservative Government, on the advice of the Bank of England, restored the pound to the gold standard at its pre-war exchange rate, it brought Britain's fragile recovery to a virtual standstill. The resultant actions of British companies seeking to reduce their costs to make their products and exports less expensive by cutting jobs and wages, led to further discontent and unrest in an already extremely volatile workplace and laid the foundations for the biggest workers' action in living memory. O.S. Nock called it 'the tragedy of 1926' and most likely, for many reasons, he was right. The General Strike of May 1926 was a call to arms for the common working man and woman to have his and her voice heard and action felt. The voice was not listened to, but the action was sorely noticed. The strike had a severe effect on the country and part of its aftermath was a badly bruised railway industry, and a gravely damaged GWR. It left the company reeling and hurt in many ways, economically, socially, philosophically and it would not be stretching the point too far to say emotionally. It would take a long time for such wounds to heal, on both sides, and the railway industry's business recovery was a matter of fingers-crossed hope over certainty. In Swindon Works all the unions had stood together as men and women heeded the call, even in the offices. Apprentices were not supposed to strike (all men interviewed expressed this point most strongly), neither was there an expectation that they would, as was seen in the strike of 1919; nor were they considered 'blacklegs' or 'scabs' or any other name usually attached to those who crossed picket lines; nor did they receive 'a present of a gallon of tar through their letter boxes'[8] or on their front doors and windows[9] when they did. Striking, for apprentices, was hugely risky. It could mean losing their apprenticeship and their chosen future livelihood, for, having withdrawn their labour – definite misconduct – and purposefully broken the terms of their apprenticeship, it was highly unlikely they would be offered another apprenticeship elsewhere. Political activist and local supporter Angela Tuckett writes in her chapter 'Swindon', published as part of the book *The General Strike (1926)*, of a surprising and somewhat astonishing encounter between apprentices and management during the second day of the strike. It is so incongruous it is worth repeating in full:

The morning of Tuesday, 4 May, pickets went to all the gates, but they were not needed. The unions had agreed to allow apprentices to clock in if they wished that first morning and issued instructions to the pickets accordingly. One of these was L V Parker, a vehicle builder and one of the young ILP enthusiasts. He describes what happened next. 'We let them through but we took their names and noted which shop they worked in. But there was no work done by them as the men were out and the machinery stopped. After they had gone inside they organised meetings during the morning, gathering their fellow apprentices together from all over the works. They decided they would go out. When they reached the 'Tunnel' entrance in London Street, the manager W A Stanier, was there. To prevent them leaving he had a hose turned on them. For a time they held back. Then one tall ginger-haired chap decided he was not going to put up with that. He got in amongst the boys and they decided to rush the exit in a body. And they did. Some got soaked through, but the manager was swept aside, his hat knocked off his head, and the boys swept out to the cheering of the men. It was quite a sight to see the manager treated like that'. By 12.30pm a notice appeared at every entrance signed by C B Collet, the Chief Mechanical Engineer: 'In view of the large number of men who have failed to report themselves for duty these works are hereby closed until further notice'. There was no doubt, the battle was on.

Battle indeed it was and one in which hostilities continued after the 'peace' had been agreed, so Swindon Works' men claimed. The Company was slow to reinstate many of the men, choosing who they wanted, withdrawing seniority of service, whilst rescinding or limiting earned privileges on a seemingly ad-hoc basis. 'Victimisation' was the word on the men's lips, which the company vehemently denied. Undoubtedly there was great bitterness on both sides which lasted for a long, long time. Many railwaymen left Swindon to seek employment elsewhere, never to return. One lad who came out in support of the men and paid the consequence was young apprentice Sidney Frank Hayward, who had not long started working in the Steamhammer Shop. He never went back. He was given his notice: 'your services are no longer required.'

One immediate after-effect of the strike was that once again the GWR needed to drastically reduce its working costs and quickly. It took stringent and hard-edged measures to do so and acted fast. Swindon Works was immediately placed on a four-day week, with all shops shut on Mondays and Saturday indefinitely.

Short-time working was a feature of GWR's Swindon Works right through its lifetime but particularly so through the 1920s and 1930s. It was also a feature in other Works, as mentioned by Harold Holdcroft.

GREAT WESTERN RAILWAY.

CHIEF MECHANICAL ENGINEER'S DEPARTMENT.

Extended
Short Time Working.

It has unfortunately become necessary to extend the short time working to include the Mondays as well as the Saturdays off, and the Workshops will be closed for these lengthened periods commencing Friday evening, 12th September.

C. B. COLLETT

SWINDON,
29th August, 1930.

TWITCHER & CO., PRINTERS, SWINDON.

'Shortening hands' became the order of the day; this was to have a marked and ongoing effect on all stages of apprenticeships:

EMPLOYMENT OF BOYS

In addition to the men we have discharged, due to the necessity of reducing our staff. We have also lost 49 men through completion of apprenticeship or retirement on reaching 70.

I think the time has arrived when we should engage a certain number of lads to partially fill these vacancies, in order that our proportion of apprentices may be maintained.

I shall be glad therefore to receive your permission to take on say 40 lads, during the next few week to fill these vacancies, and also engage lads as similar vacancies occur.

By this means we shall be enabled to reduce our staff to the number required, and at the same time maintain the balance in the workshops.

Further correspondence returns again to the reduced numbers of apprentices, stating:

Although it is of course understood that the number of the apprentices has still to be reduced so that the ratio may be the same when the discharges have been completed, it does not seem advisable to completely stop putting on apprentices until this minimum is reached, owing to the stagnation that occurs.

This is specially so in the Fitting, Turning and Erecting apprentices, as in the preliminary stages of apprenticeship embracing the group of nut, bolt heading and parting lathes, on which 35 apprentices spend the first 6 months of their time, no movement can take place until new apprentices are put on, and this re-acts through the whole of the machine groups and in a more modified form in the Fitting and Erecting groups.

Official evidence shows that on 16 August 1926 just seventeen office boys were transferred to their trades:

B Shop	5	Fitting, Turning & Erecting
K Shop	3	2 Coppersmiths & 1 Tinsmith
V Shop	6 }	Boilermaking
AV Shop	1 }	
J Shop	1	Moulding
Q Shop	1	Angle Iron Smithing

By 1927 and 1928, however, the GWR was, Nock says, in much better condition than some of the other railway companies and enjoying their 'engineering eminence'. They had introduced new designs in engines, not least the magnificent 4-6-0 4-cylinder 'King' class (1927), which put them ahead of the competition. Yet a record book entitled *Great Western Railway Fries [Fridays] Report. From: 1.1.27 To: 31.12.27*[10] shows the GWR were definitely still laying off men and letting go large numbers of apprentices, at least at Swindon Works; the latter may have been a knock-on effect of the 'inflation' of apprentices Cook had talked of. The book records the numbers of men and boys leaving and the reasons for their doing so. The word 'leaving' is being used very flexibly here. Being asked to leave, given no option but to leave, it being suggested you leave, using any excuse to make one leave – all come under this 'leaving' umbrella. Under their heading 'Causes for Leaving' are listed:

Advanced Age / Age Limit [most were aged 70 or thereabouts]
Continued illness [this suggests the management took the decision]
Deceased [there were a surprising number under this heading – 114 in all]
Discharged unsuitable
Discharged physically unfit

Discharged services no longer required
Manager's instructions – absent without leave
Marked off – WCA case/awl
Own accord
Resigned – under notice to leave
Resignation – ill health
Reducing / Shortening hands [i.e. laying off men]
Transferred to – [other departments in the Works, to permanent staff, or elsewhere along the system]

In respect of apprentices and those in training there are several headings:

Termination of apprenticeship by resignation [usually premium apprentices]
Discharged – apprenticeship terminated
Discharged – apprenticeship completed
Discharged – training completed

The numbers given for those 'leaving' are:

Year	Men	Boys	Total	
1927	382	18	400	
1928	443	16	459	} total 1,275
1929	397	19	416	

Those who had completed their apprenticeships would have been counted as 'men', having by that time attained their majority. The number of apprenticeships completed were: 1927 – 145; 1928 – 169; 1929 – 192; making a total of 507. Of these there were only eighty-nine who were retained, with 317 being discharged.

The number of 'terminated' apprenticeships was eighteen. Reasons given include 'absent without leave' and 'lateness'. Timekeeping was one of the 'Ten Commandments' of the GWR. It was almost written on tablets of stone, so immutable was it. It was included in their rules from the earliest of times, and was a stipulated requirement in the apprenticeship indentures and agreements. 'Lateness' led in the first instance to loss of earnings and repeated lateness to further loss and disciplinary action, such as suspension, which could be up to a number of days, and finally even dismissal. Tight hold was kept on timekeeping. At the beginning of the day, and after the lunch-break, the men and boys would 'check in'. Each workman and apprentice had his own brass ticket, a small metallic disc with their work number stamped on it; later this became known as 'the check'. It was unique to each individual. This precious 'check' had to be placed in the check-box before the 'checky' (the timekeeper) closed it. In 1876 the rules stated that if you did not deposit your check you would be 'paid half time only for that particular portion of the day'. In the early half of the twentieth century, if unfortunate enough not to make it before the slamming down of the lid on the check box, for whatever reason, you were docked a quarter of an hour's wages. If you came even later you risked being sent home again. Should, as an apprentice, you repeat any lateness again during the week, you would be brought up before the shop foreman. Being brought to the attention of the shop foreman for the wrong reasons was something which any apprentice would have feared, greatly. Foremen wielded powers that could make or blight your path through the workshops, your pay increments and your future employment prospects. One did not want to get on the wrong side of them! In Samuel Carlton's time, premium apprentices who lost two-quarters in one week had to be personally conducted by one of the head foremen to see him – a head foremen and a Works Manager added up to any apprentice's worse nightmare, especially as it meant that their apprenticeship might be in serious jeopardy. One does not know how often these 'terminated' young apprentices of the 1920s had been late, but when the company is looking to lose men, then it is obviously not a good practice to test them. One or two unfortunates were also marked up in red 'not to be re-employed'.

Surprisingly, amongst the 'Termination of Apprenticeships' are a goodly number of premium apprentices, some of whom are two, three or even four years into their time, whilst one, N.M. Freeman, had almost six years under his belt. Whilst no explanations are given for these particular terminations, economic pressures of meeting the premium payment must be the primary consideration. Some of these lads may have had fathers in the Works who had been laid off, or were now on 'short-time', so could not find the required money. 'Outside' premium apprentices could also have had fathers (or mothers – as census records show where there is no father it is the mother, as head of the household, who would be responsible for the payment) who were similarly affected. Over this time unemployment in the country was high and by time Labour took office after winning the 1929 General Election it had been running at around a million men out of work for some time.

Amongst the twenty-nine 'Discharged Training Completed' were listed:

W. Scull	Planer		D.O.B.	19.10.1905
Ent. Ser. 10.02.1920	R Shop	5/-	Dischgrd.	11.11.1927
A.N. Porter	Machinist			
	(Oxygen Metal Cutting)		D.O.B.	25.08.06
Ent. Ser. 31.01.1921	AM Shop	35/-	Dischrgd.	12.08.1928
C.H. Hughes	Machinist (Gen Joiner)		D.O.B.	08.09.1906
Ent. Ser. 14.03.1921	D¹ Shop	35/-	Dischrgd.	12.10.1928
W.F. Tremblew	Machineman (Shaper)		D.O.B.	30.09.1906
Ent. Ser. 02.01.1922	R Shop		Dischrgd.	09.11.1928
A.J. Snell	Machineman (Driller)		D.O.B.	10.11.1906
Ent. Ser. 4.10.1921	AM Shop	35/-	Dischrgd.	07.12.1928
H.J. Varney	Machineman (Grinder)		D.O.B.	06.01.1907
Ent. Ser. 12.09.1921	AM Shop	35/-	Dischrgd.	01.02.1929
P.E. Alexander	Machineman (Driller)		D.O.B.	06.12.1906
Ent. Ser. 19.10.1921	G Shop	35/-	Dischrgd.	04.01.1929
W.G. Gardiner	Machineman (Auto)		D.O.B.	19.11.1906
Ent. Ser. 15.06.1921	T Shop	35/-	Dischrgd.	04.01.1929
E.F. Parsloe	Holder-up		D.O.B.	18.05.1908
Ent. Ser. 22.10.1924	AV Shop	37/-	Dischrgd.	21.06.1929
F. Haynes	Fitter		D.O.B.	30.05.1907
Ent. Ser. 23.04.1923	O Shop	46/-	Dischrgd.`	
S.W. Humphreys	Machineman (General)		D.O.B.	13.07.1907
Ent. Ser. 23.04.1923	AM Shop	35/-	Dischrgd.	16.08.1929
H.R. Humphries	Machineman			
	(Planer & Slotter)		D.O.B.	07.07.1907

Ent. Ser.06.06.1922	R Shop	35/–	Dischrgd.	16.08.1929
A.J.H. Hatherhall	Wheel Turner		D.O.B.	14.08.1907
Ent. Ser. 28.09.23	AW Shop	35/–	Dischrgd.	13.08.1929
J.W. Hawkins	Holder–up		D.O.B.	28.09.1908
Ent. Ser. 12.03.1923	V Shop	37/–	Dischrgd.	25.10.1929
D.A. Sheppard	Machineman (Slotting)		D.O.B	11.10.1907
Ent. Ser. 21.08.22.	AM Shop	35/–	Dischrgd.	08.11.1929
R.W.J. Beale	Metal Machinist		D.O.B.	21.10.1907
Ent. Ser. 14.08.1922	AM Shop	35/–	Dischrgd.	22.11.1929
R.A. Webb	Wood Machinist		D.O.B.	09.11.1907
Ent. Ser. 11.09.1922	D¹ Shop	35/–	Dischrgd.	13.12.1929

I have not itemised all those discharged after training, merely a sample to highlight the many different types of work that fell within 'training' and also 'machineman' or 'machinist' – a specialised and defined skill group, and one that raised some dispute and debate in the twentieth-century Works' workshops when what was 'skilled' and what was 'semi-skilled' still defined the man and the level of his rate of pay.

The earliest mention of machinemen for the GWR is the Fawcett List, whereby seven 'Men at Machines' are cited. At this time (1843) these men would have been considered to be 'engineers', amongst the elite of tradesmen in the railway world. In these earlier years the artisan machinists were held as superior to engineers, who were considered by some as a nonentity trade and not worthy of a mention in *The Book of English Trades, and Library of Useful Arts 1818*. The machinist, however, is described as being 'of very recent introduction' but embodying in his profession 'the chief principles of the Mechanics'. A machinist, it was claimed, 'possessed of considerable ingenuity and great mechanical knowledge, his employment being of a very complicated kind'. He also 'requires the talents and experience of the joiner, the brass and iron founder, the smith and the turner, in their most extended variety'. The awe the machinist was held in is summed up by the long listing of the 'most important articles he manufactures', some of which we would not nowadays recognise as being within a machinist's domain, such as 'machinery constructed for experimental and scientific elucidation, steam engines both of condensing and high pressure to any power, philosophical and gas–light machines, garden engines, hydro–static engines and hydro–mechanical presses', whilst also including some that we would recognise as being of their work: 'cutting engines for screws, wheels, cylinders and boring bars, stamping and cutting presses with dies and punches … all sorts of turning in iron and steel.' By 1831 some already held there to be a distinct difference between the operative mechanic and the British machinist, as written by civil engineer John Nicholson, who claims his practical guide book is 'adapted in every possible way to be of use to the Mechanic *and* Machinist' – two separate entities. Come 1851, with the birth of the Amalgamated Society of Engineers, Machinists, Millwrights, Smiths and Pattern Makers, there appears to be agreement of some very clear differentiation. Why, how and when did this separation occur? How subtle was it or was it a biblical Red Sea parting of the waves? I have found nothing to enlighten us on this aspect; however, a logical rationale is that differentials would have started to occur when engineering became more theoretically based and more conceptualised in design and operation, whilst also expanding to take on work of wider dimensions. Machine work, however, was and remained more specific, i.e. related to output and production. It was about producing specific parts already designed and thought through. Another factor that would have reinforced the differential was economics. Factory work, especially machine work and fitting, turning and erecting (engineering), was paid by rates, usually piece rates, and employers and crafts guilds/societies, and later unions, would have been keen to keep specialised rates separate to be used as bargaining tools. One early document that highlights this separation and magnifies the differentiation in status is that of the submission to the Board of Trade for 1886 and 1891 previously cited. 'Machinist (Iron and Wood)' is a quite separate category to that of 'Mechanics – (Metals & Wood)'. The weekly wage rate of each grade shows the wide divide. Mechanics (metals) ranged from 19s up to 55s and those of mechanic (wood) from 20s up to 38s. Those for the machinist, however, started at just 5s and went up to of a maximum 35s. The 5s rate was more than likely the first-step-on-the-rung training rate, as with the apprentices; however, the majority of the mechanics (metals and wood) are to be found in the middle-range wage rate, whilst the majority of the machinists are to be found in the lowest wage rate. It is quite obvious that by this time machining had become a 'relegated' trade.

It is interesting to find GWR information on training for machinists, as it is little mentioned or recorded either in official records or in books. One official document I have unearthed is one that outlines the new 'understanding' between company and the Machinist Society, arrived at in the aftermath of the General Strike. It is written to C. Aldington at Paddington, signed by C.B. Collett on behalf of Churchward (then CME) and dated 11 December 1926:

—⟨𝑜/𝑜/𝑜⟩—

Probationary Period for Machinists

Further to my letter of the 10 November, we have now come to an understanding with the Machinist Society that future Machinemen in these Works shall be trained from boys, and that the probationary period shall be arranged for five years commencing at 17 years of age.

The classes of Machinemen are arranged in six groups of varying rates of pay, according to the group, and also according to age, the full rate for the same grade being reached at 23.

At 22 years of age the probationary period is ended, and the rates shown below are the starting rates for Machinemen of the grades mentioned. These rates are base rates, and do not include War Wage or bonus.

1	Universal Millers & Grinders	Loco Carr. & Wagon
2	Palin Cylindrical Grinders	" " "
3	Wheel Turners	Loco Works
4	Shapers, Planers, Slotters, Millers	
	Borers, Drillers 1st class	
	And other Grinders	Loco Carr. & Wagon
5	Wheel Turners	Loco Works
6	Drillers 2nd class	Boilers, Erecting Shop
	Drillers & Plate Edge Planers	Loco Carr & Wagon
	Millers and Drillers	Wagon Shop
	Corewers & Sawyers	Loco Carr. & Wagon

Age	1	2	3	4	5	6
17	12/6	12/6	12/6	12/6	12/6	12/6
18	13/-	13/-	13/-	13/-	13/-	13/-
19	15/-	15/-	15/-	15/-	15/-	15/-
20	17/-	17/-	17/-	17/-	17/-	17/-
21	25/-	25/-	25/-	25/-	24/-	24/-
22	28/-	28/-	28/-	27/-	27/-	26/-
22½	32/-	32/-	31/-	30/-	30/-	28/-
23	37/-	36/-	35/-	34/-	33/-	32/-

—⟨𝑜/𝑜/𝑜⟩—

One young man to go through on this new 'agreement' was Ernest John Tremblen. Whilst the agreement talks of 'probation', his certificate states he started his period of training on 28 May 1926, working on 'Slotting and Oxy Jet Cutting' and completed it five years later in May 1931. Interestingly his comments are just the same as those who had done an apprenticeship – 'Tremblen bears a good character, possesses good ability as a workman, and has conducted himself in a satisfactory manner'. Like other certificates of the time, it was signed by C.B. Collett, then Chief Mechanical Engineer.

It is particularly interesting to note the official terminology used here to describe the training years – it is not an 'apprenticeship' nor even 'a training period', but a 'probationary' period. Such terminology subtly but decisively separated machinemen from other trades, who had apprenticeships, although this was, in fact, 'training' by another name. In the twentieth century machining was known as a semi-skilled job, yet talk to any man who has worked around machinists and they will tell you that machining was/is highly skilled. Some tradesmen liked to say a machinist was to metal as a carpenter is to wood. Simply stated, a machinist uses machine tools to make or modify parts. This process is known as 'machining'. One criterion that distinguishes semi-skilled machining from skilled turners on lathe work is that with machining the tool moves, as opposed to working on a lathe where the part moves. The machines twentieth-century machinists worked with fell into four main categories:

Drilling machines – bench, floor, radial and horizontal
Milling machines – machines, horizontal, vertical and boring mills
Turning machines – engine lathe, turret lathe, vertical turret lathe and vertical boring mill
Grinding machines – surface, cylindrical, centerless and universal

Drilling, milling, turning and grinding are the operations they most commonly performed.

They also worked with other tools, such as measuring tools and cutters, including various milling cutters like face mills, shell mills, endmills and form cutters; then there are various drills, reamers, taps, countersinks, counter-bores and core drills. Machinists usually work to impressively small tolerances, and those who worked in Swindon Works' tool room (O Shop), where precision was the mantra, were top-notch workmen who, in recognition of this, received 'a bit on top' above other machinists. One such man was Tony Tucker, who did most of his training there and eventually ended his time 'Inside' as chargehand:

I started work on Loco side in July 1951 when I was 15. I'd put in for an apprenticeship as Fitter Turner & Erector. So many put in for this trade that they only selected those that went to Higher Education. I was offered Moulding or Metal Machinist, so I took Machinist, which at that time was semi-skilled. I was a trainee not an apprentice in those days. The training was for 5 years.

When I was 16 I started in the scraggery on Dave Sims gang. This was the gang that all the machinists started on, although this was not part of my training. When it was time for me to start my training I was moved to the other side of R Shop to work a Dolly drill. It consisted of drilling a hole on the end of a bolt so that a split pin could be used. The bolts were in a pile of sacks and when you picked up a sack all these mice ran out. I was only on that gang a short while when I moved to the T Shop, which was the Brass Finishing shop. Everything in here was about brass. I worked on nut flatteners and put hexagons on different shaped nuts I liked that in there, the chargeman was Ron Adams, a smashing chap and good fun.

My next move was to the O Shop or the Tool Room. That was the hallowed place to work and if your face fitted you stayed there for the whole of your traineeship. There were two machine gangs in there, the milling gang, which had drills, shapers, a planer, slotting machines, and gear cutters. The other gang consisted of all types of grinding machines. I started off on the big radial drill, and then moved onto various milling machines, and also the bevel gear shaper.

Because of the nature of the work and it being the Tool Room, the foreman insisted that I should attend night school. I went for about 18 months but it wasn't for me. It wasn't helpful. It was directed mainly on turning. Any questions I had, the instructor couldn't answer because he was a fitter, so I gave up on it. After about two years on milling I moved to the grinding gang. First job was re-sharpening taps and dies on a Cincinnati cutter grinder. After a while I progressed onto a cylindrical grinder, grinding taps and reamers to size.

Tony Tucker was lucky: on finishing his training he was kept on. In 1927–29 all of the young men leaving because they had completed their time would have received what was known

---

BR. 9276

BRITISH TRANSPORT COMMISSION

BRITISH RAILWAYS
WESTERN REGION

CHIEF MECHANICAL AND ELECTRICAL ENGINEER'S DEPARTMENT

JW

SWINDON, WILTS.

R. A. SMEDDLE, M.I.Mech.E.
Chief Mechanical & Electrical Engineer

Monday, 19th August, 19 57.

Certificate of Training

Ref: 2/M.109
11967/A
13/1

I hereby certify that

Anthony Edward TUCKER

born on the   9th July, 1936   *has been*

employed as a   Machinist   *in this Department*

as follows:-

Period of Training   five   *years*

from   21.7.52   *to*   8.7.57

Where employed   Locomotive Works, Swindon

Work upon which engaged   Machining (With experience in Shaping, Drilling, Vertical and Horizontal Milling, Surface, Cylinder and Tool Grinding, and Bevel Gear Shaping).

Chief Mechanical and Electrical Engineer.

Tony Tucker was one of the 'top-notch' machine men who worked in the tool room. Men who worked there were held in the highest respect, yet 'training versus apprenticeship' spoke volumes in terms of hierarchical status.

'inside' as the DCM – 'Don't Come Monday'. On the Friday one would receive a letter stating very bluntly, 'your services will no longer required after 5.20 pm [and the date]'. The very lucky few would also get another letter stating 'please start Monday …' and thereby have no loss of service, an important factor in terms of seniority and privileges. In these circumstances, however, the DCM had the extra edge of being an easy way for the company to reduce the numbers of men without actually technically laying them off. The DCM was not an uncommon occurrence. Indeed, it was a long-practised tradition – an economic measure used by all manner of trades down the ages to keep the numbers of men on qualified wages under control and supply a replenishing steady stream of cheap labour for the company, big or small.

The percentage of apprentices to journeymen, whilst having an 'authorised' number, often varied according to the circumstances of the time. Sometimes the number of apprentices was very small, such as with plumbers or maintenance painters, so an adjustment of an additional just one or two, or a similar loss, could make a significant difference. These Company records give us some indication of the fluctuations:

Locomotive Works June 1938
Percentages of Apprentices to Journeymen

Grade	1926	1930	1931	1932	1936
Fitters, Turners and Erectors	22	22.2	24.1	28.6	23.3
Boilermakers	34	36.2	33.8	32.1	26.2
Bricklayers	10	11.7	12.9	20.0	16.0
Carpenters	27	23.6	25.9	36.2	21.6
Painters (Maintenance)	26	16.6	27.8	35.7	4.8
Painters (Engine)	24	34.6	34.0	48.6	48.4
Plumbers	20	20.0	20.0	25.0	33.3
Blacksmiths	12	15.6	15.9	14.0	25.0
Gas Fitters	25	28.0	31.8	47.1	31.2
Patternmakers	8.8	14.7	16.7	28.6	20.0
Moulders (Iron)	17	20.1	21.5	24.1	20.2
Moulders (Brass)	55	40.0	44.4	75.0	45.4
Coppersmiths	31	28.4	29.4	40.2	39.0
Tinsmiths	21	17.0	18.8	26.9	16.7
Angle Iron Smiths	25	27.2	27.3	28.6	44.4

Percentage of Apprentices to Journeymen, 1936 & 1938

Grade	No. of Apprentices		No. of Journeymen		Percentages		
					Actual		Authorised
	11/7/36	1938	11/7/36	1938	1936	1938	
Fitters, Turners & Erectors	261	266	1122	1130	23.3	23.6	25
Boilermakers	122	120	465	442	26.2	27.5	35
Engine Painters	16	14	33	29	48.4	48	25
Blacksmiths	9	11	36	39	25	29.7	16

Gas Fitters	5	5	16	16	31.2	31.2	25
Patternmakers	5	5	25	24	20	20.8	10
Moulders Iron	19	31	94	119	20.2	26	20
Moulders Brass	15	31	33		45.4		50
Coppersmiths	32	30	82	80	39	37.5	35
Sheet Metal Workers	5	5	30	31	16.9	16.1	20
Angle Iron Smiths	4	2	9	8	44.4	25	25
Plumbers	1	1	3	3	33.3	33.3	20
Maintenance Painters	1	2	21	21	4.8	9.5	25
Bricklayers	4	4	25	24	16	16.6	16
Carpenters	8	5	37	32	21.6	15.6	25
Machine Trainees	71		361		19.7		
Welding Trainees	14		20		70		
Total	507 –		2031 –		25		
	85 =		381 =				
	422		1650				
Total 1938		(261)		(868)			

It is interesting to see in the first table, which records previous years, that 'Tinsmith' is still a trade. This long-established early craft was to later disappear and become absorbed into 'Sheet Metal Workers'. (1938 figures were added in pencil later.)

Emerging from the dark years of 'the Depression', and just when it was beginning to adjust to more relaxed conditions, the country found itself plunged back into war: the Second World War. This time the 'call to arms' was louder, quicker and better organised. The Railway Executive Committee had already been operating as an advisory body to the Ministry of Transport since September 1938, and had set up at least sixteen sub-committees to deal with all aspects of what was prophetically thought to be 'an impending national crisis'. At this time around 650,000 men were on the combined payrolls of the Big Four.[11] Although the majority of railwaymen were in 'reserved occupations', some 103,000 were eventually released for other war service. The number of Great Western men released into the armed forces was to ultimately exceed 15,000, with over 400 employees killed in action.[12]

Once again the railway workshops and their machines were converted for war work and this time round the Works' contribution was staggering: everything imaginable, from shoes and munitions to locomotives for war work, parts for tanks, planes and armoured vehicles, and even submarines, as Roy Blackford remembers, who was doing his coach finisher apprenticeship at that time:

> believe it or not, when I started as an apprentice in 2 Shop, this was in 1944, in 4 Shop they were making Chariots, the two men submarines, where they sat astride, they were actually building them in there and a lot of the mahogany they had in store was being used for that. A lot of the good timber was used up during the war. When I worked in 2 Shop first of all you had to walk through 4 Shop to get to it, these Chariots were stood up on trestles, where they were being worked on.

Albert 'Bert' Harber came from a dyed-in-the-wool GWR family with a long GWR tradition. They had been stalwarts of the Works' fire brigade over many decades. He started his five-year

2.

Shop & Tkt.No.	Name	Grade	mths final deferment proposed	Rejection proposed	Deferment refused (R.E.Troops)	Replacement.
BE.960 957	Bilkey 22.1.23 P.R. Hore 15.3.24 R.G.	Erector Dilutee " " (Yth)		X X		Will reduce output from Erecting Shop. Must either be replaced by able-bodied dilutes or re-arrangement and absorption of women. A portion of the replacements may possibly be post-poned until the flow of new manufacture and boiler position is improved.
B4.8508	Kennett 10.9.45 E.F.	Turner Dilutee	X			Dilutee ex Govt. Work or female.
E.9566 9560 9555 9515 9559 *	Harber 10.9.22 B. Rolfe 13.1.21 R.A. Allen A.H. Davidge A.W. Hicks N.A. Morris V.E. # On loan from Carr.Dept.	Wireman Trainee " " Electrician 1 Fitter " Electrician. "		X	✓ X X ✓	Accept 9 electricians and 5 youth electricians released from Govt. Contract in No.5 Shop, 9 to be regraded as additional requirements for wiring and maintenance work. Spackman and another to be put to fitting for crane maintenance.
F.2599 2587 2540 2594 2552	Bunce 31.7.23 R.A. Glover 26.4.23 GG. Marks 7.9.21 D.G. Reade 30.1.22 F.E.P. Tidmarsh 18.6.13 W.E.	Stm.Hammer } Driver(Yth) } " " " " " " " "	X X X X X			Can see no way of replacing these youths who are now upgraded to strikers. If these are taken and not replaced, new engine construction will be reduced and smiths become inoperative. Upgraded smiths will have to be reduced to striking. Other youth strikers are also being called up. Have recently lost four effective smiths, one by release, one retirement, one death, one accident.
G.3312 3355	Boots L.J.H. Angold R.S.	Fitter "			X X	Woodward – M/men upgrade & Woodward by female. Female indirectly (Miss Dolman to Williams' gang as fitter.)
K.4481 4783 4792 4790 4735 4786 4475	Rouse S.G. Davis 22.3.23 T.G. Bright 19.8.21 B.C.E. Chandler 4.7.D.C.E. Day 3.4.22 E.C. Lewis 4.4.26 A.C.W. Page 20.10.22 R.W.G.	App.C'smith. Welder Trainee " " " " " " " Jnyman. Welder Trainee	4 months	X X X X		Female trainee welders to be increased to 8 (4 by day & 4 by night to utilise maximum points available) and a further number when men are called up

Not being considered for enlistment (JWH 23/4/43)

These details of the release of young men from the forces bring home vividly the difficulties faced by the railways in maintaining their railway work in the workshops.

training to be an electrician in E Shop (maintenance) in 1938, aged 16. (In fact, he stayed in E Shop for the whole of his working life apart from his time out during the war). Although based in E Shop, Bert Harber worked all over the Works, wherever electrical maintenance was needed. Before he could be officially called up, he was sent to work on building power-lift cranes in Cardiff Docks, which were being built under licence for the war effort. 'I wouldn't have done that if there hadn't been a war.'

John 'Jack' Fleetwood worked his apprenticeship in the Brass Foundry during the war and remembers:

The war years were rough. It started with working seven days or seven nights each week but this did not last long as what with the sickness and absences, the men couldn't carry it on, so it was dropped to six nights or six days each week alternate, remember these were twelve hours shifts. Later in the war my mate in work and I wanted to join up, my mate hated the Foundry. We went to see the Personnel Officer and he hinted if we joined up we would not be allowed to finish our apprenticeships. My mate went anyway.

Under the Defence Regulations 58AA, introduced in July 1940, strikes and lockouts were illegal during the war period. Strikers could be, and were, prosecuted under these emergency anti-strike laws; strikers were even sent to prison. The unions had agreed a truce with the Employers Federation, and even the Communist Party were officially against strikes, although not necessarily against the strikers. The Minister of Labour had the powers to enforce compulsory arbitration – so the message was clear: 'no strikes'. Yet, despite the legend that 'everyone pulled together', the Second World War was a time of ever-increasing strike action, rising from 0.94 million days in 1940 and peaking in 1944 with 3.714 million days (the

The explanation to this picture says 'apprentices on strike for more money June 1915', and an entry in a foreman's (believed to be of A Shop) diary notes succinctly: 'Boys marched around the Works and through Shops (war bonus) 9.30am to 10.30. 10/6/15', which indicates something of a strike or 'downing tools' nature happened.

highest for a decade).[13] As big companies made big profits from war production, the workers' grievances grew as they worked the long, dark hours for still poor pay. The first serious wartime disputes took place in 1941, first on Clydeside and then in Coventry, Lancashire and London, and, perhaps surprisingly, it involved engineering apprentices demanding better pay. In 1943 a more significant strike broke out in the Vickers Armstrong shipyard at Barrow-on-Furness, with thousands of engineers and, again, apprentices and associated trades walking out – and staying out. Bevin's Ballot Scheme for 'Bevin's Boys', whereby 10 per cent of all apprentices were to be directed to the mines to overcome the dire shortage of coal, brought outrage from apprentices, particularly on Tyneside, and led to a cohesive action whereby these apprentices formed their own Apprentices' Guild and called a strike action in 1944. Whilst strike action had been taken previously by some groups of apprentices, mainly in the shipbuilding industry and particularly in Scotland, strikes amongst apprentices on the railways are not known of or, if they happened, certainly not widely recorded or reported; indeed, social scientist P. Ryan remarks that 'the neglect of apprentice strikes in the literature warrants discussions' and asks the question: 'Why would so salient a phenomenon have been so rarely considered by social scientists?'[14] I would also ask why not in respect of the railways. Undoubtedly for Swindon there is but 'small' evidence available, but we do know that there is a photograph purporting to be a crowd of young Swindon Works' apprentices on strike in June 1915 because their wages had not been raised whilst the men's had, though no 'official' evidence can be found to support this. There is also their participation in the 1919 Strike action and Tuckett's evidence and anecdotal legend that they came out in the General Strike. Contemporary personal recollections tell of an 'almost apprentice strike' in 1941 during the war, when apprentices on the carriage side of the Works decided to take matters into their own hands. Percy Warwick, who took part, recalls:

GWR Swindon Battalion Home Guard, Passing Out Parade, 1945, held outside Carriage & Wagon shops in Swindon Works. Many apprentices joined the Home Guard. A GWR list of Home Guard members dated June 1943 shows that 411 apprentices were registered, 202 with the GWR unit and 210 in the local unit. These volunteers carried out their duties after working a full-time day or night in the factory.

I went to my apprenticeship on Carriage side towards the end of October 1939. I went in the Army in 1941 from the Works. A lot of us apprentices went. It all started because the apprentices were asking for more money. It was only Carriage side apprentices. Loco didn't want to come in on it. We talked about going on strike. We had a big meeting in the old Smith's Shop alongside the canal, and a Union man came down from Doncaster to address us. Unfortunately it all came to nothing. So we all decided to go up to the Recruiting Office, we were all going to go as flight mechanics with the RAF, but in the meantime the Management must have had a meeting and stopped all those who didn't already have permission from going.

I had to get written permission to leave. I received a letter from Management saying that I could renew my application in two to three months which I did successfully. I went in the Army and then when I came back from the war I finished off my apprenticeship.

During the Second World War many civilian and volunteer defence groups were set up to carry out different functions. The GWR had a group of their own of men registered with the company for the protection of railway property, and a list from the Carriage & Wagon Works included D.W. Cove, an apprentice wagon builder. Another list of Carriage & Wagon men, this time enrolled as 'Local Defence Volunteers', also includes a handful of apprentices wanting to do their bit for the war effort: D.J. Carter, apprentice coach body maker in 4 Shop; E. Turner, apprentice coach trimmer in 9 Shop; and W.G.A. Robinson, blacksmith's apprentice in 14 Shop. Presumably this would be mirrored in a Loco Works' listing, if one could be found. One way or another, apprentices were determined to do their bit, and did.

Maurice Parson was a trainee machinist and had first-hand experience of adapting his work to war needs: 'The picture is taken of me when I was working in O Shop during the war. The machine in the picture is a gear cutter and it was modified to do this job cutting the gear teeth in turret rings for armoured cars.'

Notes

1 Pratt.
2 Drummond.
3 All information from and quotations from Macdermott.
4 Information and quotes on the First World War taken from Pratt, Vols 1 & 2.
5 Earnshaw.
6 National Archive RAIL.
7 Private Collection.
8 Tuckett.
9 *The GWR Magazine*, 1919.
10 STEAM Museum Railway Records
11 Figures taken from Alan Earnshaw, *Britain's Railways at War*, Atlantic Transport Publishers, Truro, 1995, p. 96.
12 Bryan, *The Great Western at War 1939–1945*, Patrick Stephens, 1995, p. 126.
13 Office of National Statistics, Working Days lost 1901–98, online.
14 Ryan, 1999.

A New Era

When the Transport Act of 1947 came into effect on 1 January 1948, nationalising all British railways, the control of the Great Western Railway passed to the British Transport Commission. Where before there had been the Big Four – the GWR, the LMS, the LNER and the Southern – now there was the massive One, and the Great Western Railway Company, which had been in existence for 113 years, was no more. Swindon Works, like every other works around the country, now came under the control of the BTC and, at first, few noticed any changes. Ernest Fischer remembers 'it didn't seem to make any difference to us. I certainly didn't notice any difference, we had the same piece prices, did the same sorts of things.' Percy Warwick remembers it too: 'After Nationalisation you didn't really sort of notice it, we just carried on as before. The only difference was when they started painting the carriages the different colours from the old chocolate and cream.' The same went for Roy Blackford: 'You wouldn't have known any difference at all, I can count myself fortunate 'cos I was an apprentice in 1946 and nothing changed until about 1950.'[1] For a while the influence of the GWR remained in place, but inevitably change came, as that was what the people and Government had wanted. Nationalisation of the railways was to bring massive upheaval and in the resulting turmoil and tumult, cut-backs and cut-downs, 'power play' became the name of the game, as not all would survive or retain their status in the dawning of this 'brave new era'.

After the war was a time for new beginnings, and new apprenticeship schemes were being initiated all over the country. Training and re-training was the discourse that permeated discussions of getting Britain back on her feet. With the shortage of manpower and skilled labour, companies were now wooing any and all young men (not just the sons of men in their employ) to join them and their schemes. The GWR had always had an extremely good reputation with regard to their apprenticeship training. It had stood the test of time, producing tradesmen and engineers that were held in worldwide regard. Despite grumblings by many that there had been unwarranted lengths of time spent on repetitive work and that they had often just been used as 'cheap labour', there were few, if any, that at the end were not proud to boast 'I am a Great Western man'. In the new fervour of looking for apprenticeships that worked, the Works received a number of requests for information regarding their schemes. The manager of the Juvenile Employment Department, Wolverhampton and The Steel Company of Wales Ltd each requested a conducted visit. What would they have found when they came? John Attwell had just finished his apprenticeship as a coach finisher. His son, academic Graham Attwell, reflectively analysed the process his father had gone through, as part of the 1990s debate on vocational education and training:

> Learning was authentic and totally situated in the work place. Despite the lack of a formal curriculum framework tasks were graded and progressive both through an ordering of progression and movement from one gang to another and through a progression from simple (and often repetitive) tasks to gradually more complex work … The model was particularly effective in developing work process knowledge through the passing on of implicit knowledge

from one generation to another. There were no written manuals or textbooks. Work teams themselves developed methods for solving the problems those particular tasks would bring with them. The knowledge of how to undertake these processes was passed on from team to team and from workers to apprentices. Individual skills were linked to carrying out particular procedures within an authentic and real work environment. Such a model encouraged the development of innovation, through the application of knowledge and skills. Incentives for innovation were making the job easier and allowing more 'free time', and increasing bonus payments through the piecework system.

The model of apprenticeship and of learning was heavily dependent on the form of work organisation. Work was ... carried out by the gang. The range of tasks carried out by each gang seems to have been relatively broad. Within this form of work organisation there was the opportunity for an apprentice to undertake the full range of work tasks needed to achieve tradesman status. It is also important to note the very high percentage of skilled workers within the shop, providing a ready pool of potential 'teachers' and a strong sense of occupational cohesion.

In the light of this analysis, it is interesting to note that although there would be a clear pathway through the shops for each trade of apprentice, the time spent and jobs done in each shop was flexible and could vary, sometimes significantly. The certificates of Lawrence John Ambrose Hersee, October 1932, and Arthur Bailey Davage, November 1937, both fitter, turner and loco erectors, show this:

		Hersee	Davage
		Months	Months
General Fitting & Machine Shop	Fitting	11	15
	Turning	17	17½
Machine Tool Shop	Turning	6	
	Fitting		2
Brass Shop	Turning	1	
	Fitting		5
Boiler Mounting Shop	Fitting	4	
	Turning		4½
Millwrighting Shop	Fitting	4	
	Turning		2
Erecting Shop	Erecting	17	14
	Total	*60*	*60*

We can see, therefore, that Hersee has had more emphasis on fitting whilst Davage has done more time on turning, and they have a difference of three months on erecting. There were reasons for this. The Millwright Shop was a 'limited opportunity' for a few more able and competent apprentices to widen their horizons because it had limited manpower capacity ,only 'the few' could do this. In the Millwright Shop they would not necessarily work on railway work but in a general mechanical engineering capacity, and on such things as plant maintenance, road motor vehicles or lifts and cranes. Such an event could not, obviously, be planned individually at the outset, but, necessarily, along the way.

After the war, with the need to reconstruct a bomb-damaged Britain and to fill its empty coffers as quickly as possible, technology and science were once again at the forefront of discourses regarding industrial development and Britain's 'place in the world'. In 1945 a Royal College of Technology was introduced and there was a proposal for 'Higher Technological Education' to elevate standards. This was followed in 1946 by 'Scientific Manpower': a ten-year plan to double the numbers of scientists in universities.[2] In that same year the North British Locomotive Company Ltd (NBL) published a twenty-four-page booklet: *Locomotive Engineering as a Career.* It was their guide and lure to aspiring apprentices. The NBL were ahead of their time in abolishing premiums, though the wage rates – from as low as 89p (17*s* 10*d*) a week for trainees, up to a maximum of only £3.19 (£3 3*s* 10*d*) – seem absurdly low to present-day eyes. The booklet stated: 'The present day out-look for the industry is unusually favourable', declaring the need to replace not only those locomotives destroyed in the war but also those that were on their last legs and needed renewing. The chairman of the Board of Directors of the NBL went on in the booklet: 'It is the duty of the Company to see that every apprentice accepted receives the most comprehensive and thorough training in his trade that is possible to give him.' The booklet outlined all the requirements and conditions on offer:

Conditions of Acceptance for Apprenticeship
Physical fitness
Boys must have a sound physical standard of health … A medical examination is necessary.
No Premiums (payable to any individual or the Company)
Indenture for a five years' apprenticeship

Conditions of Employment
Every apprentice both Trade and Engineering, is expected to be a production unit in the shop.

Wages
The rates of pay for apprentices are on a scale in accordance with National Agreements.
Wages rise at the end of each year of apprenticeship.
Current rate of pay (June 1946)
1st year   £1 8*s* 1*d* per week
2nd   £1 13*s* 2*d*   "
3rd   £2 6 0*d*
4th   £2 13 7*d*
5th   £3 3 10*d*
Trainees aged 14 earn 17/10*d* per week
    "   "   15   "   23/- per week

Hours of Work
The present normal hours of work are –
Monday to Friday   7.45 a.m. to 12.15 p.m.
                          1.12 p.m. to 5.30 p.m.
Saturdays   No normal work
Apprentices may be required to work overtime.

Holidays with Pay
In common with other workers employed by the Company apprentices are entitled to a week's holiday and to 6 other agreed days on full pay every year.

Tools, Books etc.,
Certain tools of their trade must be provided by the apprentices themselves, but the cost is very low.

Books and Drawing Instruments too are purchased by apprentices on the advice of the Technical School Authorities but the total outlay is very reasonable.

Canteens
Hot mid-day meals are provided at moderate prices.

The whole tone is incredibly conciliatory and amenable, especially when compared to that of the forbidding and dictatorial tone of early indentures and company agreements. The North British also ran a separate engineering apprentice scheme, which Nigel Macmillan recalls:

> I became an *indentured* sandwich apprentice engineer at the North British Locomotive Company's Queen's Park Works [in 1947] It was called 'sandwich' because the workshop bit was sandwiched between six monthly bouts of university and vie-versa, whichever end one was looking from. Engineering apprentices were a new idea and superseded pupil apprentices, the only difference being in the latter case parents paid a fee, in the former we were paid a weekly wage like the apprentice turners, fitters, etc. I thought it was a thoroughly sporting idea. There were two of us and we were paid 29s 5d [£1 47½p] a week less 3s 6d [17½p] health stamp, with one week's holiday at the Glasgow 'Fair'. The engineering apprentices were put through all disciplines during their fives years and usually started at 18 rather than 16 as 'Highers' were a must.

Whilst Swindon Works had always prided itself on its standard of workmanship, it was not always thus in the rest of the country. After the Second World War new world market forces, market competition and new technology exacerbated fears that Britain's mechanical and technical training was becoming, if it was not already, inadequate. Steam that had dominated the railways was being phased out and dieselisation taking its place; coaches went from being all wooden structures to the use of metal frames; engines went from being built of many different components to being 'units'. In these dying days of steam and the emerging days of diesel and electrical power, it became increasingly clear that new technologies and new skills required new approaches to training. That old itch, that apprenticeships were unnecessarily long, was constantly raised and scratched, with the argument now being that more structure and a better relationship between education and training could overcome the need for this.

Whilst others waited and talked, some like Edgar J. Larkin, the then energetic and progressive-thinking Superintendent of Apprentices of the LMS, had already reached and implemented this new philosophy. He had gone ahead and introduced a bold new approach to theoretical and practical training for all grades of apprentices, including the trade apprentice who had done poorly at the LMS in previous times. Back in 1932 Larkin had started to restructure apprenticeship training and devised what he called 'the Progressive system of Workshop Training', based on 'logical and arithmetical principles', and serious attention was given to the time necessary to be spent on each level of skill required, i.e. Elementary, Intermediate and Advanced. One significance for the trade apprentice was that no apprentice received more training at another's expense. He also knew at his commencement what had been planned for him. Larkin continued to develop his training scheme, finally taking the boys out of the factory and into 'school'. Eventually, in 1947, he persuaded the LMS to established a Works Training School (WTS).

Jim Burrows was one of its early entrants and writes of his experiences and memories on the 'Bygone Derby' website:

> DERBY Locomotive Training School was opened in 1947 by the London Midland and Scottish Railway Company (LMS). When I entered the training school in May 1949, I was in an intake of about 30 15-year-old lads. Our working hours were from 8.15am to 5pm, with

a one-hour midday break, which made a five-day week of 38 hours 45 minutes. Mr Thomas[3] said this was to bridge the change from school hours to industrial hours, which were then 44 hours per week.

The workshop was divided into four sections, each with its own specialist instructor.

The sheet metalwork section was where the ancient craft of tinkering, using tinplate, was taught, together with heavier-gauge metalwork and welding. In the woodworking section, joinery, pattern-making, foundry-moulding and core-making were taught.

Tuition in the machining section was mainly on small centre lathes, plus a small amount of time on the larger centre lathes and capstan lathes. The fitting section concentrated on benchwork, where we were taught how to use hand tools on work pieces held in the jaws of a vice, plus the skill of cutting steel plate using a hammer and chisel.

The fitting section also had a blacksmith's hearth and anvil to enable the art of blacksmithing to be taught. The training programme lasted a year and every apprentice had to spend four weeks on each of the four sections to discover which craft he preferred and his aptitude for it.

This was followed by eight months of further training in the specific crafts that the apprentice had chosen. Each of the sections had its own showcase, where examples of the work done by apprentices were displayed.

In addition to the workshop training, there were two classrooms where more academic subjects were taught, such as mathematics, English, engineering drawing, science and industrial history. The latter had a distinct railway bias. The lecturers were either railway staff or teachers provided by Derby Technical College.

On Friday afternoons, we had PT on a field at the north end of Derby Railway Station, known as the Loco Sports Ground, where the instructor was provided by the Technical College. I well recall the groans from my follow apprentices as we were put through a vigorous programme of muscle-stretching and conditioning exercises. While we were performing these routines, train crews, taking their vehicles to Chaddesden sidings, used to look on in amazement! When the 'torture' was over, we went back to the training school feeling the beneficial effects of our exertions and often went into the lower classroom, which was equipped as a cinema, to watch educational films.

How radical was this? How much does it sound like a 'traditional' apprenticeship? It must have made the hairs of mature tradesmen stand up in astonishment. Such was the success of the school, however, that its reputation grew and it featured in several media articles, one entitled 'The School of their Dreams'. After Nationalisation the training school was to play an influential role in the provision of training for railway apprentices all over the country. In the early days and first flush of enthusiasm following Nationalisation, members of the BTC, accompanied by members of the five executives set up by the Commission, visited Derby to inspect and evaluate the *modus operandi* at the training school. They were obviously suitably impressed as shortly after 'a report entitled "Staff Training and Education" recommend that the general pattern of practical and theoretical training at the school ... should be developed and extended to the larger workshop centres of the five executives wherever practicable'.[4] Larkin states that by 1959 'a training school had been officially opened and was in full operation at each of the main works of the London Midland Region'.

In the BR reorganisation Swindon had lost out in the power-grab and now sat on the fringes whilst Derby dictated the state of play. Apprenticeship training in Swindon Works continued as before. Apprenticeship, in general, was in the doldrums. Despite all the talk, the situation in most of the country continued as before and most of industry remained unhappy, believing the system was not delivering the skills required to cope with current industrial requirements. Then a new and unusual fact began to impinge on the consciousness of policy-makers, a something extra that had to be factored into the equation – the looming problem of the post-war baby boom which was expected to impact, or implode, in the early 1960s. The Carr Committee (1958) decided that rather than State interference and improving or changing vocational training in situ, the better approach to deal with the 'bulge' was to concentrate resources on providing new technical colleges, whilst, at the same time, urging unions and employers to work together and voluntarily make apprenticeships shorter and more relevant to the industry's needs. One of the outcomes of this debate was the creation of the tripartite Industrial Training Council (July 1958), which sounded grand but was, academic Hugh Pemberton claims, 'effectively powerless'.

For training and apprenticeship in general, the 1950s was the time of 'the talk shops' or 'talking heads'. Not much seemed to happen. People, especially the young, were pleased to see the back of this deadly dull decade and were optimistic for the 1960s, now remembered as 'the swinging age' full of optimism, colour and brightness. The decade started well for the Works. The arrival of the 'New Rail Shop' in 1961 that supplied all the Western Region, 100 years after the last rail mills, seemed to aspire to this bright new future. Reorganisation, interpreted as 'modernisation' or 'adjusting to meet current economic needs', became the new game in town, opening the way for a diesel takeover. Despite all this upheaval, or maybe because of it, it seemed an exciting time for those still 'Inside'. Under this modernising programme a new Diesel Testing Station and new Diesel Repair Shop were opened and Loco Workshops were refurbished and refitted, but in truth, such excitement and aspirations were short lived. The introduction of the 'Main Workshops Future Plan' (1962) which, under the new theme of 'rationalisation', was really a cost-cutting and money-raising measure – when land values became part of the stay-or-go equation – called for the closure of almost half the British Rail workshops throughout the country. The reality of this rationalisation was a dramatic contraction in size and purpose for the Works, and the decisions made then on strategies regarding the purpose and focus of the Works' activities had a finally fatal effect just two decades later. In 1962 there was a slow realisation of the dark times ahead when the staff magazine *Swindon Railway News* wrote: 'Few years have broken over the Works more gloomily than 1962, but we continue to hope and plan.' In terms of apprenticeship, the Works was offering all possible connotations whilst still being very traditionally orientated, as this section of the 'Locomotive Works Annual Report' shows:

British Railways Board
Manager's Office
Locomotive Works Swindon
Annual Report 1963

Training has been given to the following personnel during 1963.

Training	Number
Craft Apprentices and Trainees	324
Engineering Apprentices	13
Sandwich Course Apprentices	7
Engineering Graduate Apprentices	4

In connection with our Apprentices and Trainees, 225 day studentships were awarded at the commencement of the current educational session. Entries were made to the International Apprentice Competition, a Patternmaker Apprentice being the most successful entrant in going forward to the final selection tests.

The continuing debate on training needs and the insistent demands of industry finally resulted in the creation and implementation of the Industrial Training Act (1964), when central government became directly involved and intervened in employers' training practices. Gone was the laissez-faire approach – now there were directives and requirements. There are those that would argue that this Act made the greatest impact on training in the UK throughout the latter part of the twentieth century, whilst there are others who believe it failed miserably to make any real impression. Dr Hugh Pemberton, examining this in his paper, 'The 1964 Industrial Training Act: A Failed Revolution', elucidates the function of the Act:

> The act had three objectives: 'to enable decisions on the scale of training to be better related to economic needs and technological developments; to improve the overall quality of industrial training and to establish minimum standards; and to spread the cost more fairly'. The 1964 act gave the Minister of Labour statutory powers to set up industrial training boards (ITBs) [e.g. Engineering Training Board] containing representatives from both sides of industry. Each was responsible for overseeing training in its industry, setting standards and providing advice to firms. Most importantly, each paid allowances to trainees that were financed via a compulsory levy on firms in its industry. This levy/grant system was designed to remedy the failure of the labour market to deliver sufficient skilled workers and to end the 'poaching'.

Dr Pemberton further explained:

> The way it worked was that a levy was imposed by the industry's training board on all firms within that industry, at so much per worker. Firms providing training recognised as meeting the ITB's standards could then apply for a rebate. So a firm that provided a good level of training would not be out of pocket. Indeed, if its training levels were better than average it could potentially make a 'profit' [i.e. receive more in rebates than the total levy paid, though obviously this 'profit' was offset by the cost of actually providing the training.]

Even before the Act was implemented, changes were in the pipeline, which were to have a significant and profound effect on apprenticeship training at Swindon Works. These changes meant that, at last, Swindon Works was able to play catch-up with other workshops. Whilst the 1958 Annual Report of the Chief Mechanical & Electrical Engineer of the Works (R. Smeddle) had declared under the heading 'Special Report' that plans for an 'Apprentices Training School' had been authorised by the BTC on 21 November 1957 and 'are now being finalised', the 'finalisation' took some time as it wasn't until three years later, in September 1960, that an article in *The Evening Advertiser* informed Swindon readers that:

> Work is due to begin on Monday on an £180,000 school for railway works apprentices in Swindon The school is the first of its training type to be built in the Western Region. It is hoped the building will be ready by spring 1962.
>   It will incorporate a single storey workshop covering 11,000 sq feet fully equipped to prepare the boys for the type of work they will do when they pass on to the Works. Other facilities in a storey block include a lecture room, a library, a common room, and staff accommodation and a combined assembly hall, gymnasium and cinema.
>   A railway spokesman said the normal annual intake of apprentices to the Works was about 120. Remaining vacancies would be filled by boys from other parts of the region. The school will cater for boys entering either the locomotive or carriage and wagon works who will attend for 9 or 12 months. They will learn all types of work and be given the chance to choose the jobs which they intend to follow. Though their studies will include further education, the accent will be on introducing them to their future work.

It would be a cataclysmic change. Tradition was to be thrown away. The delivery of training, constant in the Works for over a hundred years, would now change completely and in so doing alter the dynamics of the workforce and the ethos of the Works itself. To the men it was a loss of something intangible, a loss of a role that had had a value that could not be quantified. Now

Left: The new 1960s architecturally styled pre-apprentice training school was built in Newburn Crescent/Dean Street on the site of Newburn House. The school was formally opened 24 April 1963 by H.O. Houchen of the British Railways Board.

Below: The first intake of Western Region apprentices (also known as the baby boomers) 1962–63, who, according to the White Paper 'Better Opportunities in Technical Education', would 'be given the best possible opportunities for Technical Education and training'.

they were no longer 'all things' – teacher, guide, mentor, protector, even father-figure – to the brand new young lad on the threshold of his working life, taking his first steps into adulthood; that role had been taken away and given to just a chosen handful, at the new training school.

The new pre-apprentice training school was a brand new school with a brand new approach – a holistic approach, tackling all aspects of the apprentice's training and development. A Western Region information sheet explained what the new thinking was. The 'Objects' of the Pre-Apprenticeship Training School, of which there were seven, included some surprises: d) 'to ascertain the boy's natural aptitude and thus try to place him in a trade in which he is considered likely to be successful' being the most radical departure from the thinking and practice of before, and: f) 'to give the boy every encouragement to develop into a useful citizen', these encapsulating the new 'holistic' attitude yet resonating with the thinking of the founding fathers of earlier movements, such as the Mechanics Institution and the RSA. The year was to be structured into three four-month periods, with the first being a probationary and assessment one. One new and additional aspect of the apprenticeship was that now it was compulsory to take first aid classes and pass St John's Ambulance exams in order to gain a certificate and an afternoon a week, usually Fridays, was given over to this. First aid, already significant in the

The 'shop floor' in the training school was nothing like that in the factory workshops – here, bright, clean and orderly; there, smells, noise, dirt and grime of many decades. Here there were four sections: nearest front is machining; next is fitting; further back electrical fitting; and sheet-metal working. Behind the back door (left) was welding and behind the right, moulding.

Works, now became a big part of the inter-training schools' activities, with annual competitions, shields and cups. Once or twice a week a session of PE (previously unheard of) took place. On a good-weather day this was held in Wescott Place Rec. and on a bad day in the gym within the school. At least one day a week was given over to work in the classroom and regular instruction in industrial safety measures became part of the syllabus.

There was, explains Roy Hazell, who was involved with the training school from its beginnings (a full-time lecturer on engineering drawing and workshop theory from 1969 and finally training assistant in the WTS in 1972), 'a new element of "nurturing" throughout, helping to instil a sense of self-discipline and responsibility'. To this end there were numerous incentives offered by way of annual prizes for the first year's efforts – 'Apprentice of the Year', 'Best Safety Poster', 'Robert Alfred Smeddle Memorial Award for Academic Ability', 'Foremen's Association Prize for the Best Craft Apprentice' and numerous others. Hazell remembers that all the instructors involved at the school were excited to be part of the new way of thinking.

The major step-change introduced by this new approach to training was that the first year was 'off the job' and 'in the school', and the philosophy and methodology had changed from 'learning through practice' to 'learning by instruction'; now the apprentices were formally taught, right from the beginning, the why together with the how – indeed, now learning and not production was the prime motivation. Some old bits remained, albeit somewhat changed. As before apprentices were taught by qualified craftsmen from the Works, but now in a squeaky clean school workshop; also now it wasn't an add-on to the instructor's day job – it was their full-time occupation, their *raison d'être*.

For those who had served their first year of 'hard labour' or 'relentless grind', as some had called it, in horrendously noisy and dirty conditions, having been tossed head first into the chaos and pressures of factory life and left to find one's feet as best as one could, this first 'hand-held' year with school-type hours in unimaginably clean and bright conditions and no production quotas must have seemed a very lightweight endeavour – not 'the real thing' at all. As many men commented to me: 'they hardly got their hands dirty!' This is a comment with many layers. Traditionally, as we have seen previously (see Chapter 4), apprenticeship had been all about 'hands on experience', 'learning to live with the grime' and 'getting dirtied'. It was all part of the rite of passage into the railway workplace. It was also one of the 'testing' elements of apprenticeship – testing endurance, ability to take the punishment, commitment both to yourself and your gang. In most of the older men's eyes, it was not until after this flimsy first year was finished and the boys arrived inside the Works that 'the real stuff' started. In truth, I think this is what the proponents of the school thought too – why else call it the 'Pre-Apprenticeship Training School' and talk of transferring 'to the main works for completion of their apprenticeship proper'? This was not, however, how it was generally portrayed or spoken of.

Geoffrey John Fletcher, born 4 November 1947, was one of the second in-take into the ATS starting in September 1963. He recalls that prior to starting you indicated what type of apprenticeship you preferred and, depending on how you did during your probationary period, the decision was taken by the instructors as to whether or not you were offered your first choice. 'The majority were lucky in being offered their first choice,' says Fletcher, 'including myself being offered fitting, turning and locomotive erecting.' Roy Hazell remembers that these choices were, as in GWR times, also based on the needs of the Works, whether they needed so many fitters or so many electricians. This was communicated to the principal/chief instructor of the ATS, who would implement it.

After this initial year's training period in school, it was down the tunnel for the rest of your training in the Works. Alan Philpott, who had been training officer for the Loco Works and then again for the combined Works, had the task of overseeing the training when the boys came across – it was a demanding task. Geoffrey Fletcher remembers reporting to him regularly. Fletcher's 'Record of Practical Experience' for the next four years shows his progress in the Works going from shop to shop:

Fun, but with serious intent – Sid Smith, Works' fire chief, foreman in the Works' fire station, second from left, training apprentice lads in fire drill (July 1964). *Roy Hazell Collection*

Winners of the Cecil First Aid Cup competition (1980–81), run by the local St John's Ambulance. Presenting the cup is Roy Hazell, training assistant. Left to right: apprentices I. Farhal, M. Luszcz, C. Whelan. *Roy Hazell Collection*

Works Training Scl	basic craft practice
Machine Shops	general turning including automatic, turret, centre lathes, etc.
Fitting Shops	general locomotive detail fitting including diesel engine repair shop
Erecting Shop	diesel locomotive erecting and repair
Diesel Training Scl	Diesel traction (mechanical) course
Diesel Testing St.	engine and transmission testing
Welding School	basic welding practice

Also recorded in the book are the 'Technical Studies' he had undertaken at the local college during this period on day-release and one evening night school. Geoffrey Fletcher finished his time on 3 November 1968, which, including the probationary period, meant it had taken the same five-year period.

In 1965 the Works' Annual Report records, under the heading '1.5 Apprentices Training', the number of apprentices and trainees as at 31 December 1965:

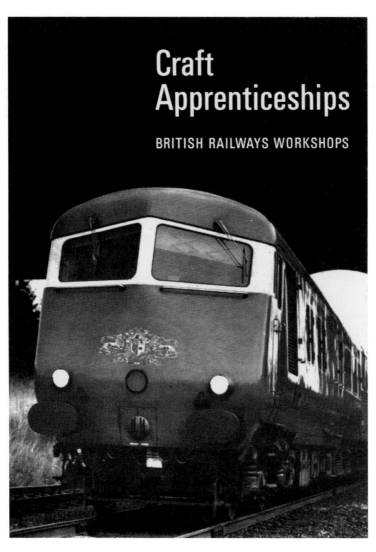

Craft Apprenticeships

BRITISH RAILWAYS WORKSHOPS

The 'British Railways Workshop Craft Apprenticeships' handbook dryly explained what would happen in the new Apprentice Training School: 'Practical exercises have useful end-products such as screw-drivers, set-squares, clamps, calipers and tool boxes ... The classroom subjects ... are Mathematics, English, Engineering Science, Engineering Drawing, Industrial History and Geography and Workshop processes and materials.'

Apprentices & Trainees 31 December 1965	Loco	C & W	Total
Blacksmithing	–	3	3
Boilermaking	2	5	7
Carpentry & Joinery	4	3	7
Coch Bodymaking (with Finishing experience)	–	8	8
Coach Finishing (with Bodymaking experience)	–	7	7
Coach Painting	–	3	3
Coach Trimming	–	2	2
Coppersmithing	9	3	12
Electrical Fitting	24	1	25
Engineering	4	1	5
Fitter, Turning & Erecting	179	5	184
Gas Fitting & Plumbing	2	3	5
General Fitting & Turning	–	31	31
Moulding	2	–	2
Painting (C.E.M.)	2	3	5
Painting (Engine)	2	–	2
Painting (Maintenance)	1	–	1
Patternmaking	2	–	2
Sheet Metal Working	1	–	1
Wagon Rivetting	–	3	3
Wood Wagon Building	–	7	7
Total	234	87	321
TRAINEES			
Holding-up	–	1	1
Metal Machining	9	10	19
Wheel Machining	–	1	1
Wood Machining	–	4	4
Welding	3	–	3
Total	12	16	28

It also identifies another five apprentice 'graduates' and 'scholars' and four 'Sandwich Course students'. The report records that 336 apprentices were taking City & Guilds courses on day-release classes at the college. Under section 1.2, it is recorded that there are '451 apprentices and juniors', and that the number of 'wages-grade', including these 451, is 4,702, with 333 workshop supervisory staff. At this time the number of apprentices at the ATS for transfer to the Works was fifty-four. Apprenticeships seemed to be in a reasonably healthy state.

Whilst the teaching and mentoring parts of the new approach appeared to be working, with training still taking a five-year period the issue of length of training had obviously still not been adequately addressed, so in 1967 the Engineering Industry Training Board introduced the 'modular training system', with eight basic principles, the three most significant being:

Flexibility – that training must be broadly based … [so that] craftsmen are equipped with a range of specialist skills which they can use in a *flexible* way.

Length of Training – the length shall be based on what has to be taught – and the rate of learning … [giving] an incentive to trainees to become qualified *as quickly as possible*.

Further Development – It is to be expected that whilst the initial training as a craftsman *could be as short as three years*, most craftsmen will need to return to the training system at intervals throughout their careers to learn new skills. [my italics]

This new 'new' training would contain three main elements: 1) Basic training under full time instructors; 3) Experience in an industrial environment. One and three were as before but it was No.2) – Selected training in specialised craft skills grouped together in 'modules' – that was the significant difference. It is interesting to note that now the words 'apprentice' and 'apprenticeship' have disappeared from the EITB information regarding this modular system, instead the words 'trainee' and 'training' appear.

Andrew ('Andy') Martin Binks was one of these new 'trainees'. He left school aged 15 years and started his training to be a fitter in September 1970. His employer was BREL (British Rail Engineering Ltd), who had taken over from British Railways Workshops Division. Binks' first year was at the now Works Training School. Here he was issued with not a BREL log book, but an EITB log book. The book was issued for two reasons: a) to provide a record of training and

Opposite below: Right from the beginning the new training included the 'what' and the 'why' with the 'how'. Arthur Angel explains technicalities of sheet-metal work to attentive and rather scrubbed-up looking apprentices.

Right: The boys gather round eager to get going on this rather clean Gardiner engine used on DMUs, as explained by instructor Harold Fletch. (These photographs, taken for PR purposes, highlight the differences between the school and the factory.)

Extracurricular activities included swimming challenges and football matches. Later, field trips with out-of-school team-building activities, such as a day's horse trekking as here in Codford, Warminster, were added. *Roy Hazell Collection*

Technical studies during apprenticeship

Year	Course	Result
1964/65	Mech.Eng.Technicians 1	Failed
1965/66	Mech.Eng.Craft Practice 2	Passed
1966/67	Mech.Eng.Craft Practice 3	Passed
1967/68	Mech.Eng.Craft Practice 4	Passed
1968/69	Mech.Eng.Craft Practice 5 (Diesel Engine Fitters)	PASSED

Educational attainments:—
City & Guilds of London Institute;
Mechanical Engineering Craft Practice,
1966 – Part I, 2nd Class Pass
1968 – Part II, with Distinction.
1969 – DIESEL ENGINE FITTERS
WITH CREDIT

Record of practical experience

Works Training School – Basic Craft Practice

Machine Shops – General Turning including Automatic, Turret, Centre Lathes etc.

Fitting Shops – General Locomotive Detail Fitting including Diesel Engine Repair Shop.

Erecting Shop – Diesel Locomotive Erecting and Repair.

Diesel Training School – Diesel Traction (Mechanical) Course

Diesel Testing Station – Engine and Transmission Testing

Welding School – Basic Welding Practice

Left and above: Geoffrey Fletcher's training records are interesting on many levels. They show that people can fail in one area and it is interesting that 'technical studies' are separate to 'educational attainments', although both regard mechanical engineering.

Cricket match challenges were popular between staff and apprentices at the ATS (1969). Sat front: A Hicks; kneeling, left to right: G. Blake, K. Morgan, Fisher; standing back, left to right: A. Crocket, D. Jones, A. Curtin, R. Evans, L. Freeman, D. Smith. *Roy Hazell Collection*

The new BTC Apprenticeship Agreement still talks of 'Guardian', 'craft', and 'binding' and 'service', but no longer a 'Master', now an anonymous 'Commission'.

References to the British Transport Commission herein shall be read as references to the British Railways Board.

BR.391

BRITISH TRANSPORT COMMISSION

BRITISH RAILWAYS

APPRENTICESHIP AGREEMENT

This Agreement made the Twentythird day of April 19 64 BETWEEN Herbert William MEAR Locomotive Works Manager, Swindon, Wilts.

on behalf of the BRITISH TRANSPORT COMMISSION (hereinafter called "the Commission") of 222, Marylebone Road, St. Marylebone in the County of London of the first part, and Harold FLETCHER of 99 Morris Street, Swindon

in the County of Wiltshire (hereinafter called "the Guardian") of the second part, and Geoffrey John FLETCHER of 99 Morris Street, Swindon in the County of Wiltshire (hereinafter called "the Apprentice") of the third part.

WHEREAS—

1. The Apprentice has completed a period of probation from the Sixteenth day of September 19 63 to the Third day of January 19 64 and has attained the age of 15 years.

2. The Commission are willing to accept the Apprentice to be taught and instructed in the craft of Fitting, Turning and Erecting.

3. The Guardian having enquired into the nature of the business conducted by the Commission desires that the Apprentice shall learn the craft of Fitting, Turning and Erecting in the service of the Commission.

Now it is hereby AGREED as follows:—

(1) The Apprentice, of his own free will and with the consent of the Guardian, hereby binds himself as Apprentice to the Commission in the craft of Fitting, Turning and Erecting on the conditions hereinafter appearing.

By the 1970s the 'apprentices' had all become 'modular trainees' in the new jargon of the day and they now undertook 'modules' of learning. Andrew Binks (centre front) sits proudly amongst his fellow modular trainees for the 'Year of 1970–71' WTS photograph of the Swindon intake. All but eight (back row from the right) went on into the Works.

performance which was then used by the EIBT to assess his work; and b) to record the details of the tasks undertaken. The inside cover explained the 'trainee's responsibilities for keeping log book up-to-date', mainly that entries must be made regularly and initialled by supervisor; that it must always be kept at place of work during the training; and all entries, except sketches, must be done in ink. It then explained the 'scheme of module training', informing that some set tasks had to be 'specially checked by your supervisor to ensure that you have reached the required standard of skill' and that these were known as 'phase tests.' Lastly, it instructed the correct way of 'recording': 'sketch the main jobs you are set to do, list materials and tools used and note time taken.' When this had been completed satisfactorily and initialled by the supervisor, 'the Job

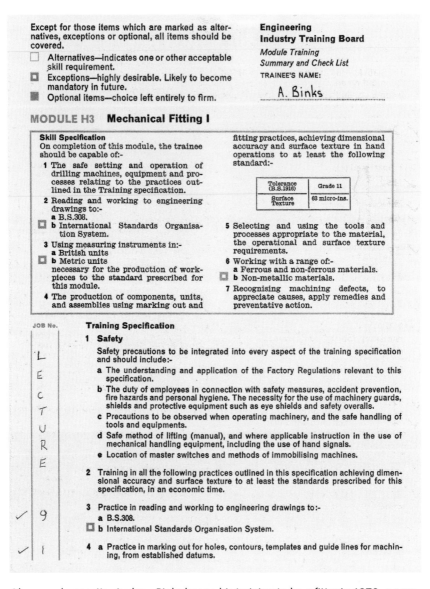

Above and opposite: Andrew Binks began his training to be a fitter in 1970, a new decade with yet another new approach for training. These sample modules that Binks had to complete show that it is also very much the age of health and safety as its message is reinforced by repetition in each module.

Number would then be entered against the relevant part of the Training Specification', which had been covered. If the job being carried out was a phase test, the supervisor had to write 'phase test' against it and also enter the assessment. Phase tests required the trainee to produce a 'piece', for example a tool, for inspection and show they knew the theory behind the process (this was not a new aspect, it had been done previously). The facing page carried two samples of 'specimen entry', showing the way to illustrate the technical drawings, list the materials and tools, and note the time. It also gave an example of a supervisor's assessment: 'QUALITY – satisfactory, ACCURACY – satisfactory, TIME – satisfactory. Signed and dated.' The book, A4 in size, was of cm-squared paper, split into headings: 'Date ... Job No. ... Brief Description ...'

Except for those items which are marked as alternatives, exceptions or optional, all items should be covered.

☐ Alternatives—indicates one or other acceptable skill requirement.

◻ Exceptions—highly desirable. Likely to become mandatory in future.

▪ Optional items—choice left entirely to firm.

Engineering
Industry Training Board

Module Training
Summary and Check List

TRAINEE'S NAME:

A. M. BINKS

MODULE H25   Mechanical Fitting II

Skill Specification
On completion of this module, the trainee should be capable of:-

1 The safe setting and operating of machines, ancillary equipments and processes relating to the practices as outlined in the Training Specification.

2 Reading and working to engineering drawings to:-
   a B.S.308.
   ◻ b International Standards Organisation System.

3 Using measuring instruments in:-
   a British units
   ◻ b Metric units

   necessary for the production of workpieces to the standard prescribed for this module.

4 Selecting and using correct tools, feeds, speeds, coolants, lubricants, and processes appropriate to the operational requirement, materials being worked, and surface texture requirements.

5 The production of components, units and assemblies using fitting practices, achieving dimensional accuracy and surface texture in hand operations to at least the following standards:-

Tolerance (B.S.1916)	Grade 8
Surface Texture	32 micro-ins.

6 Working with a range of:-
   a Ferrous and non-ferrous materials.
   ◻ b Non-metallic materials.

7 Recognising machining and fitting defects, to appreciate causes, apply remedies and preventative action.

JOB No.

L
E
C
T
U
R
E

3

Training Specification

1 **Safety**
   Safety precautions to be integrated into every aspect of the training specification and should include:-

   a The understanding and application of the Factory Regulations relevant to this specification.

   b The duty of employees in connection with safety measures, accident prevention, fire hazards and personal hygiene. The necessity for the use of machinery guards, shields and protective equipment such as eye shields and safety overalls.

   c Precautions to be observed when operating machinery, and the safe handling of tools and equipments.

   d Safe method of lifting (manual) and where applicable instruction in the use of mechanical handling equipment, including the use of hand signals.

   e Location of master switches and methods of immobilising machines.

2 Practice in reading and working to engineering drawings to:-
   a B.S.308.
   ◻ b International Standards Organisation System.

3 When this module is preceded by "Machining for Toolmaking and Experimental Work (Module H.1)", the following sections from "Fitting 1 (Module H.3)" should be covered to the standard laid down in the Training Specification:-

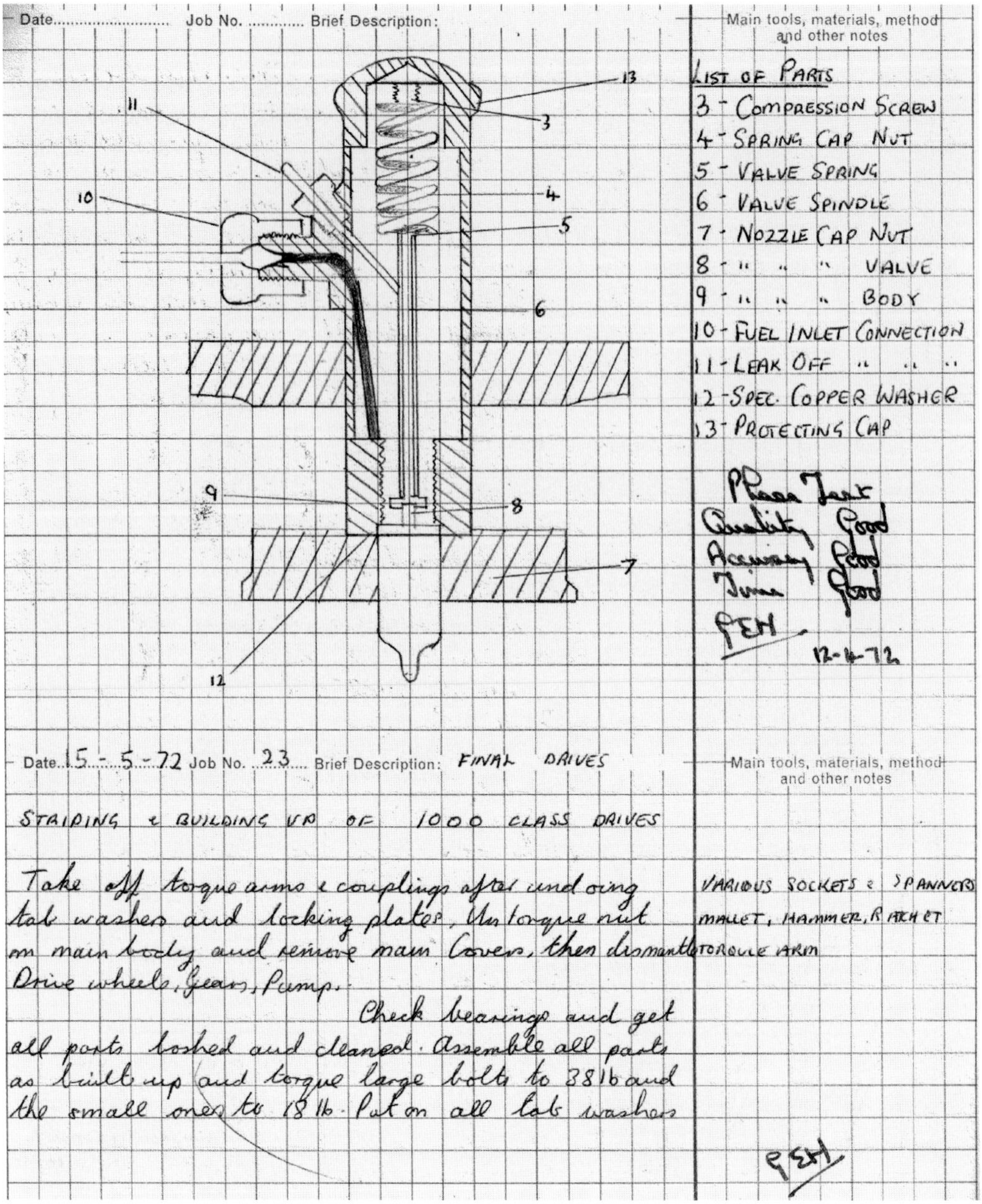

Date........................ Job No. .... Brief Description: Main tools, materials, method and other notes

LIST OF PARTS
3 - COMPRESSION SCREW
4 - SPRING CAP NUT
5 - VALVE SPRING
6 - VALVE SPINDLE
7 - NOZZLE CAP NUT
8 - "   "   "   VALVE
9 - "   "   "   BODY
10 - FUEL INLET CONNECTION
11 - LEAK OFF "   "   "
12 - SPEC. COPPER WASHER
13 - PROTECTING CAP

Phase Test
Quality   Good
Accuracy   Good
Time   Good

PEH.
12-4-72

Date 15 - 5 - 72   Job No. 23   Brief Description: FINAL DRIVES   Main tools, materials, method and other notes

STRIPING & BUILDING UP OF 1000 CLASS DRIVES

Take off torque arms & couplings after undoing tab washers and locking plates. Un torque nut on main body and remove main Covers, then dismantle Drive wheels, Gears, Pump.
     Check bearings and get all parts toshed and cleaned. Assemble all parts as built up and torque large bolts to 38 lb and the small ones to 18 lb. Put on all tab washers

VARIOUS SOCKETS & SPANNERS
MALLET, HAMMER, RATCHET
TORQUE ARM

PEH

Binks' work is cleanly and clearly presented throughout the book. The phase tests were also well executed, often, initially, earning Binks not just 'Good' but also 'Very Good'. It has to be owned, however, that towards the end of the course they had lapsed into 'Average' and even 'Fair'. Binks completed his first year satisfactorily, earning his EITB Certificate F202476. In his second year (7/09/1971–4/09/1972) he undertook Module H3 Mechanical Fitting 1, finishing with H25 Mechanical Fitting 2 in his third and final year (7/09/1972–24/9/1973). For each module there was a 'skill specification'. It is interesting to note in these days of heightened awareness of health and safety, that number one in the training specification for both modules relates to safety, highlighting five practices to be learned and understood.

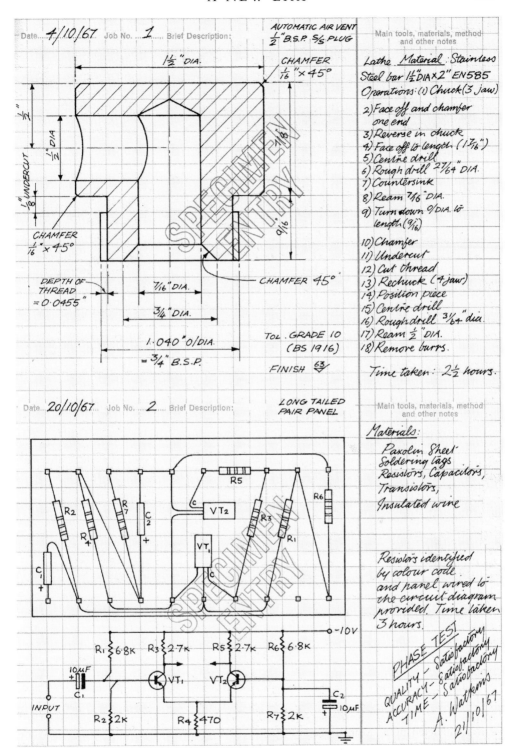

Date 4/10/67. Job No. 1. Brief Description:
AUTOMATIC AIR VENT
½" B.S.P. S/S PLUG

Main tools, materials, method and other notes

1½" DIA.
CHAMFER 1/16" x 45°

Lathe. Material: Stainless Steel bar 1½" DIA x 2" EN58S
Operations: (1) Chuck (3 jaw)
2) Face off and chamfer one end
3) Reverse in chuck
4) Face off to length (1⅞")
5) Centre drill
6) Rough drill 27/64" DIA.
7) Countersink
8) Ream 7/16" DIA.
9) Turn down 9/16 DIA. to length (9/16)
10) Chamfer
11) Undercut
12) Cut thread
13) Rechuck (4 jaw)
14) Position piece
15) Centre drill
16) Rough drill 31/64" dia.
17) Ream ½" DIA.
18) Remove burrs.

CHAMFER 1/16" x 45°
DEPTH OF THREAD = 0·0455"
7/16" DIA.
3/4" DIA.
1·040" O/DIA.
= 3/4" B.S.P.
CHAMFER 45°
TOL. GRADE 10 (BS 1916)
FINISH 63

Time taken: 2½ hours.

Date 20/10/67. Job No. 2. Brief Description:
LONG TAILED PAIR PANEL

Main tools, materials, method and other notes

Materials:
Paxolin Sheet
Soldering tags
Resistors, Capacitors,
Transistors,
Insulated wire

R5
R6
C VT2
R3
VT1
R1
C1

Resistors identified by colour code. and panel wired to the circuit diagram provided. Time taken 3 hours.

PHASE TEST
QUALITY - Satisfactory
ACCURACY - Satisfactory
TIME - Satisfactory
A. Watkins
21/10/67

-10V
R1 6·8K   R3 2·7K   R5 2·7K   R6 6·8K
10µF
C1
VT1   VT2
INPUT
R2 2K   R4 470   R7 2K
C2 10µF

Opposite and above: Right from its earliest 'educational' times, it had been a requirement of Works' apprentices to present one's study work in a clean and tidy manner. Binks' new EITB logbook made this easier with its helpful layout and squared paper. It is interesting to compare the nature of the task and approach to that of Gordon Ing's back in the 1930s (see Chapter 4).

Kevin Weaver, who had joined the Works from 'outside' and gone into the ET Shop (electrical traction) as an electrician, was invited to become a training instructor for the second part of the new course, which took place in the factory. He was sent to Leeds on an instructors' training course in 1978. His new job, along with two other instructors, was to assist the progress of the trainees through their modular time in the Works. He still has his B.R. 205/1 book, which is a record of the module he oversaw from September 1978 until December 1985, shortly before the closure of the Works. The units identified are:

Correcting Distortion in Shafts	(C Wood) 9 Shop
Marking out rough castings etc	(G Ponting) WTS
Using inserts	(D Hunt) 20 Shop
Rotary files, sanders stores ordinance	(R Arnold) Welding School
Safety Lecture & Film Show	ATS
Mechanical lifting	17 Shop
College Course	
COA (completion of apprenticeship)	

One of the major differences to previous apprenticeship training was that, once in the Works, no longer did the apprentice/trainee work only within the production needs of the factory workshop; rather, the workshop had to accommodate the trainee's training needs. Kevin Weaver remembers having to remind foremen about allowing the apprentices time to complete their designated tasks, even if it was not the work required by the foreman at that time. This created tensions between old-school trained tradesmen and the new modular trainee; disrupting production would have not been permitted in the old days. Interestingly, Andy Binks and his fellow trainees still considered themselves 'apprentices' and had no idea they were doing anything 'modular' at all. Binks just remembers working on gangs all over the Works in two-week or four-week slots. Day or 'block' release at the local college of further education was still integral to this part of the training, but some had to travel further afield for their day courses if there was nothing suitable locally; sign-writers went to Slough, painters to Willesden College and blacksmiths to Stroud. The whole of Binks' training was achieved in four years, which Kevin Weaver remembers as being about the norm at this time. This new 'rapid through put' training may have been the solution to skills shortages but it did not sit well with many of the men who had been through the traditional five-year route.

As with the policy of taking outside work into their workshops, BREL also now took in 'outside' apprentices from other non-railway companies (even taking girls), giving the WTS an expanded lease of life with the Youth Training Schemes (YTS). BREL offered three courses: 1) General Maintenance; 2) Electronic and Mechanical Assembly; 3) Warehouse and Storekeeping. One lad who took up this latter course of training was Nigel J. Hockin, who had been the only one in his first year to do so back in 1970. Hockin remembers he was to be one of just four undertaking the course, but on the day it was only he who turned up. The idea behind the new course was, he says, to fast-track people into stores management. The first part was spent in the WTS doing parts A, B and C Mechanical Engineering with the other apprentices, to familiarise him with engineering tools and terms. He also did some foundry and welding work. Hockin clearly remembers each piece he made as he went through the sections:

Section	Work Pieces
Woodworking	ring type towel holder
Turning	a screwdriver
Fitting	fitter's clamp
Tin plate working	a tin mug
Sign writing	paint Inter-City logo and number as on a diesel engine
Electrical	buzzer
Trimming	a cushion with piping stuffed with horsehair

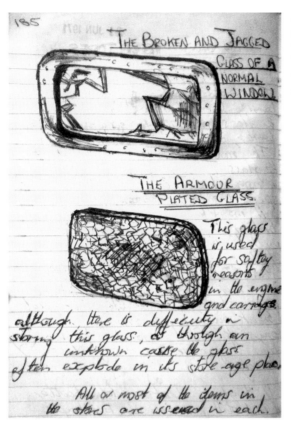

Left: Nigel Hockin undertook a 'rare' training scheme – he was the only one doing it in his time – offered by BREL under the new 'Youth Training Schemes'. Unlike with EITB course there was no helpful logbook but back to the days of an ordinary notebook.

Below: To be a storesman one had to be a walking encyclopaedia of parts to be really good at the job.

These pieces could then be bought at scrap value prices and taken home. The second part of the course was, as usual, in the Works with day release to the college to study 'Communication', 'Clerical Duties', 'Commerce' and 'Storekeeping'. In the Works Hockin rotated around the stores and those offices dealing with stores procedures. Like other trainees, he had to keep a meticulous notebook, which now makes fascinating reading as many of the buildings and sites no longer exist.

His BREL 'Certificate of Training' of September 1970 to August 1972 gives his record of training as covering 'Basic Engineering Craft Course/Warehouse Practices/Administrative Procedures/Stock Control; Ordering; Progress; Receiving'. It was a course that embodied the new thinking in terms of breadth of training and length of time, but it was, for Hockin, to no avail. Upon finishing he had expected to step into a position that leapfrogged over several grades – heavy gang (basic labourer), warehouse staff, warehouseman, foreman, office personnel, deputy purchaser, senior purchaser – to become a deputy purchaser. Such a situation would have been anathema to the unions (and those men waiting to step into dead-man's shoes in the intermediary grades) who, Hockin believes, blocked this; and so instead of a job, he, like many apprentices before him, was 'let go'.

From what through-put apprentices have said and others have written, the training school, whether as the ATS or the WTS, appears to have been a good experience. Those fortunate enough to have been there have good memories of it and of the people who instructed them over the time. Writing of his time in 1976, Gordon Dickinson recalls this good feeling:

Life in the training school was fun, hard work, but really interesting. For the first six months we all spent a period of time on each of the different trade sections i.e. Sheet metal, carpentry,

Certificate of First Year Training

ITB The Engineering Industry Training Board

certifies that   J. N. HOCKIN

completed a course of
First Year Training
for Craftsmen and Technicians
in the Engineering Industry
at an approved centre
during the year   1971

The training course consisted of PARTS A AND B, AND PART C (9 WEEKS)
(MECHANICAL ENGINEERING)
OF THE APPROVED SCHEME

Name of firm   BRITISH RAIL ENGINEERING LTD.

Certificate number   F203194   1034/8221

Ah. Ally.

Nigel Hockins'
certificates of training
are a delight in their
differences.

British Rail Engineering Limited Swindon

Certificate of Training

I hereby certify that

NIGEL JAMES HOCKIN

born on the 23rd September, 1953 **has been**
employed as a Stores Trainee **in Swindon Works**
as follows :-

Period of Training Two **years**

from 7th September, 1970 **to** 25th August, 1972

Record of Training
Basic Engineering Craft Course

Warehouse Practices

Administrative Procedures -

Stock Control; Ordering; Progress; Receiving.

Thowell

for . **Works Manager**

electrical engineering, machining, etc. Each section being run by an experienced tradesman, who would have spent several years in 'The Works'. These were special people, they were all strong characters with high morals and exacting standards, which had to be met, and the discipline was firm. I recall during one task which involved hour upon hour of filing and scraping at a block of steel to get it as perfectly flat as humanly possible, our tutor (ex army) was telling us the various terms and names for the tools, he held up a file and announced that this one is called a 'Bastard' and if any of us so much as smiled we would be punished accordingly. Most of us laughed out loud, resulting in half an hour of marching round and round the workbenches in silence.

After some months we got to choose our particular trade, I chose to become a Vehicle Body Coach Builder. It appealed to me because it was a sort of mishmash of all the other trades, giving me several strings to my bow, a choice that I am happy about to this day. The following six months were spent preparing us for the remainder of our apprenticeship in the Works.

As the first year progressed a strange thing happened, a rapport or bond seemed to develop between the teachers and the pupils a kind of mutual respect became apparent.

At the beginning of its existence, the training school had anticipated an intake of apprentices at around 120 a year. A 'historical note' on the 1980 prize-giving programme informs those attending the ceremony that since its opening in April 1963, 1,500 'pupils' (as they identified them) had passed through the school – an average of around eighty-eight pupils a year. The

Above: Ninety-three new BREL trainees, August 1978. Training and administration staff, front row, left to right: Jack Bevan, Len Snook, Les Cowley, Cyril Jefferies, Bob Yeats, A. McGovern, David Deacon, Chris Soady, Jack Packer, Doreen (secretary), Vic Baker (acting head), Pam Drewitt (canteen), Doug Whittle, Jack Luker, Dave Peel, Ron Clack, Tom Smith, Kevin Weaver (module controller), Alec Stacey. *Roy Hazell Collection*

Right: 'Apprentice of the Year' S. Sadler and other prize winners standing proud with Roy Hazell, training assistant, in 1984. *Roy Hazell Collection*

programme was all very upbeat and positive. Indeed, all seemed to be going well, but just a couple of years later on 19 April 1982 the *Evening Advertiser* carried graphic headlines: 'No More Train-ing', quoting a BREL spokesman from Derby (not Swindon) as saying: 'We are not going to recruit any apprentices at Swindon this year ... it is not considered prudent to take on any youngster.' Later, in November, it was confirmed that no new apprentices would be taken on for 1983/84. The final outcome of the Works was already on the cards. When the Works did close in 1986, those still goings through 'apprenticeships' or 'training' were helped to find positions with other local companies where they could finish their time.

Notes

1 Matheson, *Railway Voices.*
2 'A History of Technical Education 1940–69' – technicaleducationmatters.org.
3 Thought to be Mr Harold Thomas. Probably then the chief instructor at the school.
4 Edgar J. Larkin (1979), p. 52.

8

Doing the Time

Many of the debates around apprenticeship were focused on issues of time – too long, too short, a waste of time. Time informed the language of apprenticeship, in that it was talked of as 'doing my time' and 'coming out of my time', 'having served my time'. Starting one's apprenticeship or time was a momentous occasion, a heart-in-the-mouth experience, which, if the son of a GWR man, one had been waiting for virtually all of one's life. Where would you start? Who would you work with? Whose gang would you be on? Would they like you? Would you like them? Which charge-man and, more importantly, which foreman would you be under? All scary questions, yet edged with the thrill of anticipation which would not be answered until the day.

Ken Gibbs captures the excitement of his moment in his own memoir *Apprentice in Steam*:

> This was the big day … [21 January 1946] and I was excited and apprehensive … Start in the B Shed Monday morning 7.30 … The start of an apprenticeship in steam, probably pre-determined by my father on the day I was born 16 years before; the bustle, the rattle and noise of mechanical work and movement, the shouts and conversation, the areas of smoky mist around the rivet fires and the quieter areas of the stores and drillers in the far right-hand corner of the shop, and, over all, the distinctive 'smell' of the workshop, a mix of warm air, coke fumes, oil, metal, and a rather pungent smell which wafted across now and again and was yet undefined.

Maurice Parsons went into the Works in 1936 when he was 14½ years old. Like other boys he did not know where he was going to be put. 'I went into R Shop and my dad was relieved. He thought I might have been put in the Bolt Shop – "the Devil's Den" it was known as, it was so dark, black and dirty.'(Seen here in 1935.)

In later years, when the ATS came along, the thrill of anticipation did not diminish. The excitement of 'the start' was not lessened, even having spent a whole year in preparation for it, because even then, the feeling was that the 'real' apprenticeship didn't begin until you were inside the factory. Gordon Dickinson writes of the headiness of it for him in 1977:

> The training school was connected to the Works by an underground tunnel. Toward the end of the year it was announced that we would be going through the tunnel and emerge in the 'real world' for a tour of what was to become our work place for at least the next four years. This, for me this was probably the most exciting day of my whole apprenticeship … I was not disappointed … It was fantastic … The enormity of everything, the sounds, the smells, the machines, the buildings, but most of all the men.

Both men mention 'the smell' and indeed the smell of the factory is one of the dominant memories, mentioned often by Works' railwaymen in the course of conversation or interview. The distinctive smell of each shop and shed was part of the 'essence' of the Works and one that permeated the consciousness and became embedded in the memories of the men throughout the decades. Roy Taylor also remembers the smell, especially of the scraggery in the 1930s: 'The overwhelming memory of there, was it smelt like anything. It was that "white water" they used to work the machines, a mixture of water and rape oil.' John Charlesworth was in the scraggery twenty years later, but very much agrees with Roy's sentiments: 'It was unbelievable. It had a smell of its own that scraggery with the white water you know. You could smell it a mile away.'

In the 'factory days' of one's apprenticeship part of beginning was learning the rules, regulations, practices and habits, not just of the company, but of your chargeman and foreman and shop or shed. Everyone got their little rule book, which had to be personally signed for – and supposedly read – but it was much more than that. It was also learning 'how to take a joke' and 'who you didn't cheek'. John Fleetwood remembers back in the 1930s that the hidden agenda of the first job was to 'break you into discipline and taking orders without question', whilst William Bullock, a premium fitter apprentice also in the 1930s, soon realised that 'as a fitter's mate not only was my job to learn but I had to become a general dogsbody, fetching tools as and when required from the stores'. Many shops had their own 'initiation rites', sometimes done by the men on the lads – such as when sending them to stores for a rubber hammer or bucket of steam – sometimes by older apprentices on those newly arrived 'in shop'. Roy Hazell remembers his in B shed in 1947. He was asked to go inside the tank to 'get the fish out'. Once inside the men shut it up and banged merrily on the sides with their hammers. He can still remember the terrifying din to this day. Trevor Tremblen still vividly remembers being dunked in the water trough in A Shop by the older apprentices already there, in 1961. 'You knew it was coming,' he said, 'but once it was done, that was it!' It was important to grasp the mettle of this situation as soon as possible and to adjust to it accordingly, if one was to have a smooth passage.

Jobs for apprentices remained fairly constant over a long number of decades. They always started off as menial and mundane and over time progressed in complexity. Bullock gives a good example of this: 'then commencing to do simple jobs such as chasing the oil grooves in the white metal of the axle bored-out bearing before moving on to actually scraping the surface of the bored-out bearing to assist in the smooth running of the axle when it was bedded onto the wheel axle.'

Harry Holcroft captures the challenges of being an apprentices in the early railway years. He writes of one of the jobs he did in the 1890s:

> Another job was cutting holes in saddle tanks for hand rail pillars, for it was not possible to rig up a drill on the curved surface. A chalked string was attached at hand rail level and a flick of it produced a white line on which the centres of the hand rail pillars were marked

and centre popped. A circle was drawn at each with compasses and marked with pops on a diameter which would admit screwed ends of the pillars. What I had to do then was to gouge out a deep circular groove within the boundary of the pops with a round-nosed chisel until a circular piece of plate was cut out. The hole then had to be filled to size. Next the pillars were inserted and I had to wriggle myself into the tank, provided with the requisite number of nuts and washers. To provide a water-tight joint, the washers were faced with 'grommets', rings of spun yarn impregnated with red lead mixture.

Over a half a century later, in the 1950s, Patrick 'Pat' Sullivan remembers making those grommets and wriggling into the tank too:

you'd go to the B Shed and work on tenders … your job was making 'gromits' which were out of hemp string, you wound it round your finger to the size of the bolt you were going to put it on and made like a ring of it and that went on the bolt so that when the bolt was tightened up it made a water seal. When you'd done it you had to get inside the tank and push the bolts in from the inside, so you were inside the tender, cos the chap you were working with, he wasn't going to get in there was he? Ha ha ha. So you would go in there and people would bang the side with a hammer or something just to make sure you were still awake. There was no electric light, you had to go in with a candle … normally ordinary candles would just fit into a 5/8 nut, so you would screw the candle into a 5/8 nut and you could stand it up there while you were doing your job inside the tender. Inside the tender it just little holes, its not just a big expanse in there like a room, there's all sheets of metal at different intervals through it to stop the water flowing through, baffle plates with holes in and you had to crawl through these holes, and the holes weren't in line, so you'd go in a hole this side and then you'd go in a hole the other-side of the tender.

Sometimes your apprenticeship took you to places, that given the choice, you would rather not go, as Percy Warwick remembers only too well:

One of the first jobs I had as an apprentice was to go 'up top' in the Stamp Shop with Bert Packer, who was the fitter. We had to do a gas main leak over the top of the furnace. Ladders were put up with a plank that had been fitted up ,just an ordinary plank, Mr Packer, made sure that I went first, he made me got up first and followed me up. That was my first experience of working so high up, up in the Stamp Shop roof.

And other times it took you into shops where you quite enjoyed the work, as Pat Sullivan recalls:

Then I was in R Shop making mud plugs. They're tapered bolts, like a bolt, that you screw in tight in the fire box. That was the apprentice's job making those. The R Shop was a machine shop. I worked on a lathe in there. You had some good jobs in there, one was turning the piston rods which were four foot long, I think. That was a good job because when you were turning those rods that used to take twenty minutes to cut. To do one cut of it took about twenty minutes so that was an easy job, you know. It wasn't a dead size, you didn't turn it to the finished size because it was ground to the finished size. You turned it right down to … I don't know how many thou it was. On the same gang there was what they called banging down. That was on the actual piston itself. The piston is hollow, it's not a solid lump of steel. It's like a sandwich. You have like bolts that go right the way through to strengthen it in the middle. There was four of them and you used to have to screw them in til they were really tight and then rivet them, rivet both sides of them on a big anvil. There was two of you doing this job and that was an alright job too. You felt that you were doing something that you could recognise what was going on, on a steam engine.

John Charlesworth remembers 'the best job' during his apprenticeship was in AE Shop:

> My best time during my apprenticeship was working on Stan Lewington's gang in AE Shop.
> Stan was a character, well known for his shiny brown boots, and us apprentices knew to look
> out for them and get started! You worked with a journeyman who would be one side of the
> engine and you would be on the other side. First job was fitting crossheads into the motion
> bars, scraping the white metal to get a clearance of 20 thou. Working on Castle and King locos
> was hard and heavy lifting as they had inside gear which meant you were working underneath
> in the engine pit, on pit planks and just a light lead or, if that didn't reach, just a candle in a
> nut. Hard work but happy days too. I especially remember Christmas Eve Carol Service in
> AE Shop. We had a band playing Carols and all the apprentices were sat on the locos – magic!

Other times you could be incredibly lucky to be in at the beginning of something new, as
Jack Harber was. (Jack was older brother of Bert Harber, who had gone to work in the docks
in the Second World War.) Jack started his FTE apprenticeship in July 1932, aged 16. He was
fortunate to see the introduction of a 'new approach' to working and it became part of his
apprenticeship training:

> During my apprenticeship the erecting shop work practice was altered from a 'strip-and-rebuild
> on the same pit' and by the same erectors, to a sectionalised system of four sections. Apprentices
> spent two months on each section working on one side of the locomotive fitting the repaired
> parts. By this time the apprentice was now a skilled workman and capable of working with
> minimum supervision. The final section was the 'finishing off and trial' section – and these
> trials were generally to Dauntsey and back. The locomotive was run in steady on the outward
> journey, checked for any overheating, if all bearings were OK – a fast run back to Swindon.

Roy Blackford and John Atwell both did their apprenticeships in the Carriage Department,
both starting in No. 7 Shop (as a general rule Loco-side shops had letters attached and Carriage-
side shops had numbers), both in the same period – the 1940s. John Atwell found that:

Another moment of 'magic', especially for apprentices, was the photograph after the naming
of completed locomotives. On 15 November 1950 the 'New Work' erecting gang assemble for
theirs after the naming of the last Great Western Castle Class *Swindon* 7037. Twenty-year-old
apprentice Ken Gibbs is kneeling (third from right) on the platform along with the other
apprentices within the gang. *Kenn Gibbs Collection*

What we learnt depended totally on what a particular shop did. In fact our work was similar to a cabinetmaker. We were expected to achieve a tip-top finish. Inside 7 Shop we were mainly working on a bench. The men working on the next bench would show us how to do each job. When we were working outside the shop we were put with an individual tradesman who would teach us the job. Obviously some were better than others were.

Later I was sent 'up the line' to work outside the shop with the door gang. That was where I got my first interest in crossword puzzles. The tradesman was called Ted Quinn. The door gang was responsible for hanging the interior doors in the carriages. There is an art to hanging doors and making them slide – a knack to it. We had to screw a quarter inch rod with brackets above the door. The doors hang and rolled along the rod on wheels. If they were too high they would lift off the bottom guide rail, if they were too low they would stick or come off the rollers. Ted Quinn would get it right every time. He was fast enough that he would do a little work, then settle back to his crossword puzzles. If an apprentice mastered the skill he would be kept on the gang but some could never get the knack of it.

Whilst Roy Blackford recalls:

Another thing we did in that shop was to make all the flag poles for the guards. We had a machine called 'a rounder'. You put the square pieces of timber in and they'd come out at the other end, it was a barrel like. I remember the blind sticks. When they had blinds in the carriages [at the windows] they had round sticks at the bottom. Well they were cut out of ash and they were 3" square and you'd sit there on this 'rounder' with a bundle of them, feeding them through and they would go through and then you gathered them up. Then you had a pencil sharpener type thing which you just pushed them in and you'd finished up with a point on one end. Boy's jobs monotonous, boring then, but looking back it was quite interesting.

It is not often one comes across a programme of apprenticeship for different trades, but circa the late 1930s, for whatever reasons, the GWR produced a series of information sheets on some apprenticeships, including plumbers.

—◦◦◦—

Plumbers' Apprentices

The number of Plumbers' apprentices is only one or two, and the term of apprenticeship varies from 5 to 6 years.

In order that thorough training is obtained in the trade, the work is divided into groups as shown below, which also shows the time spent in each group.

Group	Time spent in each group		Class of work
	5 year appr. Months	6 year appr. Months	
1	6	9	Working with Journeymen. Taking off and redressing of lead on roofs etc.
2	6	9	Working with Journeymen. Fixing and repairing roof water guttering, stack pipes etc.
3	12	15	Pressing and fixing new lead work. Fixing water taps and all classes of lead piping.
4	12	15	All classes of lead work on roofs.
5	24	24	All classes of general plumbing work such as lead joint wiping on pipes. Water tanks and lavatory arrangements. Lead tanks etc.

Owing to the small number of apprentices the distribution will entail no special arrangements but each apprentice will pass into the next group as he finishes his period in the previous one.

Engagement and records of apprentice will be dealt with in a similar manner to the Turning, Fitting and Erecting, and kept on the attached card.

There is also one for 'Tinsmiths', or 'tinkers' as they were known in general, a very ancient trade but now 'modernised' and working on a larger scale in a trade now known as sheet metalworking. The number of apprentices is identified as 'about 5'; the wording of the rest of the document is the same as the plumbers:

Group	**Time spent in each group**		**Class of work**
	5 year appr. Months	**6 year appr. Months**	
1	30	36	Repairs to lamps and all classes of Sheet metal work.
2	18	24	Light plate work.
3	12	12	General Sheet Metal work, such as fire extinguishers, machine guards and welding.
G1	9–12	12	Coremaking.
2	21–28	28	Moulding all classes of small work.
3	30	32	All classes of general moulding, including cylinder moulding (see note).

Note on Group 3: During the time in the last group, apprentices who have shown considerable ability and have a good report from their Foreman will be given an opportunity of gaining experience on the Cupola stage of melting and mixing irons.

SHEET METAL WORKERS APPRENTICES

NAME	BORN	COMMENCE AK	A+G	COMMENCE APPRENTICESHIP	EG	A+G	EG
G W Johnson	16-9-32	9-8-48	9-8-48	16-9-48	20-11-50	9-9-52	
R. M. Townsend	26-9-34		49	28-12-49		7-12-51	20-2-56
R. Young	17-1-36		1-1-51	11-4-50		14-12-51	
R Johnson	10-12-34	26-3-51		1-1-51			
A J Hayward	13-4-35	17-4-50			17-7-55		Complete 13-4-57
R J Bright	16-12-35	31-12-51		25-3-52			Completed 15-12-
D. Oliver	24-8-37	27-7-53		21-9-53	23-7-56	25-3-57	to 23-8-58
R Kinnear	4-1-38	24-8-53		4-1-54	4-1-57	26-8-57	to 3-1-59
A Probert	8-1-38	16-11-53		8-1-54	25-3-57	31-3-58	to 7-1-59
F. Turner ?	13-12-37						
Alan Simms	25-5-38	11-1-54	11-1-54		26-8-57	5-8-58	In Forces 30/1/60
A Rose	26-4-38	1-3-54	1-3-54		31-3-59		Completed 5-4-6[illegible]
G E. Wallace	27-6-39	18-4-55	4-9-59		5-8-58		

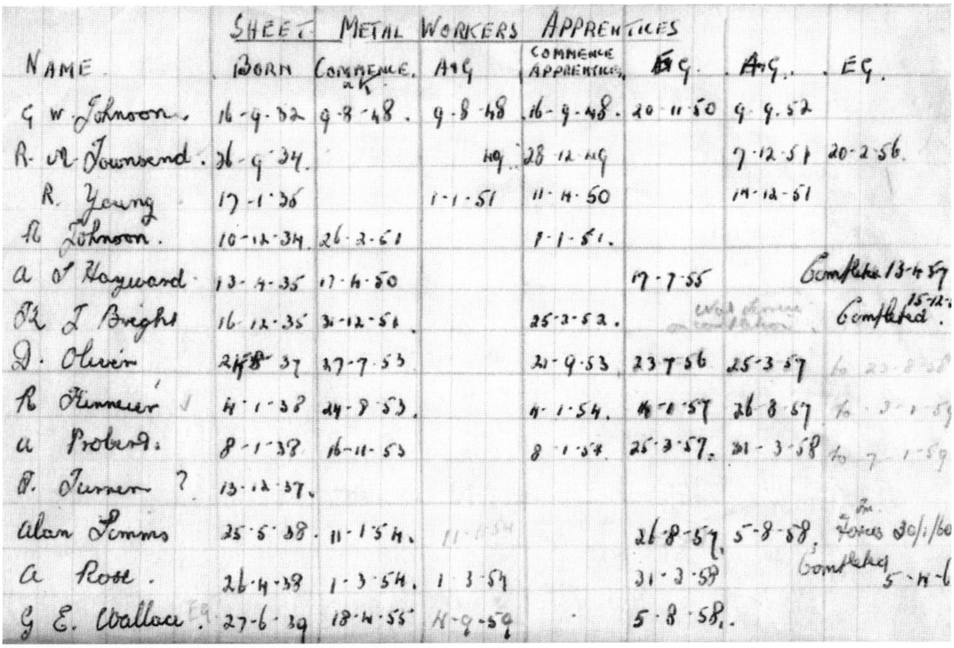

Shop record, kept probably by a shop clerk, noting apprentices, their probationary period, start time and progress of apprenticeship.

Whilst 'tinsmiths' disappeared, coppersmiths were still a separate trade to that of sheet metal workers, although coppersmith apprentices also had to learn sheet metal working as Trevor Tremblen remembers of his apprenticeship (1961-66). 'The difference between the two trades is all about the thickness of the material being used,' he explained.

Another trade identified is one that began in early times and lasted over the decades, changing little until the mid-twentieth century – moulding. Moulding was a second-class trade, but, at the time that John 'Jack' Fleetwood was signed up by his father (1938), it got *2s* higher on the rate than a rough painter or low grade machinist – the two other options his father, a tractor driver in the Works, was offered. Fleetwood believed that had his father had any idea of the conditions his son was to work in within the foundries, he would never have made that choice. 'But what was done was done, and that was the end of it,' he explained. Moulding had started as an 'intuitive craft' and, even in the early twentieth century, just as in the early years of the railways, a lot of the time a moulder still went on gut feeling, learning to trust his instinct to tell him when something was wrong in this very dangerous work. 'And many times it saved me from a lot of trouble,' Jack Fleetwood told me, 'trouble such as serious explosions and their fall-out!' Despite being a second-class trade there was a lot to learn and it is quite amusing to see this work reduced in nature in the description of 'class of work' in their apprenticeship plan:

There were no night school classes for moulders; the way they did their extracurricular learning was by 'listening to old hands talk about the problems they had during different casts … and what they did they next time to make it better – and then trying to remember it!' One of the things that moulders had to learn was about the metals they worked with: their nature, their behaviour and what they were best used for. The GWR had a special mix of metals for each type of casting, but in BR days this was reduced to about ten or twelve. Fleetwood, who spent his apprenticeship going between the J1 iron foundry and U Shop brass foundry, has written of these in his personal memoirs. They are interesting because of their 'antiquity' just as is the fact that their early moulds were made using a mixture of sand and horse dung, collected from the GWR horses and kept in 'dung boxes' outside the workshop. Also used as a binding agent was pig manure (later replaced by oil) – how health and safety would have loved all that!

1938 –1984 Metals used
BRASS METALS USED IN BRASS FOUNDRY
BRONZES
No. 1 Phosphor Bronze   – liners and bushes
No. 2 Phospor   – "   "
Gear Bronze   – gear wheels of all types
Turn Table Bronze
Aluminium Bronze
Leaded Bronze

GUNMETALS AND OTHERS
No. 1 Gunmetal   SCB3 Yellow Brass (Stink Metal)
No. 2 Gunmetal   No. 3 Soft Brass – general work
No. 4 Gunmetal   SCB6 Copper for steam flanges
Leaded Gunmetal
New Gunmetal   no scrap added
Hydraulic Gunmetal   hard wearing – good for pressure testing
Bell metal   for signal box bells, ships bells
Nickel Gunmetal   clips for overhead electric cables
Pure lead   weights for lifts on stations
Nickel pure   for pumps at Severn Tunnel Pumping Station
Copper 99% pure   for welding blocks (BUTT)
Semi-steel   for ingots on 2 ton reclamation furnace
Cast Iron
Aluminium   7 types of aluminium
Maganese bronze   high tensile brass
Nickle silver   used for carriage lock parts (doors)

The list gives an idea of the range and variety of the work undertaken by moulders, and reminds one that the GWR had, at one time, its own fleet of ships. What is also interesting is the language used by moulders to describe different things and situations in their daily routine:

Moulders' Terms
Scrap castings are called 'Shitters'.
A ladle is known as a 'Shank'.
A fresh mix of sand – 'Fat'
Box parts (2) are 'Cope and Drag'
A rough casting is as – 'rough as a badgers…'
Not enough metal for a mould – 'a short cast'
A strained casting with excess metal around it – 'a flyer – shut the windows!'

A casting with a 'swelling' – 'he's pregnant'.
A mould that leaked metal while pouring was called – 'Welsh Riser'.
There is a moulders' saying that 'Iron will eat a certain amount of sand, but molten brass will not' and that is a fact!

Most apprentices, unless interrupted by exceptional circumstances, followed a set path to emerge with a trade at the end. Maurice Parsons, however, had a somewhat unusual experience of training and, it could be said, apprenticeship. His father, a labourer who worked in the factory for forty-two years, had put him up for training as a machinist. Parsons recalls:

> I started my training at 17 years, which was the usual time. First I was in O Shop, then AM Shop and then T Shop. Just at the end of my training the Management sent for ten of us machinists, we were all twenty two I remember. He said 'we don't want you chaps anymore, but if you would do erecting, we will train you up as Erectors and keep you on'. So, that's what they did. They trained us up for about a year, I think and I went on erecting. I worked six years as a Loco Erector in B Shed. I was in the Works thirteen years and left in 1949.

No doubt this more than unusual behaviour was the result of desperately needing skilled men as quickly as possible after the losses of the war. It was a portent of things to come, when men trained in one trade had often to adjust, adapt and extend their skills in order to stay in work in the ever-changing world of railways over the next handful of decades of the Works' life.

Moulding was, right up to the middle of the twentieth century, dirty, unhealthy and dangerous work, which, even after training, required an intuitive instinct to know when things were going wrong. Starting an apprenticeship in such conditions was 'quite horrendous', as Jack Fleetwood remembered.

Learning about moulding in the moulding shop in the mid-twentieth-century Apprentice Training School was quite a different proposition to what had gone before – sanitary and safe, goggles and gloves, and no roaring fires.

Out of time

Whilst one can be sure that there are few things that one can be sure of in life, for apprentices and trainees there was one: just as there was a beginning so there would also be an end – a 'coming out of time'. When this happened, suddenly one had ceased to be an apprentice and become a journeyman, and, as one man said to me, 'it was the first time you were recognised as a human being rather than a lower-life'.

In the pre-ATS era, it was, as John Attwell remembers, the foreman who decided whether one had 'proved satisfactory'. This was a long established practice, as a circular of July 1888 from Samuel Carlton to the foremen headed 'Apprentices Advances' shows. In those days it was the foreman's report that affected what went on the final certificate, as we can see from the comments for Raymond Edward Reeves. Reeves' apprenticeship in 'Railway Carriage Building' ended 13 May 1899. Under 'comments' it states: 'and the foreman under whom he has been employed reports that he is a good workman. Signed W Dean.' In fact, Atwell remembers, everybody 'passed'; he did not know of any that did not.

At this momentous end there were three 'rites of passage' for the now young man of 21 (in usual circumstances), taking that step from boy to man, from apprentice to qualified journeyman. One of these was receiving that special, much treasured sheet of paper, headed up with the company/BR name that

'Almost journeymen' – fitter, turner and erector apprentices on the third (and final) part of their apprenticeship, posed outside AE Shop (1950). These apprentices would have been spread out over all the different gangs in the shop – 'New Work', stripping, frame, boiler, erecting, or the finishing gang. Front, left to right: Ray Howell, John Ireland (on loco), Ian Ribbons, Dave Owen, Roy Hazell; middle: Ray Eburn, Ken Hammond, Les Raves, Gordon Stroud, Brian Lornick, Randy Dunbar, Peter Barnes; back: Ian Williamson, John Godfrey, Titcombe, Jim Starley.

carried the immortal words of 'Certificate of Apprenticeship' or 'Certificate of Training'. The certificate became a treasured possession and even today many ex-railwaymen still have theirs. In GWR days, for example, it would state:

Name	Alan Stanley Peck
Date of birth	7 September 1919
Period of apprenticeship	5 years from 19 September 1936
Where employed	Swindon Locomotive Works
Trade	Fitting, Turning & Locomotive erecting

Under the heading 'Work on which employed' would be a brief outline of what one had done and the time spent doing it. Peck's details were recorded as:

General Fitting & Machine Shops	Turning –	16 months
	Fitting –	10 months
Brass shop	Turning –	4 months
Millwrighting	Turning –	4 months
	Fitting –	1 month
		35 months

[Peck had a 'modified' apprenticeship because of his time in war service.]

Then there were the 'comments'. Undoubtedly these comments were seen as important, but, having seen a number of certificates that cross many decades, it is amusing to see that the words varied very little between each person or over the years. The comments on the certificates of Stanley Joseph Smith (1892) and those for Alan Stanley Peck (1941), who went on to have the letters C.Eng., F.I.Mech E. after his name and to hold senior posts of management in the Works, are exactly the same: 'bears good character, possesses good ability as a workman and has conducted himself in a satisfactory manner.' In truth one should not expect otherwise as, if the now to be qualified journeyman had not met the criteria as stipulated, they would have had their apprenticeships terminated. The significant difference between Peck's and Smith's certificates is that Peck's also declares: 'During Sessions 1937/39 was awarded a Free Day Studentship granted by this Company at the College, Swindon', indicating he had been a 'top-of-the-pile' academic apprentice. It was all pretty standard stuff except, as we saw previously, during the war periods when comments such as on Peck's would appear: 'Served in a technical unit whilst on Military Service from 1/9/39 to 6/5/46. During this period he was engaged on duties associated with his trade.'

Although the certificates themselves changed in style and presentation over the years, the essence remained the same as can be seen from those of Ken Gibbs and his father. With three decades between them and despite not being the GWR, but 'The Railway Executive (Western Region), the comments are much the same as ever (see Chapter 1).

For Geoffrey John Fletcher, in the new era of apprenticeship, his certificate took the form of a 'little red book' called 'Record of Apprenticeship'. Apprentices during British Railways Workshops era also received a special printed message card from the general manager.

The second 'rite' was the leaving ceremony, which could differ according to which shop one finished up in or the era of the apprenticeship. Dennis A. Cole writes of this in his personal memoirs when he left the factory:

In the great AE Shop, the 'leaving ceremony' always occurred just before the end of the last day's shift, usually on a Friday. The 'victim' after handing-in his railway provided tools … previously checked by the 'bay' foreman, would roll his overalls into a bundle under his arm and proceed to the East door at the far end of the shop, which was quite a long walk. Then he was 'given-the-bells,' namely, the steel buffers of all locomotives adjacent to that final walk 'peeled-their-chimes' as fellow workers struck the buffers with their hammers – a fond farewell for another poor blighter going out into the cold hard world!

The last of these 'rites' very much signified what a cold, hard world it could be as the lad also received the almost inevitable 'your service will not be required' letter that was the 'DCM'. For the majority it meant looking for work elsewhere, whether in Swindon, a different part of the country or even abroad. One would go off and get experience before, hopefully being taken back on when a job arose. Mrs Joyce Murgatroyd clearly remembers this of her husband Henry 'Harry' Murgatroyd.

Once he'd finished his apprenticeship, like other apprentices, Murgatroyd went to work as a journeyman in another company. Many of the young men then would go in the Merchant Navy and do some turns as an officer. They were welcomed as it was known they would have been well trained. He went on a couple of long trips, on the main route to Australia.

A sign of the new times – not a certificate but a 'little red book' and a message of congratulations.

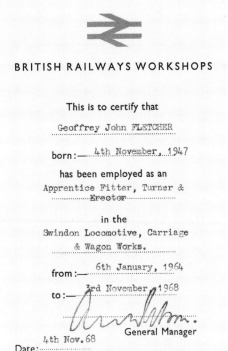

BRITISH RAILWAYS WORKSHOPS

This is to certify that

Geoffrey John FLETCHER

born:— 4th November, 1947

has been employed as an

Apprentice Fitter, Turner & Erector

in the

Swindon Locomotive, Carriage & Wagon Works.

from :— 6th January, 1964

to :— 3rd November, 1968

4th Nov. 68
Date:

General Manager

A MESSAGE FROM THE GENERAL MANAGER
BRITISH RAILWAYS WORKSHOPS
ON COMPLETION OF YOUR APPRENTICESHIP

May I congratulate you on attaining your 21st birthday and completing your Apprenticeship, for you have now reached one of the thresholds of your career in achieving Craftsman status.

You are now part of a team with responsibilities to yourself, your colleagues and your employer, a team whose success depends upon the ability and sincerity of each individual member including yourself.

In meeting the challenge of your future, it is up to you to learn all you can and develop your skills and knowledge. Furthermore, remember that throughout your Apprenticeship many were prepared to help you, and in the same way you should now be willing to assist others during their training.

Your future lies before you. Make it your intention to be a good Craftsman and Citizen and derive satisfaction from a job well done.

My best wishes to you for a very successful career.

No.   (3305)

BRITISH RAILWAYS (W.R.)

Swindon   5.11.   68
.... Works,....................... 19

Mr. G. J. Fletcher .... *Your services will not*

be required after ..... 4.30 p.m. Friday, 8 Nov 68

for H. W. MEAR

Manager.

'Your services will not be required' – commonly known as 'the DCM' – don't come Monday!

For a lucky few, at the same time as receiving their DCM, they were also informed that they 'can be re-engaged as a … (trade) on Monday'.

After the introduction of National Service, the dismissal tradition changed slightly, as those who had decided for the option to stay on and finish their apprenticeship would hang around and wait to receive their call-up papers for the mandatory period with one of the armed services.

Ryan Conduit believes he was the last apprentice to 'come out of his time' in Swindon Works. He recalls that time, his end, and that of the Works too:

> It's true that there were apprentices after me but I was the last to actually finish his time *at the railway works,* the others going to finish theirs at other factories like Press Steel as it was then.
>
> At 16 (in 1982) I was lucky enough to get a 1st year Apprenticeship Training through the then Manpower Service's Commission. It had been announced that due to government policies very few firms in Swindon would be having apprenticeships. Vickers, Square D, Lister were some that did, and we worked alongside these at the training school getting our government pay cheque of £25 a week. As Swindon was the main training facility for 1st year Apprentices, there were, of course, other rail apprentices from other regions.
>
> As our first year was coming to a close the future of Swindon Works was still unknown and they were still not taking any apprentices … all I know is that a total about face happened, and BREL offered a selected few of us who applied and had the grades, full apprenticeships for the next 3 years, I being selected as a plumber pipe fitter apprentice.
>
> So here it was we reported to the Works to the two men that held our training in their hands. For me Jerry Pontin and above him Ken Dann. I don't remember too much about that first day, only being taken down in a group and dropped off in 19 Shop pipe fitters and

Possibly the last intake of apprentices at the training school in 1985, although none for the Works. Whilst the Works closed on 26 March 1986, the training school continued until the end of the school year. Front row staff, left to right: Bob Wright, Roy Arnold, Tony Berry, Linda Telling, Roy Hazell, Pam Drewitt, Bert Goddard, D. Nipress, Charlie Affleck, Ron Shipton. *Roy Hazell Collection*

plumbers, in charge Brian Bowden, a guy that I have the deepest respect for to this day. As apprentices we travelled around to different sections of the Works learning every aspect.

On 26 April, 1986 that 'Last Day' I had been called up to the training department too finish my Apprentice Log Book and hand it in. I can remember being there all day before finally finishing it, then handing it in to Gerry Pontin who took it to Ken Dann for final signing off. As he came through the door the final long hooter that was ever to sound started too blow, 'Well', he told me 'you're the last in a very long line. The last apprentice this Works will ever produce'.

Looking back over the whole history of apprenticeship in the Works, it can clearly be seen that although there was a 'norm', there were also many kinds of exceptions to it. Apprenticeship carried the status of being the 'elite' method of training, but it was not the only training carried on within the Works, and, as we have seen, at one period 'apprenticeship' found itself also termed 'training', alongside the other models. Whilst some went through a designated period of training and evening-class attendance and came out with a 'Certificate of Apprenticeship', others went through a designated period of training (and some evening class) and came out with a 'Certificate of Training'. Apprenticeships were undertaken for both first-class and second-class trades, whilst training was designated for semi-skilled work. Once again it comes down to that old debate: 'what is skill, who defines it, who has it and to what degree?' Undoubtedly,

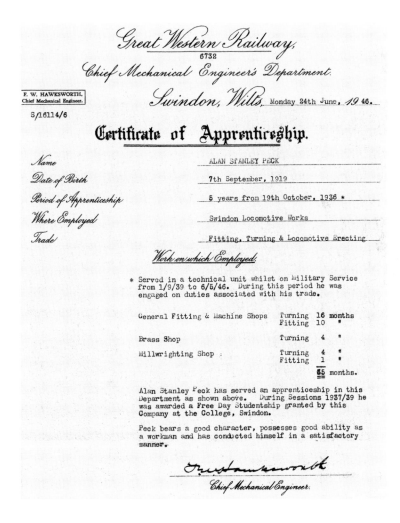

BRITISH RAILWAYS BOARD

Draft ✓

TRAINING CERTIFICATE

𝕿𝖍𝖎𝖘 𝕮𝖊𝖗𝖙𝖎𝖋𝖎𝖈𝖆𝖙𝖊 records that

DAVID JOHN GALLAGHER

born 5TH March 1963 has been trained as

an Electrical Fitter.

from 28th August 1979 to 23rd May 1983

Record of practical training and experience :

12 months Basic Craft Engineering Practices

24 months Engineering Industry Training Board Modules

J01 - Mechanical Maintenance and J02 Electrical Maintenance

on Rail Traction - Rolling Stock and Plant Maintenance

9 months applied electrical Traction and Rolling
Stock experience

Record of further education :

City and Guilds - Craft - Engineering 200 - General (Credit)

City and Guilds - Craft Engineering 200 - Electrical (Credit)

City and Guilds Electrical Craft Studies 2. Parts I II (Credits)

City and Guilds Electrical Craft Studies Part III

Signed

( )

the majority of those who came out of Swindon Works considered that they had had the best training available, but also undoubtedly, those with 'apprenticeship' on their papers came out with a certain edge. Completing an apprenticeship or training was an achievement, but that was only part of the story. As Ken Gibbs, a one-time apprentice, cleverly puts it: 'Finishing an apprenticeship (or training) is like completing a university degree, although celebrated it's not the end, it's the beginning of the rest of your life!'

Notes

1 Some of the oral evidence given in this chapter can also be found in Matheson, *Railway Voices*.

Appendix

Apprentices who did not return to Swindon Works, Loco and Carriage & Wagon sides to finish their apprenticeships, having died during the First World War, as recorded by the GWR:

Casualties Amongst GWR Men Serving With The Colours

L.H. Cole	apprentice fitter	killed in action
F.J. Morgan	apprentice fitter	died of wounds
A. Watson	apprentice Loco	killed in action
F.T. Holley	apprentice Loco	killed in action
A.E. Read	apprentice Loco	killed in action
G.C. Dadge	Smith's apprentice Carriage	killed in action
J.F. Vickery	frame builder's appr. Carriage	killed in action
C.E. Stroud	premium apprentice	died of wounds
K.C.F. Cann	apprentice Loco	killed in action
G.T. Hack	apprentice Loco	died of wounds
H. Walton	apprentice boilermaker	killed in action
V.G. Cumnor	boilermaker's apprentice Loco	killed in action
A.E. Paynter	frame builder's apprentice Loco	killed in action
W.H. Singer	apprentice fitter	died of enteric
E.J. Williams	smith's apprentice Carriage	killed in action
J.P. Price	boilersmith's apprentice	killed in action
S.T. Corner	boilersmith's apprentice	accidentally killed
A.W. Sellars	boilersmith's apprentice	killed in action
A. Cooper	angle iron smith Loco	killed in action
F.C. Haylock	boilersmith's apprentice	killed in action
F.J. Chander	coppersmith Loco	died after operation
R.W. Heap	fitter apprentice Carriage	killed in action
A.C. Ellis	fitter's apprentice	died of pneumonia
A.B. Grellier	premium apprentice	killed in action
G.L. Hatcher	premium apprentice	killed in action
S.A. Sinnet	fitter's apprentice	killed in action
W.W.M. Dulin	apprentice	killed in action
F.E. Duck	apprentice	presumed killed in action Aug 1917
N. Day	premium apprentice	killed in action
H. Taylor	premium apprentice	killed in action
G.H. Osborn	gas fitter's apprentice	killed in action
T.D. Evans	apprentice	died of influenza
H.A. Greer	coach body mkr apprentice	died of influenza
C.H. Wiltshire	apprentice	died of fever
N.R.W. Dixon	apprentice Loco	died of wounds
J.C.H. Fisher	coach painter's apprentice	killed in action

W.A. Hayward	apprentice boilermaker	killed in action
S.G. Lee	apprentice painter Loco	killed in action
T.A. Lewis	apprentice fitter Loco	died
R.C. Lord	apprentice fitter Loco	killed in action
F.C. Whatley	coach bldr's apprentice C	died of chill

Others recorded elsewhere:

G. Gill		killed in action
P.C. Matthews		
W. Shakespeare		died
A.F. Woodman		

Note: This is not a definitive listing, only those I have come across.

Bibliography

Books

Bagwell, Philip, *The Railway Men – The History of the National Union of Railwaymen*, George Allen & Unwin Ltd.

Bonavia, Michael, *The Four Great Railways*, David & Charles Newton Abbott, 1980.

Cattell, John & Faulkner, Keith, *Swindon: The Legacy of a Railway Town*, HMSO, 1995.

Cockbill, Trevor, *This is Our Heritage: An account of the central role played by the New Swindon Mechanics' Institution in the Cultural, Educational and Social Life of the Town and District over One Hundred Years*, The New Swindon Mechanics' Institution Preservation Trust Publishing Group, Swindon 1997.

Cook, Kenneth J., *Swindon Steam 1921–1951*, Ian Allen Ltd, 1974.

Crittal, Elizabeth, *Engineering and Railway Work's, A History of the County of Wiltshire*, Vol. 4, 1959.

Crittal, Elizabeth, Rogers, K.H. & Shrimpton, Colin, *A History of Swindon to 1965*, Institute of Historical Research & Wiltshire Library & Museum Service, Trowbridge, 1983. This book was reprinted from *The Victoria History of Wiltshire Volume 1X*.

Durrant, Anthony E., *Swindon Apprentice: An Inside Portrait of the Great Western Locomotive Works*, Runpast Publishing, Cheltenham, 1989.

Freebury, Hugh, *Great Western Apprentice, Swindon in the Thirties*, Wiltshire County Council Library & Museum Services, 1985.

Gibbs, Ken, *Swindon Works: Apprentice in Steam*, Oxford Publishing Company, 1986.

Head, Francis B., *Stokers and Pokers* (1849), David & Charles, reprint 1968.

Holcroft, Harold, *Locomotive Adventure: Fifty Years With Steam*, Ian Allen Ltd, 1962.

Holland, James, *The Battle of Britain: Five Months that Changed History. May–October 1940*, Bantam, 2010.

Larkin, Edgar J., *Memoir of a Railway Engineer*, Mechanical Engineering Publications Ltd, 1979.

Macdermott, E.T., *History of the Great Western Railway*, Vols 1 & 2, Great Western Railway Company, 1927.

Macmillan, Nigel S.C., *Locomotive Apprentice at the North British Locomotive Company Ltd, Glasgow*, Plateway Press, Brighton, 1992.

Matheson, Rosa, *Railway Voices Inside Swindon Works*, The History Press, 2009.

Nock, O.S., *History of the Great Western Railway*, Vol. 3, Great Western Railway Company.

Peck, Alan, *The Great Western at Swindon Works*, Oxford Publishing Co., 1988.

Platt, Alan, *The Life and Times of Daniel Gooch*, Alan Sutton, 1987.

Pratt, Edwin A., *British Railways and The Great War*, Vols 1 & 2, Selwyn & Blount Ltd, 1921.

Rolt, L.T.C., *The Mechanicals: Progress of a Profession*, The Institution of Mechanical Engineers, Heinemann, 1967.

Scott Burn, Robert, *Mechanics and Mechanism: Elementary Essays and Examples*, 4th edn, Ward, Lock & Tyler, London, 1850.

Simmons, Jack, *The Victorian Railway*, Thames & Hudson, 1995.

Simmons, Jack & Biddle, G., *The Oxford Companion to British Railway History*, Oxford University Press, 1998.

Snell, J.B., *Mechanical Engineering: Railways*, Longman Group Ltd, 1971.

Unacknowledged, *The Town and Works of Swindon with a Brief History of the Broad Gauge*, Victoria Press, 1892.

Academic Papers & Articles

'Collective Trade Union Action and Repression in British Railway Company Workshops, 1840–1914', 5th Railway History Congress, Palma De Mallorca, 2009.

Attwell, Graham, 'Rediscovering Apprenticeship? A Historical Approach', 1997.

Chaloner, W.H., 'The Skilled Artisans During the Industrial Revolution 1750–1850', The Historical Association, 1969.

Deakin, S., 'The Contract of Employment: A Study in Legal Evolution', ESRC WP 203, 2001.

Drummond, Diane, '"Specifically Designed?" Employers' Labour Strategies and Worker Response in British Railway Workshops, 1838–1914', *Business History*, Vol.31 No.2, April 1989.

Eversley, D.E.C., 'The Great Western Railway and the Swindon Works in the Great Depression', *Historical Journal*, 1957.

Jocelyn, Olive, 'English Apprenticeship and Child Labour – a history', University of Michigan, 2005.

Minns, Chris & Wallis, Patrick, 'Rules and Reality: Quantifying the Practice of Apprenticeship in Early Modern Europe', London School of Economics.

Ryan, Paul, 'The Embedding of Apprentices in Industrial Relations - British Engineering 1925–1965', King's College, Cambridge, 1999.

Wallis, Patrick, 'Apprenticeship and Training in Premodern England', London School of Economics, Working Papers No. 22/07, 2007.

Warnes, Alice, 'Elementary Education in Swindon', B.Ed., University of Bristol, 1985.

Yarbrough, Anne, 'Apprentices as Adolescents in Sixteenth Century Bristol', *Journal of Social History*, Vol.13 No.1, Autumn 1979, pp. 67–81.

Newspapers & Journals

Mechanics Magazine, Museum Register, Journal and Gazette October 1829 (online).
Steam World, July 1992, 'Swindon Apprentice', William Bullock.
The Daily Chronicle.
The Evening Advertiser.
The Great Western Railway Magazine.
The Railway Gazette.
The Swindon Advertiser.
The Wiltshire Gazette & Herald.

Primary Sources

STEAM: the Museum of the Great Western Railway.
Swindon Central Library Local Collection.
National Archive – RAIL 253/451, RAIL 250/765, RAIL 264/295, RAIL 264/284, RAIL 264/279.
Newton Abbot Railway Centre.

Private Collections

Ken Gibbs; David Hyde; Roy Hazell; Andrew Binks; Nigel Hockin; Geoffrey Fletcher.

Websites

North Wilts Online Census Project, http://www.pope-genealogy.me.uk/nwocp.htm.
Engineers & Engineering, www.design-technology info/engineers.
Derby Evening Telegraph, Nostalgia Section, www.bygonederbyshire.co.uk.